LOCK DO

CW01429652

OUTLAWS, LAWMEN, AND FRONTIER JUSTICE IN JACKSON COUNTY, MISSOURI

By David W. Jackson and Paul Kirkman

"...it was old, built in a time when people took time to build even jails with grace and care and he remembered how his uncle had said once that not courthouses nor even churches, but jails are the true record of a county's, a community's history..."
William Faulkner, Intruder in the Dust

COMMEMORATIVE SOUVENIR EDITION

1859 JACKSON COUNTY JAIL

Owned and Operated Since 1958
by the Jackson County Historical Society
as the
1859 Jail, Marshal's Home & Museum
217 North Main Street
Independence, Missouri 64050

Publisher's Cataloging-in-Publication Data

David W. Jackson, (1969-); and, Paul Kirkman, (1961-)
Lock Down: Outlaws, Lawmen, and Frontier Justice in Jackson County, Missouri /
   by David W. Jackson and Paul Kirkman.
   190 p. 29 cm.

1. Jails–Missouri–Jackson County–History. 2. Sheriffs–Jackson County (Mo.) –Registers. 3. Independence (Mo.) –History. 4. Cross, Asa Beebe (1826-1894). 5. Jackson County (Mo.) – History. 6. Crime–Missouri–History. 7. Criminal justice, Administration of–Missouri–History. I. Jackson, David W., (1969-) author. II. Kirkman, Paul, (1961-) joint author. III. Title.

Sixth Edition, April 2012

Library of Congress Edition, December 2009 (ISBN 0-9741365-6-5)

Published in the United States of America by:

Jackson County Historical Society
P. O. Box 4241
Independence, MO 64051-4241
816.252.7454
info@jchs.org
www.jchs.org

Cover art of the 1859 Jackson County Jail cell block provided courtesy Nick Vedros.

TABLE OF CONTENTS

INTRODUCTION

The State of Missouri was admitted to the Union in 1821. Six years later, Independence was designated as the County Seat when Jackson County was formed on December 15, 1826. Less than ten miles to the west was "Indian Territory," or "The Great American Desert," and it would remain the western edge of the U.S. political boundary for another quarter century.

The historic Jackson County Courthouse Square anchors the Missouri River town of Independence. Today, the building resembles Independence Hall in Philadelphia, Pennsylvania. Interestingly, this landmark building contains within its walls the remnants of five previous courthouses, including the original nucleus that dates to 1838.[1] Over the last 170 years, each successive courthouse was expanded—rather than being demolished—the last renovation taking place in 1933 under the leadership of Jackson County's then Presiding Judge Harry S Truman.

The Independence Courthouse was surrounded by general stores, saloons, hotels, and blacksmith shops outfitting travelers embarking on the Santa Fe, Oregon and California Trails. Today, late-19th century buildings are occupied with boutiques, restaurants, museums, and professional offices. These modern-day tenants greet visitors from nearby Kansas City suburbs, as well as tourists from all over the world attracted to Independence to see Truman's hometown, and/or to see the spot where the famous westward trails began. Little do they know that Independence is home to many interesting sites with unexpected stories relevant to American history.

One such place numbered 217 North Main Street, is a solid, two-story, brick, Georgian-style home. But, why build a residence flush with the sidewalk along a commercial block? And what about the "jail" and "museum" parts of the placard signaling the, "1859 Jail, Marshal's Home, and Museum?" You don't see these other buildings from the street until you tour the site.

Discover real-life stories about early-day Independence, Jackson County, Missouri, and how the lawlessness of the frontier was dealt with . . . even if it seems crude and rustic when looking at it today.

This book commemorates the 50th Golden Anniversary of the Jackson County (Mo.) Historical Society's operation of the 1859 Jail and Marshal's Home as a local history museum. In a larger part, we commemorate in 2009 the sesquicentennial (150th anniversary) of the 1859 Jackson County Jail and Marshal's Home. This publication documents the origin and evolution of the oldest structure on Independence Square . . . and the inhabitants who lived on either side of its barred doors. Here is a commentary offering "skeleton keys" to "unlocking" an overview of the early structures, of those who defied frontier justice, and the systems and strongmen (and women) who tried to keep law and order in Jackson County, Missouri, from 1826 through 1933.

Readers with family connections to the former occupants and workers at the Jackson County Jail are invited to donate original, relative materials to the Historical Society for preservation and potential exhibition at the Museum.

Visitors to the physical site enjoy self-guided tours of the facility, and the Marshal is available for guided, group tours with advance notice. Additional information to complement this publication is available online at jchs.org.

---

[1] The walls of the 1838 Courthouse remain, and stand upon the foundation of a short-lived—and failed— 1828 brick Jackson County Courthouse. Wilcox, Pearl. *Jackson County Pioneers* (Independence, Mo.: Jackson County Historical Society, 1991), 136.

CELL

1

FRONTIER FOUNDATION FULFILLED (1804-1827)

Although Jackson County, Missouri, officially organized December 15, 1826, European-Americans had begun settling in the area for at least a half a century before. When the Lewis and Clark *Corps of Discovery* expedition made its way upstream along the Missouri River in 1804, watching them were Native-Americans of the Osage Nation who had already established trade with rugged mountain men and French-American fur trappers and traders migrating from St. Louis and into the wilderness.

With organization came the notion of "civilization" and the fluctuating distinction between what was considered lawful and unlawful.

Officials recognized rather early the need for a system and structure to detain frontiersmen who exhibited unsavory (or illegal) behaviors.

Meriwether Lewis

Capt. William Clark

Le Soldat Du Chene
"Soldier of the Oak"
Second Chief of the Little Osage Nation

1827 JACKSON COUNTY JAIL (MADE OF LOGS)

Jackson County government, led by a panel of three officials comprising the Jackson County Court (predecessor of today's Jackson County Legislature), reserved Lot 2 in Independence, on September 3, 1827, for the site of a "common jail."[2] According to specifications set forth by the County Court:

> "The jail is to be built of square timber to square one foot the building to be 20 feet square on the outside and 16 feet high above the top of the stone foundation, so as to form two stories each seven feet in clear or thereabout, the walls of the upper story to be single and the walls of the lower story or dungeon to be double, with a space of one foot left between the outside of the inner wall and the inside of the outer wall, which space is to be filled up with square bolts of split timber, round pealed, poles, placed upright or with loose rock beat into small pieces.
>
> "The foundation wall to be of stone three feet thick and let in the earth two feet and to extend above the surface six inches, the part which extends above the surface to be faced and pointed with lime mortar on the outside, the logs for the outside wall to be 20 feet in length and the logs for the inner wall to be 16 feet in length, the lower, middle and upper floors to be laid of square hewed timber the same as used for the body of the building.
>
> "All the floors to be rabbitted into the outside wall on the inside of the same, so as not to show on the outside. The middle floor to be covered with strong oak plank jointed and well nailed down, a trap door to be left in the center of the middle floor and shutter made strong with necessary fastening.
>
> "The roof to be of rafters and covered with lathing and good oak or walnut shingles, the gable ends studded and weather boarded, and large boards along the gable ends.
>
> "One window in the lower room and two in the upper room, the windows to be one foot in height (sic) and 18 inches in length well secured by strong iron bars or grates.
>
> "One door in the upper story with two strong door shutters. One to open on the inside and one on the outside of the building and having good strong iron hinges.
>
> "A pair of coarse rough steps and platform on the outside to lead up to the upper room.
>
> "The building to be raised with a half dovetail and notched down close, so that there will be no cracks between the logs. All the work to be done in a strong and work-manlike manner."[3]

The allotted cost for this structure was $400.

From the description above, the only way to enter the jail was by a stairway on the outside to the upper room, known as, "the debtors room." Below it, was the dungeon for criminals, that was reached by means of a trap door. Staples with rings attached were driven into the logs for the purpose of fastening the shackles of desperate men.

"A runaway negro was placed in the old log jail for safe keeping one night, and his master, who resided in Lafayette County, came on to claim his property. The owner identified the fugitive, left him in the care of the jailor, and retired to the hotel for the night. On the morrow he ordered the stage driven around to the jail, to get the negro, but on entering, they were surprised to find him stone dead, and hanging by his neck so low that his knees touched the floor. He had managed to find a piece of rope, with which he committed the rash act."[4]

Block house (at Fort Osage) resembling 1827 Jackson County Jail; image digitally enhanced.

The Sheriff and the County Court were tied together from the start. The Court required him to be taking care of grounds, posting bounty notices for wolf skins, acquiring tables, and chairs for court, making repairs, selling off the grass around the courthouse, etc.[5]

There was a natural desire to establish law and order early on in Independence stemming from the frontier circumstances, where there was a transient population, mostly male, almost all armed and some potentially dangerous.

"Patrols" and "constables" instituted in smaller communities had been assigned by the County Court and were part of how law worked on different levels.[6]

On the following pages is a description of the everyday duties of Jackson County's sheriffs and later marshals, and the various types and levels of law at work on the frontier. We begin with Jackson County's first lawmen…the sheriffs.

---

[2] This lot was from the very first sale of divided lots. Eventually, as other plats were recorded, this first Jackson County "subdivision" became "Independence Old Town." Jackson County Court minutes (1:10).

[3] Birdsall, Williams & Co. *History of Jackson County, Missouri: A History of the County, Its Cities, Towns, etc.* (Kansas City, Mo.: Union Historical Company, 1881), 639-640. Hickman, W. Z. *History of Jackson County, Missouri.* (Topeka, Ks.: Historical Publishing Co., 1920), 141-142. *An Analytical Index to the Jackson County, Missouri, County Court Minutes*, indexed and annotated by Annette W. Curtis, reveal in Book 1 that a plan was presented along with probable cost for a log jail (1:33-34:80120); a description of the log jail (1:35); money was appropriated for its construction through the sale of lots by the County (1:36:80121); advertising for proposals was published (1:44:80149); James King agreed to build a log jail for $388 (1:45:80150); an August 1828 report that it was being built with good work but not yet complete (1:46:80152); partial payment for work was ordered (1:47:80153); it was completed and two strong locks were needed (1:52:80171); and, L. W. Boggs was paid as superintendent of building the jail (1:54:80173).

[4] Birdsall, 640.

[5] Sheriff required to get 6 chairs, 1 table and 10-12 plank benches for County Court, Jackson County Court minutes, (1:138); Sheriff to post notice in 1832 that county will pay .50 cents for each wolf's scalp taken in Jackson county (1:175).

[6] Examples of 1831 Constable Appointments from Jackson County Court minutes include: Levi Shepherd of Blue Township (1:86); William Moderal of Harmony Township (1:86); William Williams of Fort Osage (1:88). Patrols were appointed for Blue Springs settlement, William Frances appointed captain (3:509); Company of patrol appointed for town of Independence, John Copeland Captain (6:172).

CELL

2

EARLY SHERIFFS OF JACKSON COUNTY, MISSOURI (1827-1859)

Early Jackson County sheriffs were a diverse lot, but most shared a southern heritage and were nearly all Democrats. At the time of taking office, they ranged from 23 to 54, with most being in their 30s. The office of Jackson County Sheriff was a political position, with the Sheriff subject to re-election every two years. For jailors and deputies, that meant their jobs usually expired when their boss lost re-election.[1] After their term as Sheriff, about one third rose in the political hierarchy to the state legislature.[2]

The Jackson County Court and the elected Sheriffs of Jackson County were keepers of the peace in the formative years of Jackson County between 1827 and 1859. These men served during exciting and momentous times in Jackson County's history:

CAPTAIN JOSEPH "JOE" REDDEFORD WALKER (SHERIFF FROM 1827-1830)

Joseph Walker was born in Roan County, Tennessee, December 13, 1798. His family emigrated to the Six Mile area of Jackson County in 1819.[3] At 21, Walker joined some trappers bound for the Rocky Mountains.

In 1820, as one of the first U.S. fur traders to Mexico, and was also one of the first jailed in Santa Fe for illegally attempting to barter with the Spanish. Five years later, he led a surveying expedition intent on marking a route which would be called the Santa Fe Trail.[4]

The History of Jackson County, Missouri, published in 1881, records that Walker was appointed by Governor John Miller, in…1827, and on the 29th of March of the same year, was qualified in office before Circuit Judge David Todd. Another source relates an election held on August 4, 1828, where 149 votes were returned for Walker; 29 for his opponent, Richard Chiles.[5] Coinciding with Walker's tenure was the creation of the Jackson County Circuit Court on March 29, 1827. (See JAIL BREAK: Blatant Crimes, Brazen Criminals.)

Walker, then 29-years-old, was already an experienced mountain man and explorer of the Great West. His reputation as a crack shot demanded respect. And, at 200 pounds and over six-feet-tall, Walker had a commanding presence.[6] Yet, he was described as quiet and humble, and was considered, "a gentleman among the mountain men of the time. He didn't cuss, didn't gamble and was only a ceremonial drinker. And, he didn't tolerate the mistreatment of Indians."[7]

Walker kept law and order for four years. Upon discovering a more lucrative career selling horses to trappers setting out from Independence, Walker refused a third term as sheriff. Besides, the lure of the West called him again.

In 1832, Walker left Independence for the Great Salt Lake, the Sierra Nevada Mountains, and the Kern River. "Walker Pass" was named for him. He stayed in California through the winter of 1833-34 and in the spring traveled along the Sierra Nevada range, through Owens Valley, across the desert, and back along the Humboldt. At some point, he began using the title of "Captain."[8]

He was daring, adventuresome, and courageous like many of the people he had represented in Jackson County. Captain Walker chose to live out his life as a successful rancher in California where he died near Walnut Creek on October 27, 1876, at that age of 77.[9]

JOSEPH BROWN (SHERIFF FROM 1831-1832)

Joseph Brown followed Walker as the next Sheriff of Jackson County. In July 1827, Brown purchased Lot No. 53 in Old Town Independence at the cost of $42.

Brown married Miss Nancy King January 20, 1828.[10] Her family had also previously moved to this area and settled.

After his term as Jackson County Sheriff, Brown moved to the unsettled Platte Purchase, north of the Missouri River in northwestern Missouri.[11]

JACOB GREGG (SHERIFF FROM 1833-1836)

Jacob Gregg was born in Overton County, Tennessee, April 9, 1802.[12] In 1825, Gregg led one of 30 wagons which started on the first trading trip to Santa Fe, Mexico. Each wagon was owned by a different proprietor, and their teams ranged from a spike team to six mules.

Gregg was in Jackson County when the first election was held in 1826. He was appointed the first surveyor, and was among those who selected the site of Independence Square as the County Seat.

Gregg was a deputy for Sheriff Walker from 1828-1830. At that time, the 1827 Jackson County Jail "became a bastion of shelter against an infuriated mob of Jackson Countians. Samuel C. Owens advised A. S. Gilbert, Isaac Morley, John Corrill, and William E. McLellin to take protection in the jail against the mobs that were threatening these leaders of the Church of Jesus Christ of Latter Day Saints. Of the incident McLellin wrote:

"I yielded myself into their hands, knowing that I had committed no offense.... [We] were taken to the most horrid, soul harrowing, lonesome, loathsome place into which my feet ever entered, before or since.

"What! To be locked, chained, and barred in a little room, only twelve feet square! And that, too, where robbers and murderers had dwelt, and forced to remain during a dark, lonesome night; and that, too, without any certainty as to the future.... Finally, grey twilight began to appear in the east, and as the sun began to mount up to shed golden rays upon the world, the jailer and two others entered our little dismal abode and said, "Now, sirs, if you will agree to remove from the county forthwith, we will release you."'

The men were liberated and given protection from further mob violence as they left Independence. This was one of many unfortunate incidents—including one tar and feathering— that became known as the "Mormon War."[13]

Gregg became the next Jackson County Sheriff.[14] He was once fined $1.00 for contempt of court for not attending. He was also commissioned to conduct at least two and possibly three population census enumerations. It took him ten days in 1826 to find and list the inhabitants of Jackson County, for which he was paid $10. Six years later, he took 40 days to complete the census of Jackson County for 1832 and was paid $2/day ($80).[15]

Gregg was a Quaker, but he made little pretension to religion. He was a man of high moral character and had the respect of the people of Jackson County.[16]

Jacob Gregg married Miss Nancy Lewis March 4, 1828.[17] They had nine children. The 1850 U. S. Census for Jackson County listed Gregg, age 48, a merchant by trade, with his wife, Nancy, 44; and their children: Samuel D., 19, teacher ; Christopher R., 17; Josiah, 15; William H., 13; Mary F. Newmanth, 8; Jacob F., 6; Nancy, 4; John L., 21, teacher; and, Martha F., 18. The 1850 Slave Schedules listed 4 unnamed, female, African-American slaves aged 40, 20, 17 (a mulatto), and 15. The Slave Schedules in 1860 list what appear to be the two older female slaves, who were then 50 (a mulatto) and 30. However, the two younger females from 1850 were no longer listed; but, rather, two young, black males, aged 19 and 10.[18]

Gregg was elected to the Missouri State Legislature as an "old-line Whig" in the lower house, in 1850. This was the last office he held.[19]

At some point, Gregg purchased the adjacent lot (Lot 3, Old Town Independence) south of the 1827/1841 Jackson County Jail site (Lot 2). It is possible that he constructed a modest home on that parcel for, as you will see below, on July 5, 1859, Henry Bugler, Jailor, was paid $11 for removing a house off of Lot 3, so that the 1859 Jackson County Jail could then be constructed.

Two of Gregg's sons, Frank and William H. served the Confederacy during the Civil War, riding with Captain William Clarke Quantrill.[20] William later became a County Deputy Sheriff.[21]

Gregg engaged in farming and mercantile pursuits settling at "Stoney Point." Samuel Majors bought the Jacob Gregg farm around 1872; by 1893 it was owned by William Lane. He was elected the first president of the "Historical Society of Old Settlers," on April 24, 1880. By 1881, Gregg was living near Grain Valley, Sni-a-Bar Township, Jackson County, Missouri.[22] His wife, Nancy, died December 29, 1885.[23] Gregg continued in business until he was long past 80, and by age 91 (celebrated in 1893), he enjoyed a "cozy home, attended by a faithful family servant of…long ago—Aunt Sallie [Clark]—who" was a former family slave.[24] The Greggs are buried in Koger Cemetery, in eastern Jackson County.[25]

JOHN KING (SHERIFF FROM 1837-1840)

In the August 1836 election, four men sought the office of Sheriff of Jackson County. John King won with 474 votes; Page Noland (212), Thomas G. Hudspeth (93), and Amos Riley (1).[26] According to the 1881 *History of Jackson County, Missouri,* King, "belonged to the numerous family of Kings most of whom removed to the 'Platte Purchase.'"[27]

Sheriff King presided at the first *legal* hanging in Jackson County, Missouri. Henry Garster was indicted for, "*not having the fear of God before his eyes but being moved and seduced by the instigation of the devil…with force and arms…in and upon one Williamson Hawkins in the peace of God….*"[28]

Garster was tried, convicted, and sentenced to hang after his neighbor, Rebecca Hawkins, paid Garster $150 to kill her husband, Williamson Hawkins. Mrs. Hawkins, a battered mother of eight had previously tried to poison her husband to death (twice). Unfortunately for Garster, his tracks in the snow led officials from the Hawkins' cabin to his front door.[29] Another prisoner, Alva P. Buckley, was being held at this same time, for a brutal altercation "urged on by whisky." Buckley was arrested for crushing William Yocum's skull with a rock at Moses Wilson's store on the south side of Independence Square. Garster and Buckley dug through the floor of the Jail, tunneled underground and escaped; it is the first recorded jail break. Buckley was never found. Garster, once again, wasn't so lucky; he was apprehended in southwest Missouri and extradited back to Independence for sentencing…and hanging.[30]

Reportedly, thousands of spectators came from far away to see the legal execution. The gallows consisting of two, large, 20-foot-long posts set in the ground, and a cross-bar connected the top, were constructed in an area between the "Temple Lot" (pictured below is Lexington Avenue and River Boulevard) and the present-day Missouri Pacific Railroad Depot to the south (or right in the image below). Garster rode to the site in a wagon, seated upon a rough, hand-made, wooden box, which was later used as his coffin. Sheriff King adjusted the noose and Deputy Joe Reynolds drew a black cap over Garster's head. With Henry Garster's wife, Ann, sitting side-saddle on a horse nearby, the wagon was driven from beneath the murderer between Noon and 3 p.m. on May 10, 1839.[31]

The next *legal* hanging, or judicial execution, in Jackson County wouldn't take place for nearly 40 years.[32]

Ruins of the Hawkins mill—the old style water mills with the great upright wooden wheel on the outside—were still visible 60 years later, as late as 1898.[33] To find out what happened to Rebecca Hawkins, and a complete account of the events leading up to and including Garster's execution, see, *Abuse and Murder on the Frontier: The Trials and Travels of Rebecca Hawkins, 1800-1860.* (Independence, Mo.: Little Blue Valley Publishing Co., 2003) by local author and historian, William B. Bundschu.

King was re-elected in 1838 to serve a second term between 1839 and 1840. At the end of his term as Sheriff, King was voted into the 11th General Assembly of the Missouri State Legislature in 1840.[34] King apparently died near Independence about 1845.[35]

JOSEPH H. "JOE" REYNOLDS (SHERIFF FROM 1841-1844)

Joseph H. "Joe" Reynolds, a native Kentuckian born on November 8, 1812. [36] He came to Jackson County in the Autumn of 1834. He served as Justice of the Peace in 1837, a post he later held in Independence in 1881.[37]

Reynolds, having gained experience as a deputy for Sheriff King, was elected to office and served two successive terms as Jackson County Sheriff. [38]

After his term as Sheriff ended in 1844, Reynolds was elected to represent Jackson County in the Missouri State Legislature.

On October 16, 1849, he married Miss Martha W. Haynes. The 1850 Slave Schedules list one, 22-year-old, female slave in their household.

In 1852, Reynolds was again elected for a term in the Missouri House of Representatives.

After Martha's premature death, Reynolds married Kentucky native Mrs. Mary C. Ward on September 1, 1859.[39] Joseph and Mary Reynolds appear together in the 1860 U.S. Census, ages 47 and 43 respectively, with four unrelated borders aged 6-70.

Reynolds died March 29, 1884, and is buried in Woodlawn Cemetery.[40]

1841 JACKSON COUNTY JAIL (MADE OF BRICKS)

Under Sheriff Reynolds' watch, the 1827 Jackson County Jail was destroyed by fire one winter day in 1841. Though we have not yet uncovered just who lived or worked next door to the 1827 Jackson County Jail, documentation indicates that a neighbor "was in the habit of piling ashes and embers by the side of the building."[41] It wasn't long until the 1827 Jackson County Jail was a mass of flaming debris.

On May 4, 1841, the County Court adopted the plans of George Rider for building a new jail, "and same be let to the lowest bidder on tomorrow at 1 o'clock p.m."[42] Then, on May 15, the Sheriff let the construction contract to Thomas Mercer, the lowest bidder, to build the 1841 Jail for $2,600.[43]

H. J. Hockensmith was selected by the County Court to value and appraise a part of Lot 2, Old Town, being the jail lot, one rod in width from the south side. The entire length of the lot was valued at $30. A two-story brick structure was constructed on the same site of the 1827 Jackson County Jail (Lot 2, Independence Old Town; today the site of a defunct fire station on the southeast corner of Truman Road and Main Street, Independence, Missouri).[44]

The 1841 Jackson County Jail had four rooms…two above, and two below, with a hall and stairway between the north and south rooms. The structure measured 45' long, 18' wide, and 30' high.

The two rooms on the north end of the building, both above and below, were lined with heavy square timbers, driven full of twenty-penny nails. Not a square inch of surface, either in the walls or floor of those rooms, was without one of those large nails, being driven firmly into the square-faced logs.

At one time, five, large, six-inch iron balls, with chain and shackle attached were listed as "relics of implements to confine prisoners."[45] (Since the Jackson County Historical Society opened the 1859 Jail, Marshal's Home and Museum in 1959, items like these once used at the Jackson County Jail (including keys, handcuffs, locks, etc.) have been donated so they may be permanently preserved and used in exhibits into the future.)[46]

The two rooms on the south of the hallway were less firmly constructed, the upper rooms being for women. Connecting the upper and lower rooms on the north end was a heavy trap door that required considerable strength to lift.[47] Later repairs included lining the hole for the stove pipe with iron.[48]

Reynolds processed the murderers of Antonio Jose Chavez, a New Mexico trader, who had been traveling from Santa Fe to Independence in April 1843, when he was robbed and murdered enroute. John McDaniel and his "band of western Missourians," most of whom were subsequently tried for murder and larceny. Josiah Gregg met with McDaniel, as well as Reuben Gentry and others who had been active in bringing about the arrest.[49] Of the convicted, McDaniel and Joseph Brown alone were executed; the others were later pardoned by the President of the United States.

Orrin Porter Rockwell is perhaps the most notable prisoner during Reynolds' term. Rockwell was charged with the attempted assassination of former Missouri Governor, Lilburn W. Boggs, who was by then a 50-year-old merchant on the north side of Independence Square.[50]

In his home in the 300 block of South Spring Street, on the rainy evening of May 6, 1842, Boggs was shot by an unknown assailant who fired at him through a window as he read a newspaper in his study. Boggs was hit by large buckshot in four places: two balls were lodged in his skull, another lodged in his neck, and a fourth entered his throat, whereupon Boggs swallowed it. Boggs was severely injured. Several doctors—Boggs' brother among them—

13

pronounced Boggs as good as dead. To everyone's great surprise, Boggs not only survived, but gradually improved.[51]

Orrin Porter Rockwell

Near the home a pistol was found and recognized as stolen from the Uhlinger bakery about a week before. He remembered that a man who called himself "Porter," who kept a stable for Mr. Ward, tried to buy it. Though "no evidence to warrant an indictment has been produced against him," Rockwell was arrested at Nauvoo, Illinois, on August 8, but escaped to Philadelphia. He was arrested again March 5, 1843, in St. Louis, while attempting to return to Nauvoo, and brought by stage to Independence and placed in the 1841 Jackson County Jail.[52]

Rockwell spent about 10 months confinement, eating corn dodger and poor meat, and sleeping on a scanty supply of dirty straw. Rockwell was confined with another man, named Watson, who had been arrested for stealing a large amount of money in New Orleans. These two prisoners were considered very desperate and brave, so the shackles were placed around their ankles. Joseph H. Jackson visited and, "found [Rockwell] with a pair of shackles on, and a lion skin overcoat—looked rather uncouth. There were however, so many in prison at this time, that I had no opportunity to converse with him."[53]

"A colored woman was accustomed to give them watermelons through the grated window, and, with a case-knife which they used to carve the melon, they sawed off the shackles from their ankles, and when the deputy came in at night to feed them, they both rushed out and locked the officer in, and ran for the woods. This is the second recorded jail break. They were, however, caught before they had proceeded far and again confined."[54]

Ultimately, Rockwell's trial was moved to Liberty, Clay County, Missouri, where he was exonerated "for want of the appearance of the principal prosecuting witness;" but, he was given a sentence of just *five minutes* for his attempted jail break.[55]

Lilburn W. Boggs

After recuperating, Boggs and his family left Independence Square in a 250-wagon train for California in April 1846.[56] He campaigned to be elected its captain, but lost to William H. Russell. When Russell resigned on June 18, the group was thereafter led by Boggs. Among the Boggs Company were most of the emigrants who later separated from the wagon train to form the ill-fated Donner Party. After another decade of public service in California, Boggs retired in 1855 to live on a ranch in Napa County, California, where he died on March 19, 1860.

Another tragic encounter happened to Sheriff Reynolds in 1843. He arrested and jailed a 70+ year-old man caught stealing clothes to stay warm. Apparently, he was returning home after venturing west, and had made it to Independence as the weather was turning cold. Destitute, depressed, and anguished from being incarcerated, the man cut his throat and nearly cut off his arm trying to sever the artery.[57] Unbelievably, he recovered. He was later released and continued his travel east with a purse of money and supplies collected for his trip by Sheriff Joe Reynolds and caring townspeople.

FATE OF THE 1841 JACKSON COUNTY JAIL

The 1841 Jackson County Jail served Jackson County until 1859 when the lot to the south was employed as the location for a common jail. The 1841 structure, however, continued in service for more than another half century.

The next spring, Sheriff Burrus announced on March 12, 1860, at the Jackson County Court, the sale of the 1841 Jackson County Jail and lot would be "expose[d] to sale by public outcry."[a] On May 2, Burrus recorded that, "Granville D. Page being the highest and last bidder" purchased at auction, "the old jail lot together with the old jail thereon situated, with exception of a strip eight feet wide off the south side" of Lot 2, for $1,520.[b] The 1881 *History of Jackson County* alludes to Page, who was identified as, "a negro trader, who carried on the slave trade there for a considerable time."[c]

By 1881, Charles E. Wilson was appointed a commissioner to the Jackson County Court to sell the property belonging to the County known as Lot No. 2 in the Old Town. The City of Independence proceeded to purchase the 1841 Jackson County Jail structure and lot and used it as a lock-up, or city jail...also called a calaboose.[d]

John Van Buren Martin, Jailor at the 1859 Jackson County Jail, "rebelled" in August 1905, declaring that, "no more city prisoners, drunks, and the like will be received at the County Jail. Only those for whom a state warrant is he obliged to receive. It has been the custom of the city officers to lodge all arrests at the county jail. These arrests are usually at night and the jailor is awakened at whatever hour. The city has no place to put them.'"[e]

By November, the street commissioner was instructed to make necessary repairs on the "City Calaboose" north of the County Jail.[f] Independence City Marshal Rice announced in December that the Independence holdover, or calaboose, was ready for prisoners, and Assistant City Marshals Price, Booth and Joseph began arresting; the result was noticed immediately and "the streets were so quite it could be felt."[g]

By the end of 1905, two prisoners were in the calaboose "helping make the foundation and move the fire department" to that site. The Independence Commercial Club began condemning the conditions of the City's jail in 1908.[h]

The Independence City Council ordered specifications for a new brick building for a city jail, "the old calaboose is unsanitary and cannot be remodeled satisfactorily."[i] The new city jail was located in the basement of the new City Hall constructed in 1909 at 200 South Main Street.[j]

The "sheet iron" or "iron clad" structure along Main Street remained in 1916 when it was part of the City Repair Shop. By 1926, while the footprint of the building remained constant on fire insurance maps, the "iron clad" identifiers were no longer present. In 1928, the Independence Fire Department constructed a new fire station at the location of the 1841 Jackson County Jail. J. E. Dunn Construction Company was awarded a $29,800 contract "for Station No. 1, contemplating the razing of the old shell at the southeast corner of Main Street and Van Horn Road and the erection of a modern, two-story structure.[k] It was thought that part of the 1841 brick structure was re-purposed into the fire house, which still stands and is presently (2009) being used as the Harry S Truman National Historic Site ticket office and visitors center. "The old frame shell that used to house fire company no. 1...rapidly is nearing demolition."[l]

[a] Jackson County Court minutes (11:354:99262).

[b] Jackson County Court minutes (11:358:99262; 393-394:99400). Page's two notes payable in six and twelve months had Albert G. Peters and Henry M. Stonestreet as his securities. In addition to the sale price was a $20 commission on $1,000 at 2 percent; a commission of $5.20 on $520 at 1 percent; and a $2 fee to be paid for hand bills.

[c] Birdsall, 639.

[d] Birdsall, 640. Hale and Beck, 7. Jackson County Court minutes (21:99).

[e] Anderson, Terry L. *Come and Spit on the Floor*, Volume 3:43 referencing *Jackson* (Independence, Mo.) *Examiner*, 4 Aug. 1905, 11:2.

[f] *Come and Spit on the Floor*, Volume 3:44 referencing *Jackson* (Independence, Mo.) *Examiner*, 24 Nov. 1905, 3:3. Also, "Work for Nightwatch Now," *Kansas City* (Mo.) *Star*, 25 Nov. 1905, 1.

[g] *Come and Spit on the Floor*, Volume 3:44 referencing *Jackson* (Independence, Mo.) *Examiner*, 1 Dec. 1905, 1:3; 11:1.

[h] *Come and Spit on the Floor*, Volume 3:44 referencing *Jackson* (Independence, Mo.) *Examiner*, 1 Dec. 1905, 11:1. See 1907 Sanborn fire insurance map, which shows the "iron clad" adjoining the "fire dept." building. Two separate "city jail/iron clad" structures set east on the lot. "This Jail is Unsanitary," *Kansas City* (Mo.) *Star*, 26 Nov. 1908.

[i] *Come and Spit on the Floor*, Volume 4:82-83 referencing *Jackson* (Independence, Mo.) *Examiner*, 15 Jan. 1909, 1:2. A hand made drawing of the calaboose is provided on page 83.

[j] *Come and Spit on the Floor*, Volume 5:38 referencing *Jackson* (Independence, Mo.) *Examiner*, 3 Feb. 1911, 1:5. "A Sheet Iron Jail to Go," *Kansas City* (Mo.) *Star*, 14 Jan. 1909.

[k] "To Negotiate Contracts Today," *Independence* (Mo.) *Examiner*, 8 Feb. 1928.

[l] "Razing Old Fire House," *Independence* (Mo.) *Examiner*, 16 Feb. 1928.

COLONEL THOMAS PITCHER (SHERIFF FROM 1845-1846)

Thomas Pitcher came from Kentucky to Jackson County and established residence on November 10, 1826. On January 3, 1828, he married Nancy Parrish, who had emigrated from Kentucky in 1825.[58] Pitcher was a prominent citizen and involved in many activities in the early development of Jackson County, including giving the site and building for the first public schools in Jackson County; the first Pitcher School.[59]

In 1833, Pitcher was a Colonel in the Missouri State Militia, and was responsible for leading the charge that forced the Mormons from Jackson County. In describing the uprising Pitcher reminisced years later about the events of November 1833; *"The Mormons concealed themselves in the woods just west of town where I met them and finally made a treaty with them, the conditions of which were that they were to surrender their arms and leave the county within ten days. They accepted the conditions of the treaty and surrendered and made a hurried flight from the county."* Pitcher was, after court action, ordered to return the munitions he had taken from the Mormons.[60]

Samuel Combs Owens

Pitcher was Jackson County Sheriff when the third and one of the most sensational jail breaks in Jackson County took place. In 1845, John Henry Harper eloped with Maria Frances Owens, daughter of prominent, early Jackson Countian, Samuel Combs Owens. It is said they were married by a Justice of the Peace on a country road "without alighting from their carriage." James C. Bean recorded having married the couple on May 29. However, on October 6, a preacher of the gospel, Robert D. Morrow, also recorded a marriage for the couple in the County Clerk's office. As local historian, Pearl Wilcox, explains, Mr. and Mrs. Owens *"were humiliated and chagrined by the union,"* and threatened to take their daughter away. *"Harper protested vigorously, threatened suicide, placed a pistol at his head, and pulled the trigger, which only snapped. 'Try this one,' suggested Mr. Owens, as he handed him one of his Colt revolvers. I have killed buffalo with them on the plains and have never known either of them to snap yet,' said the vexed father."*[61]

From all accounts, Miss Owens could do no wrong in her father's eyes, and she stretched the boundaries of acceptability for women at that time. One of her supposed flirtations with William W. Meredith, a boarder in the Owens home, aroused the jealousy of her husband. Harper asked Meredith into his office one day in 1846. Soon, a shot was heard, and Harper came running out calling for the Sheriff, saying he had killed a man. A crowd immediately collected and found Meredith breathing his last.[62]

Harper was arrested and lodged in the dungeon of the 1841 Jackson County Jail to await his trial for murder. The Sheriff kept careful watch when Mrs. Harper came to visit her husband, and allowed Harper upstairs. One day she begged the Sheriff to allow her to visit with her husband in private. When he returned, he saw the weeping woman peering down the door of the dungeon, and the shadow of the man in the dim interior.

The next morning, the Sheriff delivered breakfast to the prisoner and two delicate hands reached through the manhole. Mrs. Harper was discovered in the cell; her husband freed. Since the lady was well-connected politically and by family, she was allowed to go. Rewards were offered by Jackson County and Meredith's family in Baltimore; but, there was no trace of John Harper, who was said to have joined Colonel Doniphan in the war with Mexico.

In 1846, Sheriff Pitcher was given permission by the Jackson County Court to employ a guard for the 1841 Jackson County Jail—in addition to jailor—at rate of $1 per day and night. He was also permitted to employ the "present jailor, Davy D. Harral (probably Harrell)," to guard the jail at night along with the first guard at 62 1/2 cents per night.[63]

In the 1850 U.S. Census for Jackson County, 44-year-old Pitcher is listed with his wife, Nancy, age 39; and, their children: Gilbert S., 16; Victoria, 14; Julia A., 12; Thomas W., 8; Ardenia, 10; William G[ilpin], 6.

When the 1860 U.S. Census for Blue Township, Jackson County, was taken, Pitcher, 54; Nancy, 49; were listed with their children: Julia A. 18; Ardenia; 16; Thomas W. 13; Gilpin W[illiam], 11; Eli, 9; and John N., 1. At least three older children were already independent by that time: Gilbert S., 26, was listed in the household next to his parents, with one 6-year-old male slave. Victoria had married William Pinkston on October , 21, 1858. And, Lafayette, a miller, would return to his father's home by 1870.[64]

Pitcher was a slave owner. The Slave Schedules were listed at the same time as the Population Schedules every ten years. Slaves were only listed by age, gender, and race (black or mulatto, or mixed race). Judging from these identifies, it does not appear that Pitcher retained his slaves over their lifetimes:

1850			1860 (two slave houses)		
32	m		60	f	
40	f		40	m	
32	m		33	m	mulatto
21	m		28	m	
20	m		17	m	
18	f		24	f	mulatto
16	f	mulatto	23	f	mulatto
10	m	mulatto	10	m	mulatto
6 month old	m	mulatto	9	f	
			8	m	
			2	f	mulatto
			1	f	mulatto
			8 month old	f	mulatto
			2 month old	m	mulatto

Pitcher's large and grand house, like most in Jackson County, was destroyed with other property by marauding bands during the Civil War. Remarkably, the event was recorded years later by an eye-witness. James E. Payne, who was at one time an editor of the *Independence Sentinel* newspaper: "*As we reached Pitcher's Mill, we found that in ruins. On the opposite side of the road was Pitcher's house, the back part in flames, while from the front a gang of Jennison's Jayhawkers and Jim Lane's horse-thieves, now apotheosized into Union soldiers, were bringing out furniture, a piano and bedding, loading them into U.S. wagons to haul off to Kansas, as a testimonial to their loyalty and courage.*"[65]

Pitcher's wife, Nancy, died soon after the Civil War, around 1866.[66]

By 1870, Pitcher, a 64-year-old widower, was listed in the U.S. Census with children: Lafayette, 34; Julia, 28; Ardenia, 25; Thomas, 23; Gilpin, 21; Eli, 18; and, John, 16.

Colonel Thomas Pitcher, at 74, was listed in the 1880 U.S. Census with his two eldest, married daughters, and two granddaughters.[67]

Colonel Thomas Pitcher's once vast farmlands included present-day, historic Pitcher Cemetery along Blue Ridge Cutoff at 33rd Street. Pitcher was buried there, presumably without a tombstone, among other neighbors and kinsmen. There is also speculation that Pitcher *may* have later been re-interred into Woodlawn Cemetery.

BENJAMIN FRANKLIN THOMSON (SHERIFF FROM 1847-1848; 1853-1854)

Fugitive John Henry Harper was caught in 1847 at or near Fort Smith on the Arkansas River, and brought back to Independence for trial. Sheriff Benjamin Thomson and a guard were paid to go to Green County and back after Harper, who temporarily occupied his old quarters at the 1841 Jackson County Jail until a change in venue was made to Platte County.[68]

The defense was conducted, oddly enough, by Colonel Alexander William Doniphan, who had returned a hero of the Mexican War. Doniphan, who always took the side of the defense, had a remarkable record of never having lost a case. After an the most impassioned address ever heard in Platte County, according to competent witnesses who heard it, the jury acquitted Harper without leaving the jury box.[69]

Six years later, though, in December 1853, in Butte County, California, Harper was convicted of grand larceny and sentenced to 7 years in prison. The next month, Mrs. Harper, who claimed to have been a resident of San Francisco, California, since 1850, petitioned for a divorce. The Harper marriage was dissolved in May 1854.[70]

Benjamin Franklin Thomson was born January 19, 1817.[71] Before coming from Clark County, Kentucky, to Jackson County, Missouri, Thomson married Mariah Louisa (pronounced Mu-rI-uh Loo-I-zuh) Shortridge on September 14, 1837. There eldest son was, William S., was born in Kentucky about 1839. The Thomsons purchased a 140-acre plantation in November 1842. They were early members of the Christian Church at Independence; their membership records date back to June 1841.[72]

In between Thomson's two terms as Jackson County Sheriff , he was a State Representative of the 16th General Assembly of Missouri in 1850. Thomson's second term as Sheriff proved interesting, when in 1854, George W. Reynolds was confined to the Jackson County Jail for stabbing and killing John Blythe. Reynolds' jail break was short lived. John Reed happened to see Reynolds enter a stable loft just out of the City of Independence limits, and called an officer to recapture him. Reynolds was convicted and sentenced to five years in the penitentiary. But, before reaching the prison, a pardon was obtained.[73]

If you drive by today, the white paint has since been removed to reveal the red bricks.

18

The Thomson mansion, commonly called, "The Old Plantation," was built with slave labor in 1855.[74] The Thomson's appear to have kept a near-nuclear family of slaves, judging from Slave Schedules between 1850 and 1860 (the match in ages isn't exact, but close enough to presume they saw their two adult slaves in 1850 grow into a family by 1860):

1850		**1860 (one slave house)**	
22	m	30	m
18	f	26	f
		24	f (does not appear to be part of the family)
		9	f
		5	m
		3	f
		1	f

The Thomson home was constructed of bricks made of clay from the farm and dried in a kiln about one-fourth mile south of the house; the wood portions mostly of black walnut, were sawed on the spot. Though unoccupied, the "Old Plantation" stands today (2009) at 9802 East 40 Highway, amid a modern business district.[75] The home, originally built facing north but turned to face south many years later, served as a restaurant in recent memory. The structure is a rare example of Antebellum Jackson County plantation home (largely because of the devastation of Order No. 11; discussed below); its fate is yet to be determined.

In 1856, Thomson was Jackson County Assessor. In 1858-59, he was President of the Agricultural and Mechanical Association, an organization he helped establish in 1853. The Thomson's had eight sons and one daughter.[76] In the 1860 U.S. Census for Blue Township, Jackson County, Missouri, 43-year-old Benjamin F. and Maria (sic) L., 38, are listed with their children: William S., 21; Hanson S., 20; John H., 19; Matthew T., 16; Benjamin F., 9; Edwin H., 7; Charles H., 5; Robert B., 3; Anna M., seven months.

Benjamin Thomson died May 1, 1861, and was buried in Woodlawn Cemetery (then the City Cemetery for Independence, Missouri). His family moved from Jackson County shortly after Order No. 11 was issued (discussed below). The Thomson home became a headquarters for Union troops, and all the stock, implements and outbuildings were destroyed. Only the house was spared. Mrs. Thomson sold the "Old Plantation" in 1866 to Rev. Jacob Dunham Gossett, a Primitive Baptist minister who farmed through the week and preached on Sundays.[77]

    Thomson is the only known Jackson County Sheriff whose portrait was immortalized by famed Missouri painter George Caleb Bingham. Photographic reproductions of the original portraits of both Mr. and Mrs. Thomson were donated many years ago to the Jackson County Historical Society.[78]

GEORGE W. BUCHANAN (SHERIFF FROM 1849-1852)

    George W. Buchanan was born in Virginia in April 1814. After his education, he took up the study of law in that state. He came to "The Far West" and settled in Independence in 1839, where he taught school for two years, was postmaster for one term. He served Jackson County as Surveyor from 1844 to 1848, when he was elected and served two terms as Sheriff.[79]

    Since 1827, traders had migrated back and forth between Independence and Santa Fe, then in Mexico.

    By the 1840s, Independence, a burgeoning community, was outfitting an increasing transient group…travelers on the westward trails. The anxiety and stirring of a frontier river town like Independence yielded itself to a variety of characters. The supply-driven market of Independence bustled with activity…and less desirable behaviors. This strained local government's ability to provide law and order as the county seat swelled each spring with westward travelers waiting to "jump off" from Independence.

Missionaries Marcus and Narcissa Whitman in 1843 guided the first "Great Migration" to the West by leading a wagon train of 1,000 pioneers from Independence along the Oregon Trail to Oregon, where they had been since 1836. The 1841 Bidwell Bartleson Party and 1846 expedition of Colonel Alexander William Doniphan brought attention to Spanish California and territory that became the American Southwest.

Sheriff Buchanan's eyes must have widened, however, as hundreds of thousands of travelers began funneling through Independence beginning in the Spring of 1849 after discovery of gold at Sutter's Mill the previous Autumn.[80] (Captain John A. Sutter, by the way, had previously been a Westport merchant in Jackson County, Missouri.)

On August 2, 1849, the Jackson County Court "gave leave" to the City of Independence to use the 1841 Jackson County Jail.[81]

On November 23, 1849, Sheriff George W. Buchanan married Miss Eliza Jane Galbraith, the daughter of John and Katherine (Peers) Galbraith, who was born in Rockbridge County, Virginia, in April 1823.[82] The newlyweds are listed in the 1850 United States Census for Jackson County.

In the 1850 U.S. Census for Jackson County, Missouri, 36-year-old Sheriff Buchanan, a native of Indiana, was listed with his wife, Eliza J., a 27-year-old native Virginian, and their daughter Martha M., age 4. The Slave Schedules included two slaves: a 25-year-old female, and a 5-year-old male.

Captain John A. Sutter

In the 1860 U.S. Census, Buchanan, 46, is listed as a lawyer with is wife, Eliza J., 37, and their children: Catherine A., 9; James F., 7; Mary S., 3; and, George, about three months. Ten years later in 1870, the family unit consisted of George, 55; Eliza, 46; Kate, 19; James, 17; Scottie (female), 15; George, 10; and, Amy Ash, an 8-year-old black girl (who appears to have been free since she was listed by name in the Population Schedules). Buchanan also had a 14-year-old female (mulatto) slave, who was listed separately on the Slave Schedules.

Buchanan was on the first Board of Trustees of the Independence Female College in 1871. Only daughters Catherine A., 29; and, Mary S., 22; were living with their parents, G.W. and Eliza J. Buchanan, aged 66 and 57 respectively, when the 1880 U.S. Census was taken. And, in 1881, Buchanan was listed as a member of the Independence Bar.[83]

Twenty years later, at ages 86 and 77, George and Eliza continued to reside with their 49-year-old, single daughter, Catherine A., at 202 South Spring Street, in Independence, Missouri. A 13-year-old granddaughter, Mary E. Buchanan, was also staying with them at the time.

George W. Buchanan died in 1901. 91-year-old Eliza Jane (Galbraith) Buchanan died 22 Oct. 1914. They and other members of their family are buried in Woodlawn Cemetery.[84]

WILLIAM BOTTS (SHERIFF FROM 1855-1858)

William Botts was elected the next Sheriff of Jackson County.

He was born October 20, 1809,[85] and came from Tennessee and settled four miles northeast of Independence in Jackson County, Missouri, in October 1841.[86] He married native Kentuckian Miss Elzira Trimbell on November 3, 1842.[87]

In the 1850 U.S. Census for Blue Township, Jackson County, Missouri, Botts was listed as a gunsmith. Their children were: Emma, age 6, born in Kentucky; Albert, 4, Missouri; Susan, 2, Missouri. It did not appear that they had slaves in 1850.

Another factor escalating lawlessness in the border region of Independence, Town of Kansas, and Westport at this time was the passage of the Kansas-Nebraska Act in 1854. The Act left to the settlers of the Kansas Territory whether it would become a "free" state or "slave" state. Immediately, Missourians who had largely come to this area from the south—many with slaves—were face to face with abolitionist northeastern settlers flocking into Kansas Territory. For nearly seven years before the Civil War began, pro-slavery Missourians and Free State Kansans terrorized one another in violent and escalating guerilla warfare. Richard S. Brownlee described the situation:

"From 1855 until 1860 the situation on the border [between Kansas and Missouri] approached anarchy. Missouri gangs invaded Kansas and besieged and occupied Lawrence. To obtain arms they looted the United States Arsenal at Liberty Landing at home. Numerous fights and murders took place over land claims and these embroilments were eagerly identified with the slavery issue. Along the state line men banded together and formed protective and raiding associations, and, as usual in such twilight areas, characters of the most fanatic and vicious temperament were drawn to the scene."[88]

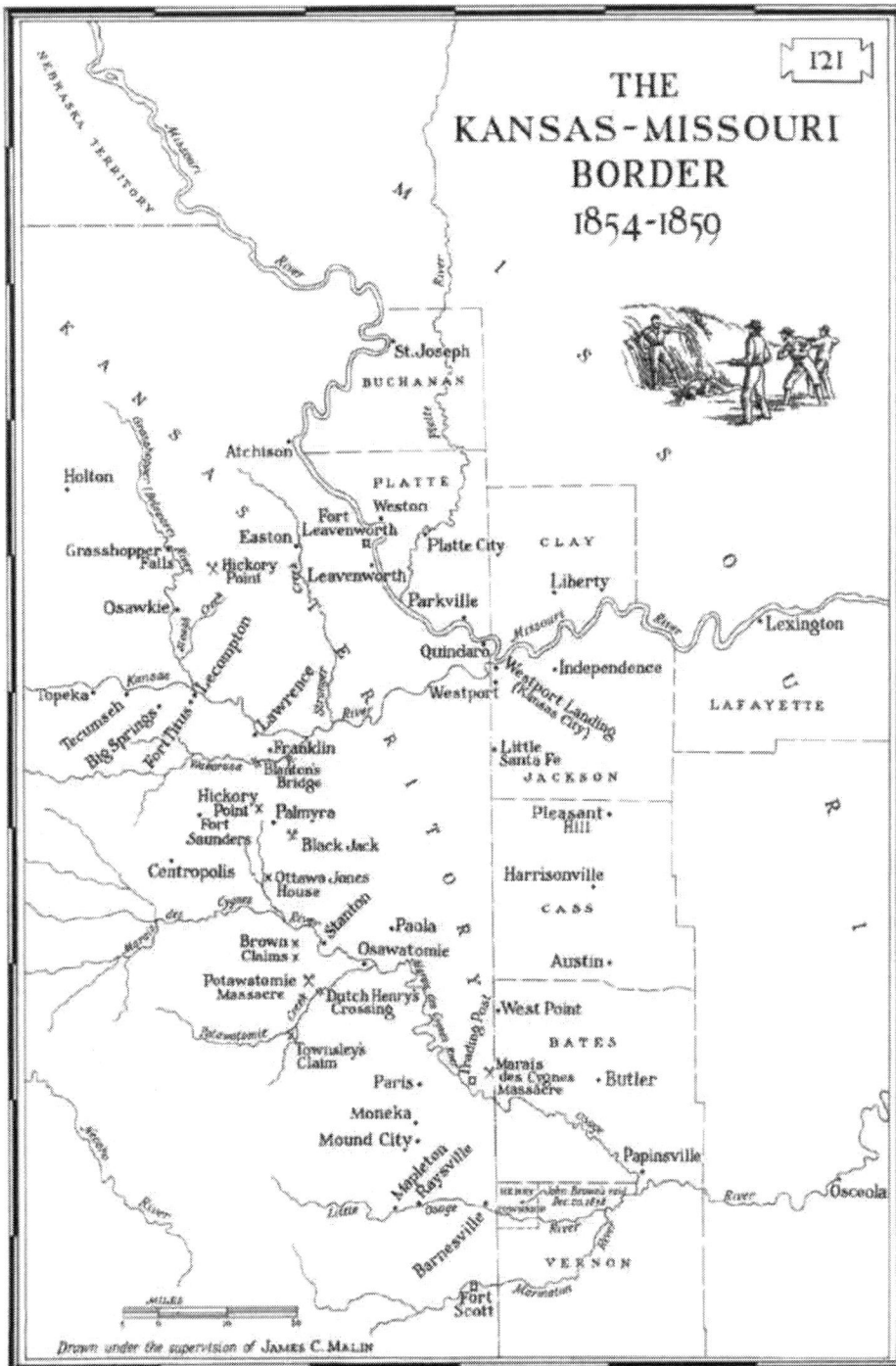

THE
KANSAS-MISSOURI
BORDER
1854-1859

Drawn under the supervision of JAMES C. MALIN.

    By 1860, the Botts family consisted of William, a 50-year-old farmer; Eliza (sic.), 35; and their children: Amy, 16; Albert, 14; Eliza, 9; Georgia, 5; Breckenridge, 3; and, Marion, 1.[89] They also had a small slave family—judging from the Slave Schedules—that list a 25-year-old male; 18-year-old female; and, a 1-year-old male. Other Botts children were: Susan A., born in 1849; Alice, 1861; William, Jr., 1867; and, Margaret Lee, 1868.[90]

    William Botts died August 5, 1889. Mrs. Elzira Botts died February 6, 1901. They are buried in Woodlawn Cemetery in Independence, Missouri.[91]

23

MAJOR JOHN W. BURRUS (SHERIFF FROM 1859-1861)

Sheriff Burrus was elected for two consecutive terms; but, he died during his second term in office. The surname is sometimes spelled Burris, but most frequently, Burrus.

The previous year when the 1860 U.S. Census for Sni-A-Bar Township, Jackson County, Missouri, was taken, 47-year-old Burrus was listed as "High Sheriff," with his wife, Mary A. [Huffman], a native Missourian, age 34; and, their children: Thomas, 14 (born ca. 1846); James W., 12; John H., 10; Taylor, 8; Ann E., 6; Elizabeth, 5; and Allen, 3.[92] According to Slave Schedules for that year, they also had eight slaves that *appear* to be a nuclear family unit living in one slave house: 54-year-old female; 34, male; 21, male; 21, female; 16, female; 13, male; 3, male; and 1, female.

Confrontations between Missourians and Kansans, rivaling events that had been escalating since 1854 and became known as the "border war," were a prelude to the Civil War.

Growing hostilities may have led the Jackson County Court to approve plans to build a new Jackson County Jail on Main Street.

---

[1] Clemenson, Gay L. "Keeping the Peace in Jackson County, Missouri, 1927-1887," (University of Missouri at Kansas City, History Department, January 27, 1998), 6. Unpublished manuscript, Jackson County Historical Society Archives, Document ID 269F10.

[2] Myers, Gwen L. "History of the Jackson County Sheriff's Department, 1827-1970." Unpublished manuscript, Jackson County Historical Society Archives, Document ID 13F17.

[3] Lauderdale, Beverly. "Camped in Yosemite: Captain Joseph R. Walker," *True West*, October (1993), 46-51, available in the Jackson County Historical Society Archives, Document ID L97F13. Elsewhere in her article, Lauderdale claims "Joseph may have been born in Virginia, rather than Tennessee." The Roan County, Tennessee, data was derived from Walker's gravestone.

[4] His brother Joel Walker was the first Justice of the Peace in Jackson County, Missouri. Lauderdale, 46.

[5] Myers, 1.

[6] Lauderdale, 47.

[7] Flinn, John. "Two Hikers Follow First White Man's Path Into Valley," Undated, unattributed article in the newspaper clipping files about Walker at the Jackson County Historical Society Archives.

[8] Lauderdale, 47.

[9] He is buried in Alhambra Cemetery in Martinez, where his headstone recounts the highlights of his career. James' son, John "Johnnie" Walker (1862-1942), remained on the ranch after his father's death, and continued in the cattle business for almost three decades. His herd numbered over 1,500 cattle. John married Margaret McDonald Walker in 1886. They had seven children, all born on the ranch created by James (mdia.org/). Birdsall, 106-108, 113, 179, 307, 316, 326, 635, 642. Hickman, 139. Wilcox, 43, 130, 234. Jackson County Court minutes (1:17, 29, 32, 43, 50, 51, 62, 65, 106, 120, 129). See also Gilbert, Bil. *Westering Man: The Life of Joseph Walker, Master of the Frontier*. (New York: Atheneum, 1983). An oral history interview between Gilbert and Sue Gentry may be accessed in the audio-visual collections of the Jackson County Historical Society's Archives. Also, Lauderdale, 51.

[10] Jackson County Marriage Records (records.co.jackson.mo.us/results.asp; viewed 8 May 2006).

[11] Birdsall, 107, 110 (Brown's middle initial might have been "C."), 179, 186, 635, 636, 642. Hickman, 148, 159.

[12] His father, Harmon Gregg, was Scotch Irish, and his mother was German. The Greggs moved to Illinois in 1811, southeast of St. Louis, where they were at the time of the famous New Madrid earthquakes. Harmon traded a horse for 100 acres of land that is today in the heart of St. Louis, including the site of the Lindell Hotel (as of 1893). He "got tired of his land in the 'little French town' and traded back. From 1812 to 1815 they were inmates at Cooper's Fort in what is now Boone County, Missouri. When the Indians became peaceful enough, they moved to Howard County, Missouri, where a creek bears their family name. In 1818, Gregg saw the first steamboat come up the Missouri River as far as Chariton. Additional details may be found in an informative article in the Jackson County Historical Society Archives, Document ID 167.38F32, by Dorothy Butler, "Lick Skillet," *Oak Grove* (Mo.) *Banner*, 22 Jul. 1971, which provides a reprint from the *Banner* from 22 Apr. 1893, "Sketch of an Old Pioneer: Jacob Gregg Celebrated His 91st Birthday April 9th."

[13] Wilcox, 430-431. For another incident surrounding the "Mormon War," see Jackson County Sheriff Thomas Pitcher's biographical sketch.

[14] A biographical note says Gregg was elected Sheriff in 1832 until 1836 (Birdsall, 316). However, another notation mentioning an August 1834 general election said that John King was elected Sheriff (Birdsall, 333-334).

[15] Jackson County Court minutes (1:8-1826 Census; 51, 52, 56, 60, 63-64, 67-69, 71, 73, 75, 78, 80, 82, 86, 88, 92-94, 97, 101, 113, 117-119, 128, 131, 135, 159, 165, 168, 173-1832 Census, 177, 180, 186, 189, 198, 206, 212). The 1881 *History of Jackson County* alludes to Gregg taking the 1836 Missouri State Census. Birdsall, 314. Results or transcriptions of these early Censuses are not known to have survived. For his fine for contempt of court see Jackson County Court minutes (1:217).

[16] Wilcox, Pearl. *Jackson County Pioneers*. Reprint. (Independence, Mo.: Jackson County Historical Society, 1990), 71, 82, 124-125, 127, 131, 137.

[17] Jackson County Marriage Records. Birdsall, 186.

[18] One slave of Samuel Gregg was Ellen Sugg. See Jackson County Historical Society Archives photograph ID jchs002942m.

[19] Birdsall, 181.

[20] *St. Louis* (Mo.) *Post Dispatch*, 24 Aug. 1902. William H. Gregg was a captain in William Clarke Quantrill's outfit, and helped organize the 1902 Quantrill reunion in Independence, Missouri.

[21] "Met After 43 Years," *Kansas City* (Mo.) *Star*, 17 Jul. 1906.

[22] Birdsall, 102, 107, 111-113, 148-149, 152, 157, 179, 181, 186, 297-298, 314-316, 320, 323, 633-636, 642-643. Hickman, 149, 157, 161-163, 265, 266, 270, 719.

[23] Daughters of the American Revolution—Kansas City Chapter. *Vital Historical Records of Jackson County, Missouri: 1826-1876*. Reprint. (Independence, Mo.: Jackson County Historical Society, 2008), 377.

[24] A clipping (likely the *Oak Grove* (Mo.) *Banner*, 13 July 1895, located in the Jackson County Historical Society Archives, Document ID 167.39F8, reads: *"SUED FOR WAGES: The suit of Sallie Clark, colored, against the estate of Jacob Gregg, deceased, appealed from probate court, was filed with the circuit clerk Friday. The plaintiff brought suit against the estate in the lower court for $1,500, which she claimed was due her for wages, covering a period of 12 years. The petition sets out that the plaintiff, prior to the emancipation of slaves, was owned by Jacob Gregg. Twelve years ago her former master, who was living at Grain Valley, sent for her, asking that she make her home with him. Under promise of remuneration she did so, but her employer died, leaving no bequest in his will, or pay for her years of toil. Her claim was disallowed by the administrator, and suit followed in the probate court, where she received a judgment of $150. From this judgment, Frank Gregg, the administrator appealed."*

[25] Daughters of the American Revolution—Kansas City Chapter, 377.

[26] Birdsall, 111. References to an August 1834 general election mentioned that King was elected Sheriff (Birdsall, 333-334).

[27] Ibid., 643.

[28] Bundschu, William B. *Abuse and Murder on the Frontier: The Trials and Travels of Rebecca Hawkins, 1800-1860.* (Independence, Mo.: Little Blue Valley Publishing Co., 2003), 130.

[29] Ibid., 106.

[30] Birdsall, 640. Also, Hale, Donald R. and Vicki P. Beck. *History of the 1859 Jail and other Early Jails Located in Independence, Missouri.* (Independence, Mo.: Blue & Grey Bookshoppe, 2001), 2.

[31] "The First Death Warrant," undated newspaper clipping in the Jackson County Historical Society Archives. Additional citations appear in *Appendix B: Legal Hangings in Jackson County, Missouri, 1839-June 1933.* Another account says that, "He [Gastell, sic.] was taken from the jail to the lot where the Chicago & Alton depot now stands [1905] in a big two horse wagon. He rode in the wagon sitting on an old fashioned wooden chair. The execution was public. The rope was tied around Gastell's neck and then the wagon driven under the uprights supporting a cross bar and the other end tied to this bar. Gastell was made to stand in the chair and the wagon was driven from under him." When this article was written, Ember Mason, a witness to this first execution, had "the chair on which the condemned man sat when hauled to the place of execution in a big wagon." "The First Hanging: A Man Named Gastell was Hung in 1839 near C & A Depot..." *Jackson* (Independence Mo.) *Examiner*, 27 Oct 1905.

[32] "The Penalty Paid. Edward Calhoun Sneed Hanged at Independence Soon after Noonday His Last Day," *Kansas City* (Mo.) *Star,* 24 June 1887, 1.

[33] "Leads in Macadam Roads," *Kansas City* (Mo.) *Star*, 2 Oct. 1898, 11, 1.

[34] Birdsall, 181.

[35] Ibid., 643.

[36] Reynolds' middle initial is a quandary. Marshall and Morrison (page 82) listed it as "**R**." His tombstone inscription reads "**N**." (Daughters of the American Revolution—Independence Pioneers Chapter. *Woodlawn Cemetery Tombstone Inscriptions*). Both his marriage certificate to Mary Ward and the 1860 Census lists his middle initial as "**H**." His birth date was calculated from his tombstone, indicating he died at age 71 years, 4 months, 21 days.

[37] Birdsall, 105, 111, 179, 181, 297, 641, 643, 664. Hickman, 92.

[38] A spot check of the Jackson County Court minutes show him as Sheriff on 20 Aug 1840 (3:265); and, on 3 Aug 1842 (4:21). He was "former Sheriff" in 1845 (5:79). As noted in the introduction to *Appendix A: Lawmen Serving Jackson County in Independence, Missouri: 1827-1933*, we've listed his span of dates to include the full years (January-December) for which he was elected, even though he obviously was in office some months prior to January 1841.

[39] Jackson County Marriage Records.

[40] Mary C. Reynolds had died the previous year on 5 Nov. 1883. Daughters of the American Revolution—Independence Pioneers Chapter. *Woodlawn Cemetery Tombstone Inscriptions.*

[41] Birdsall, 640.

[42] Jackson County Court minutes (3:383).

[43] Ibid., (3:387).

[44] Birdsall, 640.

[45] Ibid., 640.

[46] Years later, Mrs. Robert M. Anderson, assistant coordinator at the 1859 Jail, Marshal's Home and Museum, displayed a pair of handcuff keys. *Kansas City* (Mo.) *Star*, 27 Aug. 1963, 4. In September 1963, Harvey Kemper attended a public function and showed a pair of handcuffs handed down in his family that had once been used at the Jackson County Jail; the disposition of these was not mentioned in the article. *Kansas City* (Mo.) *Star*, 26 Oct. 1963, 6. In 1996, Jailor Hardin T. Hall's granddaughter donated a lock that had been used on ankle irons. A key, which had been donated the previous year by the family of another former deputy, was inserted into the ankle iron lock...and opened it. See, "New Acquisitions at Jail Museum Bring More History Back Home." *Jackson County Historical Society JOURNAL* 1996 (Summer) 36:2, 3. Another key was secured in 2005. *Jackson County Historical Society JOURNAL* 2005 (Autumn) 46:2, 27. As will be discussed later in this text, Mother Mary Jerome Shubrick's key also found its way back to the 1859 Jackson County Jail.

[47] Birdsall, 640.

[48] Jackson County Court minutes (5:91).

[49] Gregg, Josiah. *Commerce of the Prairies.* (New York: J. & H. G. Langley, 1845, c. 1844). Wilcox, Pearl. Jackson County Pioneers. (Independence, Mo: Jackson County Historical Society, 1991), 213-214. Reuben was the Santa Fe trader who spread the alarm; Nicholas Gentry had been a wagon master in this posse. Blackmar, Frank W., ed.

Kansas: A Cyclopedia of State History. Volume I. (Chicago, Il.: Standard Pub. Co., 1912), 316-317. Ball, Larry D. "Federal Justice on the Santa Fe Trail: The Murder of Antonio Jose Chavez." *Missouri Historical Review* 1986 (October) 81:1, 1-17. Eakin, Joanne Chiles. "Twenty-Year-Old Murder Mystery is Recalled in 1864," and "Some Published Accounts About the Chavez Murder," *Blue and Grey Chronicle*, Vol. 3, No. 3, p. 1-3.

[50] Boggs married his first wife in 1817 in Greenup County, Kentucky, Julia Ann Bent, a sister of the Bent brothers who founded Bent's Fort. She died on 21 Sep. 1820 in St. Louis, Missouri. They had two children, Angus and Henry. In 1823, Boggs married Panthea Grant Boone (1801-1880), a granddaughter of Daniel Boone, in Callaway County, Missouri. They spent most of the following 23 years in Jackson County, Missouri, where all but two of their many children were born. Boggs started out as a merchant, then entered politics. He served as a Missouri State Senator in 1826 to 1832; as lieutenant governor under Governor Daniel Dunklin from 1832 to 1836; governor from 30 Sep. 1836 to 16 Nov. 1840; and again as state senator from 1842 to 1846 (en.wikipedia.org/wiki/Governor_of_Missouri; viewed 2 Feb. 2009). Boggs was a member of California state assembly 19th District, 1852-53. He died 14 Mar. 1860, and is buried in Tulocay Cemetery, Napa, California. (politicalgraveyard.com/bio/boggs.html#RIO04VJWW; viewed 18 Mar 2009).

[51] Initially, Mormon prophet Joseph Smith was automatically assumed to have been behind the attempted murder, because of Bogg's tough action against the Mormons a decade before. Smith, who was later discharged, responded to a slanderous comment printed in the Quincy (Il.) Whig: *You have done me manifest injustice in ascribing to me a prediction of the demise of Lilburn W. Boggs, Esq., Ex-Governor of Missouri, by violent hands. Boggs was a candidate for the State Senate, and I presume, fell by the hand of a political opponent...but he did not through my instrumentality. My hands are clean and my heart pure, from the blood of all men,* The Weekly (Ny.) *Herald* 18 June 1842, 309. *Jefferson City* (Mo.) *Republican*, 14 May 1842. News of the shooting was syndicated all over the country. Some accounts more descriptive than others. Some even proclaimed that Boggs had died, and ran obituaries. A $300 reward was initially posted for the capture of the unknown band, *The (Maryland) Sun*, 23 May 1842, 2. *Daily Ohio Statesman*, 25 May 1842. Missouri Governor Reynolds offered a $600 reward for both Rockwell and Joseph Smith, "or $300 for either of them," *The* (Md.) *Sun*, 7 Oct, 1842, 2. Also, F.A. Sampson, ed., "A Short Biographical Sketch of Lilburn W. Boggs, by His Son." *Missouri Historical Review*, Vol. IV (October 1909-July 1910): 106-110.

[52] "Untitled," *The Daily* (La.) *Picayune*, 20 Sept. 1843, 2. Also unverified sources: *Missouri Historical Review*, 1909, 107. *Columbia Patriot*, 21 May 1842. *Jefferson Republican*, 11 Mar 1843. *History of the Reorganized Church of Latter Day Saints*, 1:360; *History of the Church of Jesus Christ of Latter Day Saints*, 6:137.

[53] "Wonderful Disclosures Respecting Mormonism: A Narrative of the Adventures and Experience of Joseph H. Jackson, in Nauvoo, Disclosing the Depths of Mormon Villainy," *The Weekly Herald*, 7 Sept. 1844, 286. Also, Wilcox, 431-433.

[54] Birdsall, 642. Watson was acquitted for want of proof.

[55] Ibid., 642. The *Southern* (Sc.) *Patriot*, 10 Jan 1844, 2. Although sentenced to five minutes imprisonment in the county jail, he was kept there five hours, while his captors tried to think of some other charge to make against him. He was finally released. Emaciated, Rockwell arrived back in Nauvoo on Christmas evening, 1843—the last Christmas day Joseph and Hyrum Smith celebrated on earth—a large party assembled at the Smith's home, and spent the time in music, dancing and a social visit. During the festivities, a man with long shaggy hair, apparently drunk, came in and acted like a Missourian. A scuffle ensued and Smith had an opportunity to see the stranger's face. To his great surprise and joy he discovered his "long-tried, warm, but cruelly persecuted friend, Orrin Porter Rockwell." The party came to order while Rockwell related in detail his experiences and sufferings while in Missouri. Smith, *History of the Church* 5:135-42. Schindler, *Orrin Porter Rockwell*, Chapter 5. Rockwell later continued to with Brigham Young to Salt Lake City, where Rockwell became one of the Utah Territory's earliest lawmen, "deputy marshal for the provisional state of Deseret in 1849." Schindler, Harold. *Orrin Porter Rockwell: Man of God, Son of Thunder* (University of Utah Press, 1966; second edition 1983); and, Esshom, Frank. *Pioneers and Prominent Men of Utah* (Salt Lake City, Ut.: Utah Pioneers Book Pub. Co., 1913).

[56] The author's maternal ancestors were also in this huge wagon train. For detailed accounts of the Campbell's 1846 migration from Independence Square, consult: Jackson, David W. *Direct Your Letters to San Jose: The Letters and Diary of James and David Lee Campbell, 1848-1852.* (Kansas City, Mo.: The Orderly Pack Rat, 2000).

[57] Birdsall, 642.

[58] Jackson County Marriage Records.

[59] Birdsall, 106, 150, 179, 185, 256-259, 261, 277, 297, 635, 643. Hickman, 148, 162, 164, 193, 240, 267, 339

[60] "Governor Dunklin Takes a Hand," www.centerplace.org/history/misc/soc/soc20.htm (as viewed 10 January 2009. Also, "Mormon History: Col. Thomas Pitcher Gives the Journal Readers His Recollections of Mormonism in this County: Events of the Memorable Year of 1833 by one of the Participants," *Kansas City Daily Journal,* 19 June 1881. Birdsall, 193.

[61] Wilcox, 433-435.

[62] Birdsall, 641.

[63] Jackson County Court minutes (6:233).

[64] Gilbert A. Pitcher married Nancy C. Johnson ,1 Feb. 1855; Ardenia Pitcher married Frank Carroll, 22 May 1870; Thomas W. Pitcher married Jennie T. Smithers, 1 Feb. 1871; Lafayette Pitcher married Mary E. Frye, 23 Aug. 1871; and, William Gilpin Pitcher married Matilda A. Parrish, 22 Mar. 1877 (he later married Flora Emilla Lewis on 12 June 1907).

[65] As reported As reported in the *Independence* (Mo.) *Examiner,* 4 Sep. 1933, and re-printed in "The Battle of Rock Creek," by Joanne Chiles Eakin, 10-11. See also, Paul R. Petersen's *Quantrill in Missouri* (Nashville, Tn.: Cumberland House, 2003), 70-71, which provides a more exacting chronology of events and the specific regiments and companies involved.

[66] Daughters of the American Revolution—Kansas City Chapter. *Vital Historical Records of Jackson County, Missouri: 1826-1876.* Reprint. (Independence, Mo.: Jackson County Historical Society, 2008), 254. The contribution of Mrs. M. A. Pitcher says that "Nancy Noland Pitcher died about 1866." The biography of E. P. Burton, who married Katherine Pitcher (daughter of Gilbert S. and Mary Elizabeth Pitcher), records Thomas Pitcher's wife as Nancy Parrish. Birdsall, 339. Jackson County Marriage Records confirm her surname.

[67] Julia Shoemaker, 38; and, Idina (sic.) Gray (sic.), 36; and, two granddaughters, Nancy Carroll, 9; and, Nina Gray, 4. [Ardenia had married Frank Carroll in Jackson County on May 22, 1870.] From this Census return, it isn't possible to ascertain clarity on the accuracy of the genealogy.

[68] Jackson County Court minutes (6:234)

[69] Wilcox, 433-435. Jackson County marriage records. Hickman, 176. Also, "Old Jail Figured in Romance, War, and Tragedy," *Kansas City* (Mo.) *Star,* 28 Mar. 1920. Also unverified sources: *Kansas City* (Mo.) *Post,* 2 Apr 1916; and, *Kansas City* (Mo.) *Star,* 30 Mar 1947.

[70] Jackson County Historical Society Archives, *Abstract of Title Collection,* the "Old Plantation," NE ¼ NE ¼ Section 20, Township 49, Range 32.

[71] Daughters of the American Revolution—Independence Pioneers Chapter. *Woodlawn Cemetery Tombstone Inscriptions.*

[72] Daughters of the American Revolution—Kansas City Chapter. *Vital Historical Records of Jackson County, Missouri: 1826-1876.* Reprint. (Independence, Mo.: Jackson County Historical Society, 2008), 123.

[73] Myers, 9. Birdsall, 642.

[74] Karl Kiekert "Old Plantation" Collection, Jackson County Historical Society Archives, Document ID L4F23. Another source in this collection says the home was finished in 1849.

[75] Jackson County assessment records show the address as 9800 E US 40 Hwy; Lots 150 and 151 of East Hollywood Addition.

[76] Birdsall, 179, 181, 229, 239, 297,643, 656.

[77] Karl Kiekert "Old Plantation" Collection, Jackson County Historical Society Archives, Document ID L4F23.

[78] The location of the original paintings is not known at the time of this printing (2009). It is hoped that they might one day be donated to the Society for the enjoyment of future Jackson Countians.

[79] [Obituary], *Jackson* (Independence, Mo.) *Examiner,* 14 June 1901, 5:2. Wilcox, 167-168, 279, 332, 419, 467.

[80] Jackson, David W. *Direct Your Letters to San Jose: The California Gold Rush Letters of James and David Lee Campbell, 1849-1852.* (Kansas City, Mo.: The Orderly Pack Rat, 2000), 1-2. Clemenson, 16.

[81] Jackson County Court minutes (7:461). The author located a newspaper article that reported the arrival to Independence on 25 Aug. 1849, Mr. Mitchell from Santa Fe, and also Aubry's and White's teams. A detachment of troops from Fort Leavenworth had also arrived, bringing with them the two Indians concerned in the murder of Mr. Norris Colburn, on the route from Santa Fe one or two years prior. The Indians "were committed to jail in Independence, and will be tried, we presume, at the next term of the U.S. District Court." *Daily Missouri Republican,* 31 Aug. 1849.

[82] Jackson County Marriage Records.

[83] Birdsall, 179-180, 236, 643, 660.

[84] Missouri Death Certificate Number 32194. Daughters of the American Revolution—Independence Pioneers Chapter. *Woodlawn Cemetery Tombstone Inscriptions.*

[85] William Botts Family Collection, Jackson County Historical Society Archives, Botts Family Bible,

Document ID 71.01F1.

[86] Birdsall, 136, 179, 643. Hickman, 247.

[87] Jackson County Marriage Records.

[88] Brownlee, Richard S. *Gray Ghosts of the Confederacy* (Baton Rouge, La.: Louisiana State University Press, 1984), 9.

[89] Jackson County Marriage Records list two marriages, though, at the time of this printing (2009) the authors are not aware of their connection to this Botts family: William Botts married Emily Parish on 21 Feb. 1865; William L. Botts married Eliza J. Botts on 29 Jan. 1868.

[90] William Botts Family Collection, Jackson County Historical Society Archives, Botts Family Bible, Document ID 71.01F1.

[91] Ibid. Daughters of the American Revolution—Independence Pioneers Chapter. *Woodlawn Cemetery Tombstone Inscriptions*.

[92] We found a "John Burriss" (sic) marrying Miss Sarah Hooper on New Year's Day in 1837. However, we did not see a marriage between Burrus and Mary A. Huffman in Jackson County. "Mary Ann Burris" became a member of the Church of Christ at Lone Jack, Missouri, on 24 July 1854. James W. Burrus was born 15 Oct. 1847 – died 3 Apr. 1919. He married Virginia M. Tucker in Jackson County on 23 Jan. 1874. They, together with James M. (23 May 1819-6 Oct. 1893) Burrus and George W. (13 Aug. 1843-16 May 1861) Burrus are buried in Blue Springs Cemetery. James W. Burrus' death certificate also revealed his mother's maiden name as Huffman. Jackson County Marriage Records. Missouri Death Certificate Number 13740. Also, Daughters of the American Revolution—Kansas City Chapter. *Vital Historical Records of Jackson County, Missouri: 1826-1876*. Reprint. (Independence, Mo.: Jackson County Historical Society, 2008), 127, 329.

CELL

3

BORDER WAR LED TO NEW JACKSON COUNTY JAIL (1858-1860)

1859 JACKSON COUNTY JAIL (MADE OF LIMESTONE)

By this time, Jennison and the Jayhawks and Red legs had gained the upper hand in Kansas and were a real threat to Independence, a town with many slave owners situated close to the border. Lawlessness on both sides contributed to fears. The need for security resulted in a solid investment in law and order with the erection of an impressive county jail. Sheriff Burrus saw the new, state-of-the-art Jackson County Jail constructed.

Peter and Sally Gastell sold Lot 3, Old Town Independence (just south of the 1841 Jackson County Jail site) to Jackson County for $600 in December 1858.[1]

On November 4, 1858, the Jackson County Court had ordered the clerk to solicit designs for a jail.[2] At the January 1859 term, the adoption of the plans of the Jail was continued to the third day of the February term when it was recorded that, *"The Court adopts the plan of ___ Cross of a Jail to be built for Jackson County, and appropriate the sum of $10,000 out of the County revenue proper for a building of the same upon said plan and specifications now on file in the office of the clerk of the Jackson County Court."* Architect A. B. Cross is identified more explicitly in a subsequent entry.[3]

Asa Beebe Cross arrived in the 1850s from St. Louis. The authors' recent discovery of Cross as the architect of the 1859 Jackson County Jail re-writes previously known data about "the pioneer architect of Kansas City." **The 1859 Jackson County Jail is the FIRST *documented AND surviving* local structure designed by A. B. Cross.**[4]

Cross' office, first door on left

Asa Beebe Cross

31

← J A I L ←

On July 5, 1859, Henry Bugler, who was employed during this time by the County to "guard the [1841 Jackson County] Jail," was paid $11 "for removing house off [the 1859 Jackson County] Jail lot."[5] This action cleared Lot 3 for the construction of the 1859 Jackson County Jail.

On April 5, 1859, Samuel J. Platt and John B. Moore, of Kansas City, were hired by the Jackson County Court as contractors to oversee the various work needed to raise the structure.

First of five pages of specifications for the 1859 Jackson County Jail.

Another bidder, J. Huston, had failed to put up a surety bond. The total cost allotted for the construction project was $12,462.[6] Judging from examined warrants for payment between 1859 and 1860, it appears the actual cost was $11,844.20.[7]

The residence portion of the site might have been completed first. On October 3, 1859, Y. W. Barker was paid $3.60 for putting glass both in the Jail and Courthouse.[8]

From Jackson County Court minutes, it appears that the 1859 Jackson County Jail was completed between February and March 1860. At that time, the last disbursements were made to the contractors, Platt and Moore, and the 1841 Jail building and lot were sold by Jackson County on May 2, 1860 (See "Fate of the 1841 Jackson County Jail" earlier in this text).

The 1859 Jackson County Jail boasted a two-story, 12-cell, limestone jail block. You don't see the cell block from the street, however. The two-foot-thick limestone structure adjoins the rear of the rectangular "Federal-Style" home (also built between 1859 and 1860), that fronts Main Street. This strategic placement likely shielded the community from the realities of 19th century crime and punishment.

DESCRIPTION OF THE 1859 BRICK RESIDENCE

The residence became the home to county employees responsible for guarding the jail, their families, and subordinate staff. Sometimes other tenants, namely paupers, were entrusted by the Jackson County Court to the care of the jailor, who received additional financial support that supplemented their family's income.[9]

The building materials of the residence are hand-made red bricks laid in running bond, and rest on a foundation of locally quarried limestone. Interior paneling of doors and window finish is typical of the "Federal Style," the most noticeable feature being the peaked lintel trim. The quality of construction of the home, high ceilings, central fireplaces, and stately exterior made it an impressive and authoritative structure at a time when few local residents enjoyed such comforts. Its appearance made clear the role of the Jackson County Jail as the mainstay of law and order in the community. "The residence resembled other houses that were owned by prosperous members of the community, reinforcing and reflecting the important social and political standing of [law enforcement officers]."[10]

The first floor west (front) façade has openings of uniform size evenly spaced in the pattern of door-window-window-window-door. Five windows on the second floor are placed directly above the first floor openings. The two doors have three light transoms, limestone lintels and thresholds. The windows have 6 over 6 light double-hung sash, limestone lintels and sills, and wood louver shutters.

The ridge roof is oriented north and south. A single chimney is located north of center atop the ridge. Both the front and rear facades feature a simple wooden cornice.

Semi-attached at the south end of the home is a one-story kitchen (or dining room) extension to the southeast corner of the Marshal's Home. Set back from the street, it is entered through a gate-enclosed entry courtyard. Since 1959, this has served as the main entrance to the Museum. The door at the rear provides cross ventilation and access to the east courtyard. A trap door along the north wall has steps leading to a full cellar underneath. A south-facing window in this kitchen/dining room—which has served as the Museum Gift Shop since 1959—looks out to a brick wall…clear evidence that when it was constructed in 1859, there were no structures immediately south.

Outbuildings and a lean-to summer kitchen once occupied spaces behind the dining room, but are no longer standing.

The Marshal's home has two entrances from Main Street.

All business-related visitors (including officials processing arrests) once entered through the north door into the Marshal's office. A north facing window looks out across a narrow alley to a brick wall of the former fire station next door (which, in 1859 would have been the site of the defunct brick 1841 Jackson County Jail). A door at the rear of the office led across an open-air corridor hallway (now enclosed) and directly into the cell block. At the turn of the nineteenth century…Alice Stewart came to live with her grandparents [Mr. and Mrs. "Mel" Hulse] at the jail so she could attend high school. Alice recalled that it was her job to lock each night the hall door that lead to the corridor of the cell block room.[11]

This corridor connected the kitchen/dining room, the Marshal's office, and the residence. The cistern providing water for the family and prisoners was also in this hall, next to the sitting parlor.

The south Main Street door was the private residence entrance that opened to a narrow hallway with a rather steep stairwell. Guests entering the residence would be greeted in the adjoining sitting parlor, furnished with the family's best available furniture. This was a multipurpose room that was used for entertaining visitors, writing letters, reading, listening to music (either a wind-up musical box, or the family's piano), and other such uses, like laying out the dead. Remember that there was no electricity at this time. The only lighting sources were kerosene lamps, candles, and the fireplace.

Notice, too, how the steep stairwell's banister in the hallway is much lower than those in use today. People in the 1800s were, on average, 4" shorter than today.

The second floor of the residence is divided into three main rooms. The Marshal's bed chamber (with a small room having the *appearance* of a large, walk-in closet over the front stairwell; but, it more *likely* served as a bath) on the south.

A small middle bed chamber (that may have served as a nursery since it has a door leading into the Marshal's bed chamber. And, another, smaller bed chamber on the north, of equal size to the room adjoining.

The small "closet" at the north end of the hall might have been fashioned at some point after construction. Another modification in the hallway is the door leading directly into the second-level jail cells. One can see that the living and sleeping quarters of the Marshal (or, Jailor) and his family were only feet away from convicts.

And what about the Dutch door leading from the upstairs hall of the Marshal's residence into the second floor jail cellblock? This doorway was presumably added *after* the 1859 Jackson County Jail was decommissioned in 1933, to facilitate easy access between the two structures.

DESCRIPTION OF THE 1859 LIMESTONE CELL BLOCKS

The limestone blocks forming the walls and floors of the mammoth limestone Jail were locally quarried along Rock Creek. Tradition has it that African-American slave labor was used in the construction of the Jail's cell block. The rusticated blocks are of notably large size, approximately 24 to 28 inches wide, 1 ½ foot high and 6 feet long. They are doweled together with 4 inch long iron rods.[12]

John Cassell recounted years later his involvement as stonemason for the Jail. The stone was quarried on the Noland farm on Rock Creek and hauled to the Jail site in wagons. A teamster would bring in two loads a day from the quarries over the old Westport Road along where the electric trolley line later ran. The exact location of the quarry has not been identified, but you can still see and drive along sections of the old Westport Road from Rock Creek towards Independence Square. A part of this pathway became the electric trolley line called Electric Avenue, later named Winner Road connecting to Lexington Avenue.[13]

The jail structure was about 30 feet square and 25 feet high.[14] There are six cells on each floor, three on each side of a center aisle, or passageway. The first floor cells have stone vaulted ceilings which support the stone slab floor of the second floor cells. The ceilings of the second story are of plate iron secured to the wood framing of the ceiling joists.

The original design of the jail provided only one restrictive entrance/exit. It was the west-facing door between the first-floor jail cellblock opposite the rear of the Marshal's office. A "U" stairway at the opposite (east) end of the cellblock was the only original access to the second-floor cellblock.[15] This stairwell was removed when the 1907 brick addition was added, and iron bars have enclosed the opening in the floor that was left. Also at that time, the east-facing doors on each level were cut out of the massive limestone blocks to accommodate the addition.

The stark, unyielding walls of each cell were lit only by what daylight filtered through the stationery louvered windows (six on the north façade; six on the south). The windows are fitted with iron frames and sash, with louvered bars on the first floor and a strap iron grid on the second floor. While allowing fresh air (they were originally unglazed), they provided little protection from the elements.

Limestone walls may have kept the cells tolerable in the summer; but the cold winter months must have been cruel punishment for those inside. A coal burning, potbelly stove in the center aisle between the cells on the first floor cellblock provided the only heat to both floors.[16] Prisoners were provided with either a straw pallet or corn shuck mattress for sleeping.[17]

Leg and wrist irons adorned some cells, and were used to restrain the movements of the more violent prisoners. Each cell's opening is outfitted with two, hand-forged iron doors measuring 2/3" x 6' 4" on heavy-duty hinges. An inner door features strap iron latticework that allowed a view to the center cellblock. Each door's lock is about eight inches square, and are an inch thick. For solitary confinement, a solid iron plate door 3/8" thick closes against the locked, latticed door…leaving those who had been caught on the wrong side of the law in total darkness.

Like most of the United States throughout the 1800s (excepting the Civil War period), the Jackson County Jail in Independence operated on a fee system set by law. Sheriffs collected set fees for arresting, transporting, for appearing in court, for housing prisoners in the jail, and for feeding them. With this, support staff like jailor, deputy sheriffs, and possibly jail matrons could be employed (though, the latter duty often befell the wife of whichever official occupied the adjoining residence of the Jackson County Jail).

The first County official moved into the house upon its completion. While definite documentation is lacking, Henry and Mary (Brady) Bugler and family were likely the *first* to occupy the residence portion of the 1859 Jackson County Jail with their children: Bridget (born 6 Sept. 1852); Mary Celia (born 12 Sept. 1854); Julia (born 17 Jul. 1856), and Sarah "Sallie" (born 8 Dec. 1857). Their three youngest sons were all born in the residence: Henry, Jr. (born 2 Oct. 1859); John (born ca. 1862); and, Thomas B. (born Dec. 1866).[18] The Bugler's could not have predicted the tragic events that would take place in their new home on Main Street.

---

[1] Stewart, Charlotte. *1859 Jail History*. (Independence, Mo.: Independence Junior Service League, October 9, 1956). Jackson County Historical Society Archives Document ID 168.13F18. More precisely, a $600 warrant issued by the Jackson County Court revealed, "The court doth order that county warrants be issued to Peter Gastell for payment of lot on wich (sic) to build a county jail payable on the last day of November 1859 with 10 per cent interest from 1st day of November1858 untill (sic.) payed (sic) to wit." Jackson County Court minutes (11:127:98599).

[2] "The court doth order that the clerk of this court solicit through the *Occidental Messenger* and *Western Dispatch* plans specifications and probable cost of building a good substantial jail with a comfortable dwelling house for the keeper for the county aforesaid, in the city of Independence. Said plans specifications and probable of the same to be submitted to the Jackson County court on the third Monday in December 1858. For the plans specifications approved of by the court, the court will pay a reasonable compensation." Jackson County Court minutes, 4 November 1858 (11:110:98566). The original specifications were microfilmed; copies are on file in the Jackson County Historical Society Archive's photographic collections; representations appear in this commemorative edition.

[3] Jackson County Court minutes (11:153: 98681). For a re-cap of the work see (11:214), which more clearly identifies A. B. Cross as the architect.

[4] Cross was born 9 Dec. 1826, in Camden, New Jersey. In 1856 he went to St. Paul, Minnesota for two years, then to St. Louis where he married Mrs. Rachel G. Taylor in April 1858. When he arrived in Kansas City, he was involved in the lumber industry in addition to starting his fledgling architectural firm. In 1890, Cross, whose office then was at 16 West Missouri Avenue (northeast corner of Missouri and Delaware Streets), advertised specializing in "Depots, Court Houses, Hotels, School Houses, Public Buildings, etc." Mrs. Cross died on 24 July 1890, when they lived at 817 Broadway. Her obituary included the detail that her son by her first marriage, William Taylor, was the architect of the Union Depot in the West Bottoms. At the time of his death on 18 Aug. 1894, Asa B. Cross he lived at 2329 Brooklyn Avenue. Their two sons, Louis and Frank died in infancy. Three daughters survived: Mrs. W. L. Ray (Lizzie G.), who lived in Cincinnati, Ohio, in 1890 and Pittsburg, Pennsylvania, in 1894; Mrs. Kate "Kitty" Barnes, whose husband was an architect in San Antonio, Texas; and, Miss Mary Emma Cross, who lived in the family home at the time of her father's death in 1894. Mr. and Mrs. Cross are buried in Kansas City's Elmwood Cemetery.

Clippings available in area archives list and describe many of his early Kansas City buildings, most of which burned, or have been demolished. A few that survive include: John B. Wornall House in Kansas City (1858; attributed); Jackson County Jail, Independence (1859; documented); Pacific House Hotel, Kansas City (1860; rebuilt and enlarged in 1868); Seth Ward Home addition, Kansas City (1871); St. Patrick's Church, Kansas City (1876); and, Colonel Harvey M. Vaile Mansion, Independence (1881).

Kansas City (Mo.) *Times*, 12 Nov. 1871; Morrison, Andrew. *The Two Kansas Citys*. (n.p., 1891), 70; *Biographical Dictionary of American Architects (Deceased)*, 9 May 1905; Bryan, John. *Missouri's Contribution to American Architecture: A History of the Architectural Achievements in This State From the Time of the Earliest Settlements Down to the Present Year*. (St. Louis, Mo.: St. Louis Architectural Club, 1928), 79; Ehrlich, George, "In Pursuit of Asa Beebe Cross: Pioneer Architect of Kansas City," *Historic Kansas City News* 1983 (July-Aug), 1-7. Sandy, Wilda. *Here Lies Kansas City*. (Kansas City, Mo.: Bennett Schneider, 1984), 44-45; Ehrlich, George, and Peggy E. Schrock. "The A. B. Cross Lumber Company, 1858-1871," Missouri Historical Review LXXX:1, 14-32 (which identifies on page 21 Cross' first building *in Kansas City* as The Mechanics Bank (2nd and Main) on which construction began in 1860. The surviving 1859 Jackson County Jail was designed in 1859 and completed between February and March 1860); Christiensen, Lawrence O. *Dictionary of Missouri Biography* (1999); *Kansas City, Its Resources, and Their Development: A Souvenir of the Kansas City Times* (1890); "Major A. B. Cross Dead," *Kansas City* (Mo.) *Star*, 18 Aug. 1894, 1; and Taggart, Kathleen Nelson. *Research Report on the Wornall House Prepared for the Jackson County Historical Society*, May 1965, Jackson County Historical Society Archives, Document ID 133.06F2, 11-14 [mentioning that his grandson's family maintained records, including a journal(s) of Cross when he was in partnership with George Rippey in 1858.]

As you will see later in this text, Cross also designed the building (hotel) that was completed as the first Jackson County Courthouse in Kansas City at 2nd and Main, as well as the second downtown Jackson County Courthouse at 5th and Oak Streets. Other clippings indicate he was also the architect of the Jackson County Jail in Kansas City.

[5] Jackson County Court minutes (11:226:98886).

[6] Ibid., (11:173:98751).

[7] Jackson County Court minutes: $1,500 (11:225, 226:98885); $1,100 (11:243:98959); $1,600 (11:256:99008); $5,000 (11:272:99075); $1,000 (11:292:99129); $600 (11:355:99252); $876.20 (11:366:99303); $168 (11:376:99344).

[8] Jackson County Court minutes (11:268:99049).

[9] For the time period most intensely studied in the Jackson County Court minutes (from 1858-1870), Henry and/or Mary Bugler were *regularly* remunerated for room and board for paupers. These are just a few of the many entries for the Buglers: (12:250:100691; March 1864), (12:265:100747; April 1864), (13:445:101948; July 1866), (13:59:102550; January 1867), (13:607:102598; February 1867), (13:634:102707; March 1867), (14:25:102887; April 1867).

[10] Bosworth, Frank M. *An Architecture of Authority: The Jail/Sheriff's Residences of Northwest Ohio, 1867-1902*. PhD. Dissertation. (Virginia Polytechnic Institute and State University, 1995), 59. As cited in Clemenson, 13.

[11] Alice Stewart married Earl Davis. She and her daughter, Pat Nell Westwood and granddaughters, Sandra and Pat Callahan, toured the Jail as its fate was being discussed by citizens. "Visit to Old Jail Brings Back a Flood of Memories for Her," *Independence* (Mo.) *Examiner*, 22 Aug. 1956. Alderman, B. J. *The Secret Life of the Lawman's Wife*. (Westport, Ct.: Praeger Publishers, 2007), 77.

[12] U.S. Department of the Interior, National Park Service, National Register of Historic Places Inventory, Nomination Form, prepared by M. Patricia Holmes, Research and Architectural Historian, Missouri State Park Board, State Historical Survey and Planning Office, April 10, 1970.

[13] "He Built the Old Jail: John Cassell Laid the Stone Walls in 1859—Still Working at His Trade," *Jackson Examiner* (Independence, Mo.) 20 July 1906, p. 7, c. 1. Another version might be found in the *Independence (Mo.) Examiner*, 17 July 1906.

[14] Stewart, 3.

[15] Birdsall, 640.

[16] Jerry Johnson, who was custodian at the Jackson County Courthouse on Independence Square at the same time as Joseph W. Potts was Deputy Sheriff and Jailor, recalled, "They burned coal in a large stove in the center hall, between each row of cells…. [Prisoners] had freedom of center hall unless they were hardened criminals." From an undated, unattributed clipping in the Jackson County Historical Society's newspaper clipping files.

[17] For instance, during a cursory survey of the Jackson County Court minutes during the Civil War era were found entries such as these: M. J. Friedsam was paid $24 in August 1863 for "blankets for Jail" (12:235:100620). In June 1865, John W. Perry was paid $29 for "mattresses and quilt furnished the County Jail" (12:359:101142). In September 1865, Christian Ott was paid $7.05 for a mattress to Jail (12:397:101297). And, in October 1865, John W. Perry was paid $10 for two mattresses to Jail; (12:423:101401).

[18] From baptisms recorded at St. Mary's Church (Church of the Holy Cross), as abstracted in Daughters of the American Revolution—Kansas City Chapter. *Vital Historical Records of Jackson County, Missouri: 1826-1876.* Reprint. (Independence, Mo.: Jackson County Historical Society, 2008), 107, 109, 111, 112, 113, 116.

CELL

4

UNCIVIL TIMES IN JACKSON COUNTY (1859-1865)

The State of Missouri was born in 1821 part of a compromise over the issue of slavery. Slavery was legal in Missouri, and many Missourians had a vested interest in keeping the nearby Kansas Territory from becoming a free state. Editorial conflicts that raged in eastern newspapers in the 1850s became bloody, violent and real along the Missouri-Kansas border. Well before the April 12, 1861, attack on Fort Sumter, Jackson County had seen its share of blood and fire.

On October 1, 1860, a committee of grand jury reported to the Jackson County Court after their examination of the County Jail and found, *"the cells in a good condition, clean and health; but recommend for better security that the walls of the cells be lined with boiler iron; some of the prisoners complain both of quantity and quality of good food furnished; but, the majority make no complaint."*[1]

On December 10, 1860, 19-year-old William Clarke Quantrill was imprisoned for "protective security" by Sheriff Burrus for one night. Quantrill had organized a group of Kansas Quaker abolitionists for a raid to liberate the slaves at Morgan Walker's farm near Blue Springs, Missouri. Quantrill turned traitor on the Quakers, informing the Walker clan of the impending raid. The result was a disaster for the Kansas group; only two of the original five made it

back across the border.[2] Andrew Walker, a friend who lived east of Independence obtained his release, only to find a large crowd on the Square demanding to hang Quantrill, but by the impassioned plea of Walker, the guerilla outlaw's life was saved.

An old document found by William Z. Hickman many years later was a coroner's jury, the "State of Mo. Jury's Verdict" in the case of a man killed by Quantrill's band during this incident, which read:

"We, the jury, after holding and in Quest over a man found dead at the Dwelling house of J. M. Walker, and hearing all the evidence that could be produced, found him to come to his death by gun shot, shot out of a musket or shot gun. He was shot in the right side with twenty buck shot and seven old shot holds n the same side, and in the right arm with three fresh shot and seven old shot holes. We found about his body one silver watch and one butcher knife and one of Allen's pattern Revolver pistols, one small flask of powder, and some pistils balls and some bullet moles, one box of gun caps, one purse with nothing in it, and one pocket knife and one belt. Give under our hands this 11th day of December, 1860. (Signed) Alfred T. Ketchum, Samuel H. Jones, Louis S. Montgomery, Elijah Parr, Joshua Dillingham, James Bowlin."[3]

When the Civil War broke out, the Jackson County Jail would be the site of more violence and suffering. During two different Battles of Independence, the Jackson County Jail was used as a hospital, in addition to confinement of prisoners by both sides.

Federal officers used the Jackson County Jail for Southern sympathizers, and "stuffed them in like sardines."[4] It is commonly relayed that as many as 15 to 20 people at a time were crowded into each 8' x 10' limestone cell; they had to sleep in shifts. Even Southern women and their children were imprisoned in the jail during the Civil War.

According to an article by Donald R. Hale in the January 1963 issue of *Real West Magazine*, the jail was nicknamed, "Prison of the Damned," during the Civil War era. One jailer known for his cruelty was Jacob Urlick, a German who supervised the jail during the Civil War when it was used by northerners to imprison southern sympathizers. Southern prisoners were thrown into the dark dungeon cells, twenty per cell. Urlick would entertain himself by taunting the prisoners and spitting in their faces.

One of Urlick's prisoners, Harrison Trow, was forced into a sparring match with a northern officer, Charles Beauregard. The understanding was that neither one would strike the other in the face. *"However, he hit me in the face the first thing and I kicked him down the stairs for it [leaving Beauregard unconscious]. For this offense I was chained down on my back for ten hours…. The provost marshal would come in once in a while and entertain me while I was chained down. He was a Dutchman and would say in broken Dutch, 'How duse youse like it?' and would sine me a song something like this: 'Don't youse vish you vas in Dixie, you damned old secess?' and dance around me."* Over the next month, Trow was forced to serve as a janitor at the jail, was sung songs of the "sweet South in a[n] insulting way…and thousands of other things that go with prison life." He was allowed only bread and water which had to be fed to him by other prisoners who were chained as well. The ordinary food rations were detestable; but, bread and water posed no real hardship. Thus, the prisoners under Ulrick's command endured the sickening stench of the latrine, vile food and the inability to move inside the dark, dank cells.[5]

Restraints that may have chained Trow for 10 hours

Beyond the guerilla warfare taking place at this time on both sides of the state line, consider the unjust treatment of free, yet unequal citizens of Jackson County. Jackson County Court minutes reveal how African-American slaves…and free men and women of color were treated. On March 5, 1861, for instance, Matt Slaughter, a free man of color, was fined $10 "for being in this state without licenses." In default of payment of his fine, Slaughter was committed to the Jackson County jail where the County Court ordered the Sheriff to hire out Slaughter for the fine plus costs. Somehow, Slaughter had gained his freedom, yet was subjugated once more. The Jackson County Court "ordered that the Sheriff of Jackson County proceed to hire out said Matt Slaughter at public outcry to the best bidder such length of timeas his hire will produce the fine and all costs incurred by this procedure." [6]

Two months later in May 1861, "Henry Jones and Lucy Jane Jones, his wife, free persons of colour [filed] their petition for a license to live in the State of Missouri. Said Henry Jones is about 52 years of age, brown colour, 5 foot six inches high and weighs about 140 pounds. Said Lucy Jane Jones, wife of said Henry Jones, is a mulatto colour aged about 39 years and weighs about 200 pounds. And, having produced in this Court satisfactory evidence they are free persons of colour and of that class of person who by the laws of Missouri are entitled to a license to remain or resided within this state, the said Henry Jones and Lucy Jane Jones, his wife, are of good character and behavior and capable of supporting themselves, by some lawful employment." Directly after their petition, William and Mary Jane Smith, "free persons of colour" also made their petition. William, was described as being 33-year-old blacksmith, 5 feet, 10 inches tall. Mary Jane was 34-years-old, and said to be 200 pounds and of "copper colour." [7]

Sheriff John W. Burrus died while in office. William B. Rogers was appointed "acting Sheriff" at an early May term of the Jackson County Court. Later that month, Oliver P. W. Bailey was appointed Sheriff.

In August 1861, a company of 400 Federal troops from Kansas City arrived in Independence, taking position in front of the Jackson County Jail. They demanded the release of four Union men. The "prisoners were confined in jail for stealing horses," said citizens. [8]

Between August 30, 1861, and March 1865, many civilian courts were eliminated and relegated to military supervision and Independence became a Federal post. [9] The State of Missouri was held in the union by military force even though the elected Governor and legislators had voted to secede from the Union on October 31, 1861.

Sheriff Bailey held his post until October 1861, when "it appear[ed] to the satisfaction of the Jackson County Court…that there [wa]s no sheriff, coroner, or other ministerial officer in Jackson County to attend to the Court, the Court appoint[ed] Tandy Westmoreland Sheriff for the time being." [10]

Even after Independence became a Federal post on June 7, 1862, Westmoreland (who had by then been appointed as Jackson County Coroner) was re-appointed Sheriff at the opening session of the Court's term that month.[11] (Other temporary officers followed in his place, as you can see in *Appendix A: Lawmen Serving Jackson County in Independence, Missouri: 1827-1933*.)

As the situation intensified, tensions erupted between families and neighbor turned against neighbor. Even women and children suspected of their loyalties to the Confederacy were arrested and placed in the 1859 Jackson County Jail under the command of the Union Provost Marshal.

FIRST BATTLE OF INDEPENDENCE

Colonel Upton B. Hays

William Clarke Quantrill returned to Independence Square on August 11, 1862, this time with reinforcements, including 25 of his men, and 375 farm boys recently recruited from Jackson County and surrounding counties by Confederate officers Colonel Upton B. Hays, General John T. Hughes, and Captain Hart (of St. Joseph). Their mission? To capture Independence from 450 Federal troops headed by Colonel James T. Buel. They rode westward into town on what is today East Maple Avenue with gunfire at four in the morning. Lieutenant Charles W. Meryhew of the 7th Missouri had a company of men stationed near the Jail, but they retreated towards Kansas City.

General Hughes, who as a private had been a chronicler of Doniphan's expedition in the Mexican War, was killed in this battle, as was Captain Hart. After a bloody hour or two around the Independence Courthouse Square and in a field west of town, Buel surrendered.

The Jackson County Jail was captured during the siege and the provost guard withdrew. Quantrill and Hays were able to free their men along with other southern sympathizers and their families incarcerated during this engagement.[12]

But the Jackson County Jail became a death house. Captain Thomas was slain.[13] And, a Federally-appointed Independence City Marshal, James "Jim" Knowles (who had previously piloted Buel into the Blue Cut neighborhood) was murdered in a jail cell for having killed a non-resisting Southern prisoner, "*an old Irishman who was drunk and cutting up a little.*"[14]

Just one month prior, Knowles and his lawyer, J. Brown Hovey, had submitted a petition for Writ of Habeas Corpus to the Jackson County Court. "*The offence for which the petitioner was imprisoned* [was] *not bailable* (sic.). *It* [was] *therefore ordered…that …James Knowles be remanded to the jail of Jackson County and be there held under the said warrant of commitment, and the jailor takes charge of him accordingly—and it is further considered by the Court here that the said State of Missouri secure of the said petitioner James Knowles her costs and charges in and above her defense in this behalf.*"[15]

46

The first Battle of Independence on August 11, 1862 (and the Battle of Lone Jack on August 15 and 16, 1862), ended in Confederate victories.[16] The Union suffered about 344 casualties. The number of Confederate deaths is unknown.

In the aftermath of the First Battle of Independence, Henry Bugler was ordered by the Jackson County Court in November 1862 to have the door and locks on the Jail repaired. Henry R. Jacob Grinager was paid $120 in February 1863 for locks and repairing locks and jail doors at the Jail.[17] In January 1863, John C. Agnew was paid $8.65 to install glass and putty, etc. to repair the Jail.[18]

That same month, Patrick Cox was paid $4 for having previously dug graves for soldiers. And, in February, Hugh Maxwell was paid $4 for also digging graves.[19] There were also disbursements at this time to individuals who had supplied wood during the winter months to stoke the wood stoves in the Jackson County Jail.

Federal control of the area was not firmly re-established until early 1863. The objective then was to rid the area of the guerrilla bands; most regular Confederate troops had already been driven out. Again, the process started of rounding up suspected Southern sympathizers. It was common practice to hold them in jail until they could pay a substantial bond (around $20,000). Upon release, they generally had to agree to leave the State of Missouri.

Quantrill returned in July 1863 with his men to free John C. Wallace, a southern sympathizer, who had been jailed, and sentenced to hang. On the day of the hanging, Quantrill and his men rode into Independence, sent the Union soldiers at the scaffold fleeing in all directions, and freed Wallace from the hangman's noose. (Wallace's daughter, Elizabeth, hosted the annual Quantrill reunions for many years after the war at the Wallace home, Wallace Grove.)

47

When the Jail overflowed with the residents of Jackson County, other buildings were used as jails. One of those buildings in Kansas City collapsed, and several young girls (some related to Quantrill's men, including "Bloody Bill" Anderson) were injured and killed. (The historical marker commemorating this location near 14th and Grand had to be moved for the Sprint Arena in downtown Kansas City.) Historians believe that this action resulted in Quantrill's infamous burning of Lawrence, Kansas in August 1863.

Three days after Quantrill's raid on Lawrence, General Ewing, in an attempt to rid Missouri of Quantrill's guerilas, issued on August 25, 1863, *General Orders No. 11* (commonly called "Order No. 11") instituting martial law in Jackson County (and other counties along the Missouri-Kansas border). The Jackson County Jail was particularly useful in enforcing control; especially after martial law was instituted, and the Federal government's military was the controlling police power.[20]

With this type of intermediary government, Provost Marshals, or military policemen, were installed. Widely employed by both sides during the Civil War, provosts served with commands in the field as well as in garrisoned or occupied towns and in military districts like those of Jackson County and Independence, Missouri. Here, the 1859 Jackson County Jail was used as a military prison and as Provost Marshal's headquarters by the Federal occupation troops throughout the War.

Provost Marshals (nicknamed the "Little Gods" for the ultimate power they had over the population) were figures of order and oppression independent of any real supervision, dispensed with a variety of duties including: investigating charges or acts of treason and arresting deserters, spies, and persons deemed disloyal; enforcing militia enrollments and maintaining troop discipline; assuming custody of and processing of prisoners and deserters;

**Union Brigadier General
Thomas Ewing**

Head Quarters, District of the Border,
Kansas City, Mo., August 25, 1863
General Orders
No. 11

I.   All persons living in Jackson, Cass and Bates Counties, Missouri, and in that part of Vernon included in this District, except those living within 1 mile of the limits of Independence, Hickman's Mills, Pleasant Hill and Harrisonville, and except those in that part of Kaw Township, Jackson County, north of Brush Creek and west of the Big Blue, are hereby ordered to remove from their present places of residence within fifteen days from the date hereof.

Those who, within that time, establish their loyalty to the satisfaction of the commanding officer of the military station nearest their present places of residence, will receive from him certificates stating the fact of their loyalty, and the names of the witnesses by whom it can be shown. All who receive such certificates will be permitted to remove to any military station in this District, or to any part of the State of Kansas, except the counties on the eastern Border of the State. All others shall remove out of this District. Officers commanding companies and detachments serving in the counties named will see that this paragraph is promptly obeyed.

II.   All grain and hay in the field or under shelter, in the District from which the inhabitants are required to remove within reach of military stations after the 9th day of September next will be taken to such stations, and turned over to the proper officers there, and report of the amount so turned over made to District Head Quarters, specifying the names of all loyal owners and the amount of such product taken from them. All grain and hay found in such District after the 9th day of September next, not convenient to such stations will be destroyed.

III.   The provisions of General Orders No. 10 from these Head Quarters, will be at once vigorously executed by officers commanding in the parts of the District, and ~~of~~ [strikethrough] at the stations not subject to the operation of Paragraph I of this Order--and especially in towns of Independence, Westport, and Kansas City.

IV.   Paragraph 3, General Orders No. 10, is revoked as to all who have borne arms against the Government of this District since the 21st day of August 1863.

By order of Brig. General Ewing:
(Sgd.) H. Hannahs, A. A. A. "G"
[Acting Assistant Adjutant-General]

administering punishment; suppressing any depredations and disturbances upon private property; limit marauding against citizens; prevent stragglers on long marches; generally suppress gambling or other vices not conducive to good order and discipline; administer and enforce the law with regard to regulating public places; conduct searches, seizures, and arrests; issue passes to citizens for movement in and out of Union lines; administration of oaths and paroles; and record and investigate citizen complaints.[21] "Secessionists, prisoners of war, aggrieved citizens, slaves seeking freedom, refugees, and common criminals passed through Provost Marshals' offices."[22]

The devastation on populations and property from enforcing "Order No. 11" resulted in terrible hardships for residents and affected Jackson County families long after the War.[23] Those who refused to vow loyalty to the North were required to leave. Many women and children (their husbands and fathers away at war) had to walk to their destinations, some as far as Texas or Kentucky.

Between 1869-1870 George Caleb Bingham, captured their misery in a stunning painting titled, "Martial Law."[24] For a second copy of his majestic painting, Bingham used what was available—two gingham tablecloths.[25] Then, in 1872, engraver John Sartain in Philadelphia, Pennsylvania, was enlisted by George C. Bingham and Company to produce a reproduction of his painting. Bingham then published and sold line and mezzotint engravings (some signed) of "Martial Law," that became better known as "Order No. 11."[26] One of Bingham's signed proofs is on display at the 1859 Jail, Marshal's Home, and Museum (and is reproduced for sale).[27]

Without local government control, most of the uniformity of society went by the wayside, including property rights and responsibilities. On the first day of its September 1863 term, the Jackson County Court ordered "that the clerk of this Court if at any time, or from any cause he believes the papers and records in his office is liable or in danger of being destroyed by a mob or the enemies of the government, that he remove the same to some place of safety—and they further order that he do so at any time by order of this Court."[28] Later that year, the Court, in an attempt to explain its delinquency in providing tax assessments, provided a "memorial" to the Missouri State Legislature during its December 1863 term:

> *"The reasons which have operated to produce these delays, have grown out of the disturbed condition of the Border Counties, and especially this County, for it seems that for the last two years, this County has been "Head Quarters" for all Guerillas of Missouri and the Marauders of Kansas. This condition of things, produced an entire suspension of law and order in the County, and resulted in relieving the County of most of its personal property, and the destruction of hundreds of valuable farm houses and improvements by them.*
>
> *"During these days of devastation, the County Assessor could not assess property, nor the Collector collect taxes; and this continued until "Order No. 11" issued by General Ewing on the 25th August A.D. 1863, swept the country of its people and their property, outside of the military posts—and Jackson County is now a County without a people, and filled with rich farms without farmers to till the soil. In view of the present ruined condition of the County, and the impossibility of making correct assessments for the years 1862 and 1863, and even for the revenue year of 1864, we would ask the Legislature to relive this County from the payment of State Taxes for the years 1862 and 1863, and grant our County Assessor further time in which to make his assessments and return his books for the current revenue year, and that the County Court further time in which to hold a Court of Appeals from assessments, and the Collector further time in which to make collections and return his delinquent lists, and for the future, with the blessings of peace, "Old Jackson" hopes to [-?-] afresh upon an honorable rivalry for wealth and high political position, among her sister counties of Missouri. And the Court doth order that the Clerk of this Court make out and certify a copy of this Memorial, and forward the same to our representatives at Jefferson City, with the request that they present the same to the Legislature, and that they requested to press the passage of Laws giving the relief therein prayed for."[29]*

In May 1864, Sheriff John G. Hayden was ordered by the Jackson County Court "to have the fence around the County Jail repaired in a good substantial manner." By June, disbursements for work completed were recorded: Henry Crump received $18 for work on the

Jail fence; Henry Bugler $10 for the same; John D. Sage received $4 for hauling plank for the fence; William M. Sage was paid $50.60 for furnishing plans for the fence; and, John Conway was reimbursed $8 for polls furnished for the fence. Robert Weston was also paid for "work done in or about the County Jail."[30]

SECOND BATTLE OF INDEPENDENCE
(PRECURSOR TO THE BATTLE OF WESTPORT)

In 1864, former Missouri Governor and Commander of the Missouri State Guard, Confederate Major General Sterling Price led more than 10,000 mounted men on a raid from Arkansas through eastern Missouri to the Missouri-Kansas border. In all, they marched 1,434 miles and fought 43 battles and skirmishes. As he neared Jackson County in October, Price gained the services of "Bloody Bill" Anderson and William Clarke Quantrill's guerillas as the Battle of the Little Blue ensued on October 21. In the Second Battle of Independence on October 21 and 22, Price drove Union troops out of Independence and their post at the Jackson County Jail. Other skirmishes at this time were at Grinter's Farm, on White Oak Creek, and on Mockbee's Farm.

Confederate Major General Sterling Price

Price was closely pursued, however, by Pleasanton's 7th Cavalry, who headed into a quickly gathered superior force at the Battle of Westport (an area that includes present-day Country Club Plaza District and Sunset Hill subdivision). This last desperate raid, after the South's losses at Vicksburg and Gettysburg, culminated in the largest Civil War battle west of the Mississippi. Sometimes called the *"Gettysburg of the West,"* the Battle of Westport pitted 30,000 men against one another. In all there were about 3,000 casualties. To put this into perspective, consider that Kansas City's civilian population at that time was only 3,000. In other words, as many soldiers gave their life in battle as there were civilians living in the frontier town at that time.

The Confederate defeat was the last of the South's many attempts to take Missouri, and it marked the end of major Civil War military action in Jackson County. In 1864, all civil offices were declared vacant.[31] This may be why the Jackson County Court missed holding several sessions in November 1864, as "neither of the justices being present."[32] In December, however, they allowed $18 as payment for previously "digging graves for soldiers."[33] Jailor Henry Bugler was paid $3 for one soldier's grave in an earlier entry. Can it be assumed that $18 would have been for about 6 soldiers? There were also notations at this time of costs for repairs to the Jackson County Jail. Although the minutes don't specify particulars, they were likely from the aftermath of the Second Battle of Independence that raged through Independence Square.

[1] Jackson County Court minutes (11:486:99622). Thomas M. Fields was chairman of the committee.

[2] Hale, Donald R. "West's Prison of the Damned." Unsourced, undated clipping in the Jackson County Historical Society Archives. The following year, on December 5, 1861, the *Leavenworth* (Ks) *Daily Conservative* reported, "On Monday last Up Hays, Renick, and Quantrill entered Independence with 200 men, robbed several stores, and took possession of the mails, coaches and horses on the Kansas City line." This incident may be the skirmish at Independence that, according to the Official Records, occurred on Tuesday, November 26, 1861. On December 30, 1861, the *Wyandotte* (Ks.) *Commercial Gazette* reported that a Federal detachment went to the Morgan Walker farm for the express purpose of trying to capture Quantrill. See "William C. Quantrill: Upton Hays Man?" *Jackson County Historical Society Journal* 2003 (Spring) 44:1, 22-23.

[3] "The First Death Warrant," undated news clipping in the Jackson County Historical Society Archives.

[4] Stewart, 4.

[5] Trow eventually escaped and re-joined Quantrill's guerillas. This event likely took place about a month before the First Battle of Independence (August 1862), which is described below. Trow was one of the persons that identified Jesse James after he was killed. Hale and Beck, 13-15. Also, McKim, Judy. "Marshal's Character Determined Lifestyle of 1859 Jail Inmates," *Jackson County Historical Society JOURNAL*, 1995 (Spring), 35:1, 6, 7.

[6] Jackson County Court minutes (11: 587:99933).

[7] Ibid., (11:612:100009; and, 11:612, 613:100010). These petitions for license were the result of a newly enacted Missouri State law.

[8] *Liberty* (Mo.) *Tribune*, 9 Aug. 1861.

[9] Clemenson, 19.

[10] Jackson County Court minutes (12:160:100247).

[11] Clemenson, 19. Jackson County Court minutes (12:164:100272; 12:168:100292; 12:171:100310).

[12] Hale and Beck, 11-13. *"Bill Basham had been a stage driver on the Santa Fe Trail, but had quit and come home to Independence about the time Knowles killed the Irishman. He had not been connected with the war in any way at that time, but someone claimed that he was a Quantrill man, and he was locked [in the 1859 Jackson County Jail]. During the battle, Meryhew, who was at the Jail, was attacked by a detachment of Quantrill's men. Meryhew and his men fired one volley and then they fled west to Kansas City. Quantrill's men then broke into the Jail and released Basham, who then and there joined the guerrillas. Captain William Gregg of Quantrill's men broke down the doors in the jail and released the Southern sympathizers imprisoned there."*

[13] Thomas had waylaid George Todd, John Little, and Ed Korger at a crossing of the Little Blue. Todd alone escaped with is life. Before he could take his revenge, another of the band slew Thomas, and, "Tod (sic.) was greatly offended as he felt he had the superior right to do the killing himself." Ironically, George Todd would later be killed at the Second Battle of Independence, in 1864. "Old Jail Figured in Romance, War, and Tragedy," *Kansas City* (Mo.) *Star*, 28 Mar. 1920.

[14] Hale and Beck, 11.

[15] Jackson County Court minutes (12:173:100321).

[16] It was claimed that Cole Younger scouted the town of Independence before the first battle dressed as an old woman. The story is recounted in *Noted Guerrillas* by John N. Edwards (St. Louis, Bryan, Brand & Co., 1877), 95-97.

[17] Jackson County Court minutes (12:180:100352; and, 12:207:100490).

[18] Ibid., (12:201:100475; and, 12:201:100476).

[19] Ibid., (12:207:100493).

[20] Brownlee, 176.

[21] Missouri State Archives. *Missouri's Union Provost Marshal Papers, 1861-1866.* www.sos.mo.gov/archives/provost/history.asp (23 Aug. 2004). The Missouri State Archives began building a searchable name/location/subject database index in 2000 from the "Union Provost Marshal Files Relating to Individual Citizens" portion of *Records of the Provost Marshal General* at the National Archives in Washington, DC. (See National Archives publication M345) At the time this article went to press, the database index represents work in 175 of 300 rolls with an estimated 40,000 Missouri-related documents. A location search for "Jackson County" yielded 370 results pointing to entries with names and activities that were recorded by the provost marshal in the western district. Another helpful, related online resource is the *Official Records*. There appear to be multiple searchable databases for the *Official Records*; one we found easy to use is posted at www.ehistory.com/uscq/library/or (23 Aug. 2004).

[22] Bradbury, John F., Jr. Introduction. "Union Provost Marshal Documents from the District of Rolla," New Series No. 27, (April 2003), *Newsletter of the Phelps County Historical Society*.

[23] For a recently published account of Order No. 11 see the Autumn 2003 issue of the *Jackson County Historical Society JOURNAL.*

[24] In the collection of the Cincinnati Art Museum, as of 2009. Also see, "Mercer Order No. 11 Frame Given Archives," *Jackson County Historical Society JOURNAL*, 1976 (August), 3, about the donation to the Jackson County Historical Society of the ornate, silver leaved frame that reportedly contained George Caleb Bingham's "canvas over wood panel" painting of "Martial Law," or, "Order Number 11" that once hung in the Colonel Joseph Wayne Mercer home in Independence, Missouri. Mercer was born in Platte County, Missouri, 22 Feb. 1845; served in the Confederate Army during the Civil War where he lost his right arm; was Missouri state treasurer, 1875-77; and, Mayor of Independence, Missouri, in 1891. He died 13 Mar. 1906, and is buried at Mt. Washington Cemetery. Mrs. Pearl Wilcox, who bought the Mercer family home at 116 South Pleasant, said the 4.5 x 5.5 foot frame was left in the attic when the heirs sold the home and moved the painting. The 55.5" x 77.5" painting hung for a while in the Nelson Gallery, and later was sold to the Cincinnati Gallery of Art, where it was restored. On first inspection, it does not appear that the painting and frame were the same size.

[25] The medium for Bingham's other known copy of this painting was on two linen (gingham) tablecloths measuring 56.5" x 78" in total. It is in the gallery of the State Historical Society of Missouri at Columbia, Missouri. Records of a third copy, most likely a "study," trace an 18" x 24" version through the 1930s; but, its present location is unknown.

[26] Ayres, William. *Picturing history. American paintings 1770-1930* (New York: Rizzoli, 1992), 123. Also, Bloch, E. Maurice. George Caleb Bingham: A Catalog Raisonne. (Berkeley, Ca.: Univ. of California Press, 1967), 123, 128, 130.

[27] "Old Copy of Picture "Order No. 11" Given to the Historical Society by a Lee's Summit Resident," *Jackson County Historical Society JOURNAL*, 1961 (June), 1,2, announcing donation of a large lithograph of George Caleb Bingham's "Order No. 11" or "Martial Law" to the Jackson County Historical Society by Willis W. Browning. The original engraving measures 21.5" x 31" according to Bloch, 223-224. The Jackson County Historical Society's reproduction was reduced to a manageable 16" x 20" version and available for sale on either egg-shell or white paper.

[28] Jackson County Court minutes (12:236:100632).

[29] Ibid., (12:248). The Laws of the State of Missouri, passed at the regular session of the 23rd General Assembly in 1865, reflect on paged 222: "An act [approved February 20, 1865] to authorize the collector [collection] of certain taxes in Jackson County. That the assessments in the county of Jackson for the years 1862, 1863 and 1864, having been returned by the assessor and received by the County Court of said county and the court of appeals held therein, notwithstanding the action of said court, is hereby legalized, and the said court shall cause the tax books for said years to be delivered to the collector of the county, who shall proceed to make his collections and returns in the manner and at the time prescribed by existing laws." Beginning on page 458 of the County Court minute book, the County Assessor began an EXTENSIVE report of delinquent tax lists for 1862, 1863, 1864, and 1865.

[30] Jackson County Court minutes (12:291:100799; 12:297-298:100822-100826; 12:301:100839).

[31] Marshall and Morrison. *Political History of Jackson County, Missouri: Biographical Sketches of Men Who have Helped to Make It.* (Kansas City, Mo.: Hudson-Kimberly Publishing Co., 1902), 82. Also, Birdsall, 643, 737.

[32] Jackson County Court minutes (12:316).

[33] Ibid., (12:318).

JAIL BREAK:
BLATANT CRIMES, BRAZEN CRIMINALS

Missouri statutes designated the County Court as the administrative and quasi-legislative arm of county government. This court's responsibility was to administer government within the county (the County Court was the predecessor of our present-day County Legislature). County Court officials were selected from those who lived in the community.

The Circuit Court, in contrast, was a judicial body with a judge who traveled the circuit, serving many communities. Criminal cases and litigation was heard in the Circuit Court.[1] On Thursday, March 29, 1827, at the home of John Young, in Independence, the first Circuit Court of the County convened. David Todd (appointed judge by Governor Alexander McNair in December 1822 at St. Charles, Mo.), served as its first judge, and he sat in both civil and criminal cases. Joseph Reddeford Walker was appointed the first Sheriff of Jackson County, and Samuel C. Owens, first clerk. The parcel at 933 S. Leslie (corner of Leslie and South) is likely the home site.

After organization of the Court, the first grand jury was drawn. It consisted of 24 men who adjourned after one day's session. In July, the court re-convened for three days and the grand jury returned its first indictment, one against William Reed, for horse stealing. He was acquitted for lack of prosecution. In November, the same year the third term of Court convened. It lasted two days after which the indictment was returned against the first woman ever tried before a Circuit Court in Jackson County, Missouri.

Hannah, an African-American slave, was convicted of assault with intent to kill. For a reason that has not yet been recovered, Hannah had tried to kill another slave in a fight that took place in the slave quarters. The fact that both parties were slaves probably had much to do with the trial and the adjustment of the punishment. Were the crime committed at that time against a Caucasian, there was only one adjudication—hanging without the formality of law or an inquiry into details. True to the customs of those days was Hannah's punishment. It was the decree of the Court that she be stripped and given 39 lashes on her bare back, "well laid on," and committed to the custody of Sheriff Walker until the costs of her case were settled. She was allowed to work for the sheriff in payment of the costs, amounting to about $5.[2]

WHAT IS THE DIFFERENCE BETWEEN "JAIL" AND "PRISON?"

Keep in mind that in the County's formative years, imprisonment was not considered punishment. Jails existed mainly to detain prisoners until trial. County jails also served as the universal lock-up for city, county, state and Federal prisoners (U.S. Marshals also used county jails when needed). Not until 1836, when Missouri built a state prison in Jefferson City, were offenders sentenced for more than one year transferred out of the County Jail; those awaiting trial or with lesser sentences remained in the County Jail. The first Federal prison at Leavenworth wasn't built until 1897.[3]

Our modern theory of reformation of criminals was unknown to the pioneers. Jails were erected simply and solely to hold bad men—and light and sanitation were not even secondary considerations. Evidence of this first era of punishment of criminals included jails with massive, solid walls with heavy grating, dungeon-rooms, and rings anchored in the floors and walls for chaining prisoners.[4]

The old-fashioned jail [was] the most sociable institution…a common meeting place where all classes from the trained crook to the misguided lad of tender years were schooled in the ways of crime. In more ways than one, the county jail [was] a rendezvous of criminals. It [was] a legitimate question to debate, whether the average county jail has any reformatory value. And it is undoubtedly true that scores of men who later [were] committed to the penitentiary [were] jail-made criminals.[5]

Jackson County's Circuit Court records indicate that the earliest crimes were assaults, larceny, betting, and the selling of liquor to Native Americans. Some infractions were settled with fines; jail time was deemed appropriate for more blatant behaviors.

At one time, punishments for assaults, betting, and liquor violations were usually fined from $3 to $6. For added insult, gamblers found the amount of the wager tacked on to their fine. Some of these fines (and the names of those who were caught) are clearly documented in a very early Jackson County ledger that was acquired by the Jackson County Historical Society in 2005. Sections of this ledger list collections made by the Jackson County Sheriff for unlawful, but minor infractions punishable by fine.

Larceny, however, was considered a very serious offense. There are records of criminals sentenced to lashes. Two Native Americans were to receive 20 stripes each for horse thievery. And, as seen above, at least one female slave received 39 lashes for assault and battery with intent to commit murder.[6]

The 1860 U.S. Census for Jackson County (at left) listed at the newly constructed 1859 Jackson County Jail under Jailor Henry Bugler's watch, eight male prisoners ranging from 18 to 40 years of age. Two prisoners were Missouri natives; two born in Ireland; one each in Germany, Iowa, and Michigan. One was identified as Native American. Five were charged with grand larceny, one with forgery, and one with murder.

Bugler's wife, Mary, five children, and house servant lived in the residence portion of the Jail.

Even the most brazen would have been discouraged by the state-of-the-art fire proof 1859 Jackson County Jail. Without considerable help from the outside, it also proved to be virtually escape-proof, too.[7] Still, there were no shortages of incarcerations...especially during the Civil War.

Some of the most notorious characters of the Civil War and the years following it were young men who hailed from the Missouri-Kansas border. Frank and Jesse James rode with "Bloody Bill" Anderson's (pictured at the left) guerillas, entering the war as teenagers. In fact, Jesse James was only 18 at the <u>end</u> of the Civil War.

Unwilling, and some would say, unable to return to civilian life, many ex-guerillas chose a life of crime. Sympathy for these former rebels was strong in western Missouri. The outlaws often targeted banks and railroads owned by Union interests.

State Historical Society of Missouri
Gen. Joseph O. Shelby

John Newman Edwards, the editor of *The Kansas City Times*, had served as an aide to Confederate General "Jo" Shelby, and was ever ready to defend the actions of the James-Younger gang. He even published a letter from Jesse James in which he claimed to take from the rich to help the poor.

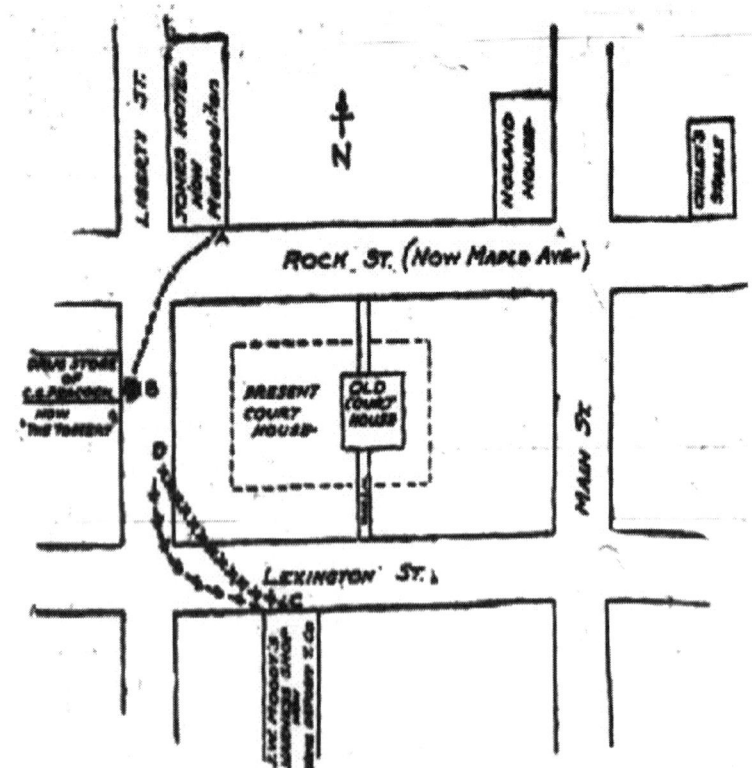

SHOWS WHERE FIGHT OCCURRED.
A-B. THE COURSE OF "JIM CROW" CHILES AND HIS SON ELIJAH TO WHERE JIM PEACOCK WAS STANDING IN FRONT OF HIS BROTHER'S STORE.
C-D-C THE ADVANCE OF CHARLIE PEACOCK AND HIS RETREAT AFTER THE SHOOTING.

Old scores were settled outside the law and those who couldn't adjust to the new order fought hard for the lost cause of the Confederacy. Many of these men came to violent ends. Harry S Truman's uncle "Jim Crow" Chiles, an ex-Quantrill guerilla, was killed by James Peacock, City of Independence Deputy Marshal, in a shootout on Independence Square on September 21, 1873.[8]

As old members of the gangs were killed or captured, new ones were brought in. In "A Dynasty of Western Outlaws," Paul I. Wellman argues that the gangs and methods instituted by Quantrill and Bloody Bill Anderson continued through the James-Younger gang, the Dalton-Doolin gang (Daltons were cousins to Younger) through the Starr gang (Belle Starr another friend of the James-Younger gang), well into the 20th Century.

[1] Clemenson, Gay L. "Keeping the Peace in Jackson County, Missouri, 1927-1887," (University of Missouri at Kansas City, History Department manuscript, January 27, 1998), 4. Jackson County Circuit Court records prior to the 1880s are quite voluminous, and are divided between two entities. Both the Jackson County Records Center and Jackson County Historical Society are in the process of preparing these files for public access at the time this publication goes to print.

[2] "Whipped for an Assault: The First Woman Tried in Jackson County Was a Slave," *Kansas City* (Mo.) *Star*, 12 Jan. 1908. Who was Hannah's master? What became of her? Did she live long enough to enjoy freedom after Emancipation? If so, what surname did she assume? Did she have children? These are questions requiring additional research. This is just one of thousands of stories waiting to be "unpacked" as the Jackson County Historical Society organizes and indexes a wonderful collection in its custody— Jackson County Circuit Court records—dating from the 1830s to the 1880s.

[3] Clemenson, 8.

[4] Cross, William T. and Charlotte B. Forrester. *County Almshouses and Jails of Missouri.* (Missouri State Nurses' Association, 1912), 3-4.

[5] Ibid., 12-13.

[6] Howard, L. Conard, ed. *Encyclopedia of the History of Missouri.* Vol. II. (New York: The Southern History Co., 1901), 167. (As cited in Clemenson, 15.)

[7] Stewart, 6-7. One escape was by John H. Harper, discussed elsewhere in this publication.

[8] Wellman, Paul I. *A Dynasty of Western Outlaws* (Lincoln, Ne.: University of Nebraska Press, 1961), 13. "Slayer of 'Jim Crow' Chiles, Bad Man, Retires from Office," Kansas City (Mo.) Star, 15 Mar. 1912, enumerates the date of the event having taken place in 1872.

CELL

5

POST-WAR PARTICULARS RECONSTRUCTED (1865-1880)

The Jackson County Jail—while damaged—survived the Civil War. In March 1865, a committee of grand jury reported to the Jackson County Court after their examination of the County Jail, "and found the outside wall and door of said jail in good order and reasonably secure; some of the partition walls are broken and very insecure; nearly all the locks of the cells are broken and without keys. The Jail appears to be clean and well kept and ventilated.[1] In October 1865, John D. Warren was paid $179 for repairs on the Jail.[2] On May 1, 1866, John D. Warren was paid $12 for putting locks upon the County Jail.[3]

The Jackson County Jail remained an important and busy place after the War because for many of these citizens, the war was not over. For this reason, peace did not come to Jackson County with the end of the Civil War.

An example of post-War violence took place at the 1859 Jackson County Jail in the summer of 1866 after an ex-guerilla and convict, Joab Perry, was arrested on Tuesday, June 12, 1866. The next evening between 10 and 11'oclock, a group of five mounted men attacked the jail to attempt a jailbreak for Perry.

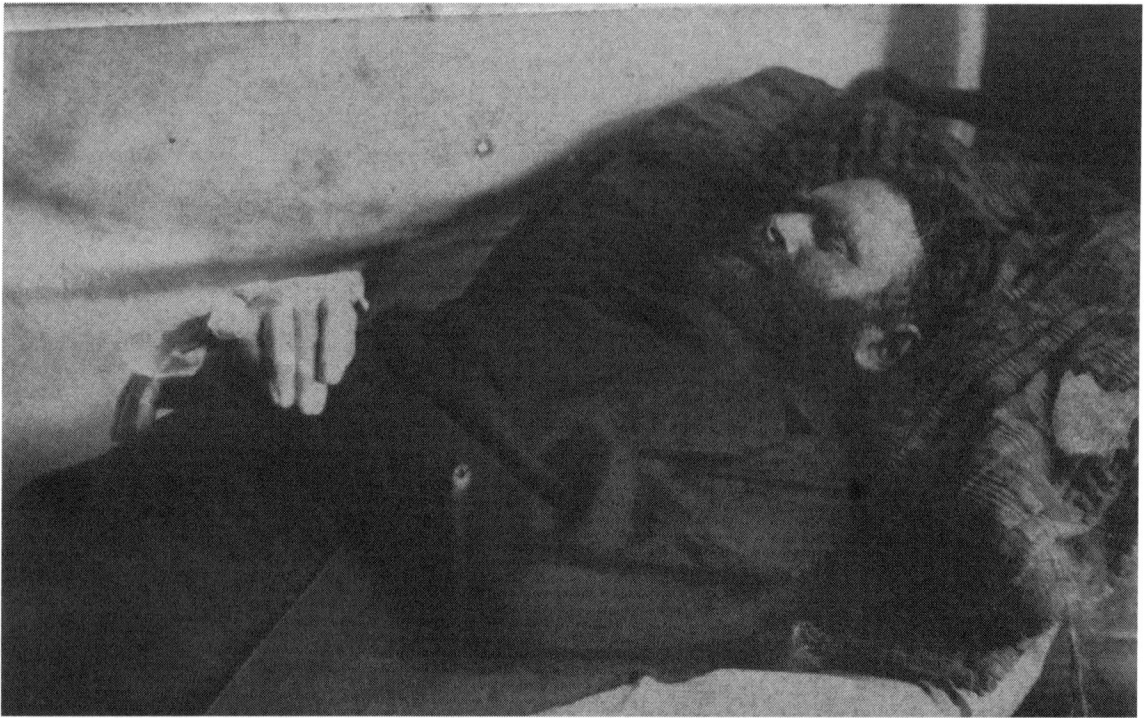

The result was the assassination of 41-year-old jailor Henry Bugler on June 13, 1866. Bugler's 4-year-old son, John, was also shot in the arm by a stray bullet during the incident.[4] Bugler, an Irish immigrant, was buried in St. Mary's Cemetery (which adjoins Woodlawn Cemetery along Noland Road in Independence, Missouri) with a descriptive tombstone of the events surrounding his death.[5] His pregnant wife, Mary (Brady) Bugler, remained employed at the Jackson County Jail. In addition to feeding and tending to prisoners and caring for her six, young children in the midst of her own "confinement," Mrs. Bugler fed and cared for from 5-10 paupers placed in her charge by the Jackson County Court for at least a year after her husband was murdered. Her son, Thomas B. Bugler, was born in the residence portion of the Jackson County Jail in December 1866. The last record uncovered showing Mrs. Bugler in an official capacity at the Jail was August 1867 (See the following endnote for a more complete history of the Bugler family).[6]

Vigilante and guerilla warfare countered with martial law—complete with immediate death penalty…executions without trial—had become more of a rule than exception. The Federal authorities had to bring 10,000 military troops back into Missouri to deal with all the ex-confederates and guerrillas as countless post Civil War-reforms began the slow process of restoring civil law.

A new Missouri State Constitution was adopted on December 6, 1865. However, its controversial "test oath requirement" by which ministers and lawyers, and anyone who wished to vote, were required to attest under oath "that they had never committed any one of 86 different acts of supposed disloyalty against the state or Union."[7] This test disenfranchised all former Confederates, southern sympathizers, and even those who had been pardoned during the War.

One who refused to take the oath was Baptist minister living in Cass County, Reverend Abner Holton Deane, who ended up in the 1859 Jackson County Jail. Deane felt his commission to preach the Gospel came not from the state, but from God. Once again, Independence artist George Caleb Bingham used his skill with a paintbrush to illustrate the desperate plight of his friend, a political casualty. "Captain Bingham," whom Deane said, "came several times…and brought me books, and once he brought his camera, and took my photograph, from which he afterward painted my portrait," actually painted two separate portraits of Deane.[8] One showed him sitting in the lobby of the jail with a Bible across his knees. The second, in his cell, reveals a dignified man on a cot by a small barred window reading the Bible. The exhibitions of the paintings and distribution of photographs brought such a clamor from the press that Deane was released on June 14, 1866 (the day after the Bugler incident described above).[9] A reproduction of Bingham's second portrait of Deane by muralist Charles Goslin is on display in the 1859 Jail, Marshal's Home, and Museum. The original of this Bingham was donated to William Jewell College in Liberty, Missouri, many years ago.[10]

Later, the U.S. Supreme Court (Cummins v State of Missouri) declared that the oath was unconstitutional as applied to members of the clergy; their right to vote or hold office could be refused, but not the right to minister.

According to the *Independence Sentinel* newspaper for Saturday, July 10, 1869, "There are now confined in jail at this place, nineteen prisoners, three charged with murder in the 1st degree, four with horse stealing and eight with other species of grand larceny; 2 with petit larceny and one with obtaining money under false pretenses. Weaver is serving out his twelve months for stealing a cow. Fox who is charged with shooting Bowling at Napoleon and who was himself shot, is so paralyzed that he cannot turn over in bed. His mother stays with him and attends his wants with great fidelity."[11]

A directive from J. W. McClurg in the Executive Department of the State of Missouri at Jefferson City dated December 24, 1869, was delivered via the Western Union Telegraph Company to Jackson County Sheriff Charles Dougherty:

"You are hereby authorized, empowered and required to at once organize, arm and equip as militia a force of not less than thirty (30) men and hold them in readiness to aid Deputy Sheriff Tomlinson of Clay County, if he require aid from you, in capturing or killing if necessary Frank James and Jesse James, the murderers of John W. Sheets, or for the purpose of aiding you in their capture or killing should they be found in your county.

"I will pay for the State five hundred ($500.00) dollars for the capture of either or each of those outlaws and delivery to the Sheriff of Daviess County or for the killing of either or each, if necessary. I will see that the State pays the expense of the organized force for actual service."[12]

It was shortly after this that Jackson County was allowed a County Marshal, as you will see in the following chapter.

In February 1877, Deputy Marshal Henry H. Hughes pursued two intoxicated men who had harassed and shot at "some colored boys." Hughes traced the men to their cabin in the woods where he was shot by Richard Green. Green was tried, found guilty, and on March 1, 1878, was hung in the courtyard of the Jail at 2nd and Main Streets behind the Jackson County Courthouse in Kansas

City. (The venue for his accomplice, Frank Miller, was moved to Lafayette County, where he was sentenced to be hung. Missouri Governor John Smith Phelps commuted his sentence to 10 years in the penitentiary.)[13] Missouri Law allowed County Marshal James W. Liggett $25 for hanging a condemned prisoner. However, Liggett's expenses were not less than $125, the ½ inch rope used having cost $15, and the building of the scaffold, $29.[14] Later that year, Cass County asked for the use of the gallows upon which Green was hanged; they wanted it for the execution of Isaacs, who was convicted there of murder.[15]

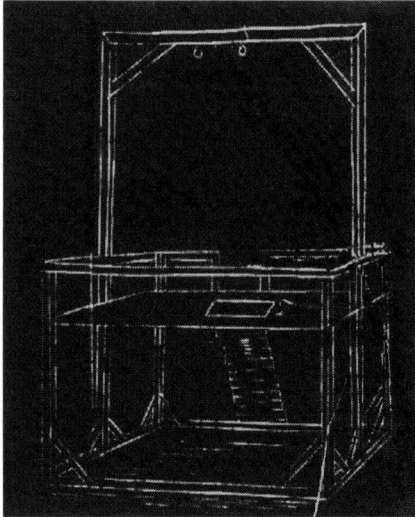

We have compiled through various sources the best available listing to date (2009) of lawmen serving Jackson County at Independence from 1827-1933 (see *Appendix A: Lawmen Serving Jackson County in Independence, Missouri: 1827-1933*). A complete listing of jail prisoners is not available. However, detailed entries were logged over time to ensure compensation for each arrest, boarding, and court appearance. Only four arrest ledgers for the 1859 Jackson County Jail are known to have survived. These have been donated over the years to the Jackson County Historical Society. The time periods covered include: 1881-1883; 1895-1900[16]; 1927-1928; and, 1928-1932. Additionally, a previously donated receipt book of William Botts provides clues to activities at the Jail from 1854-1858, when Botts served as Jackson County Sheriff. Finally, a set of more than 25 "mug shots" taken of prisoners in the late 1890s at the 1859 Jackson County Jail, tell fascinating stories in and of themselves. See Appendix E. For additional sources, Missouri State Penitentiary registers should also be investigated at the Missouri State Archives. Between December 4, 1876 (when jailor Captain Maurice Moulson Langhorne took charge of the Jail) and November 28, 1880 (when Mr. George Hezekiah Holland assumed the office), there were 409 prisoners confined in the jail.[17] Here's a snapshot of the 1859 Jackson County Jail from the 1880 U.S. Census. From the 1881-1883 arrest records, it is estimated that Jackson County's 12-cell Jail in Independence averaged about 25 prisoners per month.[18]

M. M. Langhorn[e],	45	white	male	keeps jail	born in Virginia
Anna M.	40	white	female	wife	born in Missouri
Mary	19	white	female	daughter	born in Missouri
John S.	17	white	male	son	born in Missouri
Samuel W.	13	white	male	son	born in Missouri
Anna M.	3	white	female	daughter	born in Missouri
A.J. Blackwell	35	white	male	in jail	born in Missouri
Andrew Scott	55	white	male	in jail	born in Ireland
Sam Secil	19	white	male	in jail	born in Kentucky
John Williams	25	black	male	in jail	born in Missouri
William Cooper	50	white	male	in jail	born in Missouri
Charles Arnold	19	white	male	in jail	born in New York
Julie Crandell	30	white	female	in jail	born in New York
C.E. Thompson	21	white	male	in jail	born in New York
Ambrose Shily	25	white	male	in jail	born in Kentucky
Martin Lillis	25	white	male	in jail	born in Kentucky
S.E. Thompson	27	white	female	in jail	born in Missouri

[1] The jurors were: C. W. Fairman, foreman; Jessie P. Alexander; J. M. Piper; and, P. T. Scruggs. Jackson County Court minutes (12:347:101981).

[2] Jackson County Court minutes (12:424:101406).

[3] Ibid., (13:408:101794).

[4] "From St. Louis: The Independence Murder Case…," *Chicago Tribune*, 16 June 1866, which printed a special dispatch dated June 15 of "the particulars of the murder in Independence night before last." This would make Bugler's death taking place on June 13. "The Affair at Independence: Radical Demagoguery," *Tri-Weekly Missouri Republican*, 20 June 1866, relayed a letter to the editor dated June 14 about "the peace of our community was last night disturbed…," which confirms Bugler's death on June 13 (see copies in the Jackson County Historical Society Archives, Document ID 69F28). A syndicated copy of this appeared as a, "Correct Statement of the Killing at Independence," *Liberty* (Mo.) *Tribune*, 22 June 1866, 2 (copy on file in the Jackson County Historical Society Archives, Document ID 192F6. Also, Curtis, Bill and Annette W. "First Murder of a Law Officer in Jackson County, Sheriff Henry Bugler," Vol. 8, No. 2, (December 2004), *The Blue & Grey Chronicle*, 7-9. Bundschu, Henry A. "Jailer's Death," *Kansas City* (Mo.) *Star*, 19 June 1949.

[5] Mary Bugler paid James Culbertson $25 for her husband's tombstone (you can see his name inscribed on the bottom left corner of the marble tablet); Murphy and Thompson $25 for funeral expenses; and, John T. Dunne $62 for a fence around his grave. Henry's surname is spelled "Buggler" in church records at Mary's Church (Church of the Holy Cross) in Independence; "Bugler," in Jackson County records, and on his tombstone; and, published erroneously as "Buglar," in estate settlement announcements, as found in copies of his estate file in the Jackson County Historical Society Archives, Document ID L81F15.

[6] Henry Bugler and Mary Brady were married by Rev. Bernard Donnelly in Jackson County, Missouri, on 19 Nov. 1850 (see copies in the Jackson County Historical Society Archives, Document ID L81F18). The 36-year-olds appear in the 1860 U.S. Census for Independence, Jackson County, Missouri, with their children. Mary Bugler said she was 42 when the 1870 U.S. Census taker came to her Independence home. She was 52 in the 1880 U.S. Census for Independence, Jackson County, Missouri. The Bugler's children were: Bridget (born 6 Sept. 1852); Mary Celia (born 12 Sept. 1854); Julia (born 17 Jul. 1856); Sarah "Sallie" (born 8 Dec. 1857); Henry, Jr. (born 2 Oct. 1859); John (born ca. 1862); and, Thomas B. (born Dec. 1866). For baptisms for five of the seven Bugler children, consult Daughters of the American Revolution—Kansas City Chapter. *Vital Historical Records of Jackson County, Missouri: 1826-1876*. Reprint. (Independence, Mo.: Jackson County Historical Society, 2008), 107, 109, 111, 112, 113, 116.

Bridget Bugler married John V. Hoover in Jackson County 15 Aug. 1876.

Mary Celia Bugler married Edward Matte in Jackson County 15 Oct. 1871.

Julia Bugler married John McCarty in Jackson County 28 Nov. 1882. They were listed in 1920 U.S. Census with 28-year-old son, John McCarty, and 11-year-old niece, Kathleen Bugler, in Oakland, Alameda County, California.

Sallie Bugler married Samuel Stallcup in Jackson County 10 Jan. 1873.

Henry Bugler, Jr., patented land in Grant County, Oregon, in November 1889 (see copies in the Jackson County Historical Society Archives, Document ID L81F17). Henry, Jr., appears as a farm laborer in the U.S. Census for Fresno County, California, in 1900. And, in 1910, he and his wife and daughter (both named Catherine) were in San Francisco, California. According to his death certificate, Henry Bugler, Jr., died 12 Oct. 1919, near Warsaw, Benton County, Missouri, from injuries received from being thrown from a horse. A newspaper account of the accident was not found during a cursory search; but, probate notifications began being running the week after his death in the *Benton County Enterprise*.

Thomas B. Bugler was listed in the 1900 Census in Chicago, Illinois. The 36-year-old printer married Margaret Rehberg in Kane County, Il., on July 4, 1903. They were listed in the 1910 U.S. Census in Los Angeles, California.

Ironically, sixteen years after his father was murdered, John Bugler was placed in the 1859 Jackson County Jail, suspected of participating in the Glendale train robbery at Blue Cut, Jackson County, Missouri. The indictment stemmed from a confession given by John Land. The 'confession' resulted in Bugler being charged. However, after the murder of Jesse James, prosecutor William Wallace on April 5, 1882, dismissed all charges against Bugler and thereafter, John Land recanted his confession that had implicated John Bugler. Articles about John Bugler appear in: "Full Confession," *San Francisco* (Ca.) *Bulletin*, published as *Evening Bulletin*, 1 Apr. 1882. Also syndicated as "Crime Confessed," *Inter Ocean*, published as *The Daily Inter Ocean*, 1 Apr. 1882. In December 1887, John purchased land in Grant County, Oregon; and it appears he sold it by March 1889 (see copies in the Jackson County Historical Society Archives, Document ID L81F17).

When Mary Bugler purchased land in Harney County, Oregon, in November 1894, the land transaction said that she was "of Phoenix, Territory of Arizona" (see copies in the Jackson County Historical Society Archives, Document ID L81F17). And, when the 1900 U.S. Census was listed, 72-year-old Mary Bugler was living at 337 Harriet Street in San Francisco, California. It appears from data she provided, that Mary was born in November 1828.

[7] Parrish, William E., Charles T. Jones and Lawrence O. Christensen. *Missouri: Heart of the Nation* (Arlington Heights: Harlan Davidson, 1992), 191.

[8] Deane, Rev. A. H. *Reminiscences of Half a Century*, 17. *The Pleasant Hill* (Mo.) *Union* published on 6 July 1866, a syndicated article from the *Independence* (Mo.) *Messenger* announcing, "George C. Bingham...is now engaged...upon a work which will illustrate to future generations an ignoble period of our state's history, and be a memento of the reign of radicalism." See *Independence* (Mo.) *Examiner*, 30 June 1950, for a reprint, "Old Newspaper Gives Picture of Tense Times Here in 1866."

[9] Maple, J. C. and R. P. Rider. *Missouri Baptist Biography*, III, (Liberty, Mo.: 1918), p. 101-103. Also, the *Missouri Historical Review*, January (1941), XXXV:306. Missouri, at its State Convention in St. Louis, on January 6, 1865, adopted an "Oath of Loyalty" which limited the rights of many of its citizens. "No person shall...be competent as a bishop, priest, deacon, minister, elder, or other clergyman of any religious persuasion, sect, denomination, to teach, or preach, or solemnize marriages, unless such person shall have first taken, subscribed and filed such oath." Section 14 delineates the penalty for not taking the oath: "a fine of not less than five hundred dollars, or...imprisonment in the county jail, not less than six months or by fine and imprisonment...." It is often referred to as the Drake Constitution. *Jackson County Historical Society JOURNAL* 1996 (Fall) 36:3, 5. Also, "Civil War Soldier and Preacher in County Jail." *Jackson County Historical Society JOURNAL* 1999 (Winter) 39:4, 6-8.

[10] Artist Charles Goslin of Edwardsville, Kansas, donated his portrait of Deane to the Jackson County Historical Society. It is his copy of George Caleb Bingham's portrait of Deane. Goslin said, "I painted it for the pleasure of it—because I admire Bingham so much. If it helps to stimulate an interest, then I consider my time well spent." Bingham was living in Independence when he heard of the plight of Deane. Even though Deane had served as a major in the Union Army during the Civil War, he was arrested and jailed in 1866 for defying the terms of Missouri's Loyalty Oath. Goslin understands the major's angst with this law, his loyalty to God, not the State, and his respect for all mankind, regardless of political leanings. The original "painting," in the collection of William Jewell College, is actually oil over a photograph on paper.... With Bingham's assistance, Deane was released. Later, a similar case reached the United States Supreme Court, and the Oath was declared unconstitutional as applied to members of the professions named therein. They could still be refused the right to vote or hold office, but could not be refused the right to teach or minister. "Charles Goslin Donates His Artwork to Jail Museum." *Jackson County Historical Society JOURNAL* 1996 (Fall) 36:3, 5. A lengthier article about Deane appears in, "Civil War Soldier and Preacher in County Jail." *Jackson County Historical Society JOURNAL* 1999 (Winter) 39:4, 6-8.

[11] As extracted in the Jackson County Historical Society JOURNAL 1972 (June), 14:2, 1.

[12] Baxter-Campbell-Keogh Collection of Charles Dougherty Papers, 1865-1870; Sheriff's Papers, 1869, in the Jackson County Historical Society Archives, Document ID L8F28. At the time of this printing (2009) the originals of these papers are maintained by Dougherty's great granddaughter, Barbara A. (Campbell) Magerl [granddaughter of George and Annie (O'Connell) Dougherty; daughter of William J. and Caroline I. (Dougherty) Campbell].

[13] Green's was the last public execution until at least August 8, 1881, when that issue of the *Kansas City Evening Star* reported, "Bloody Deeds: The Evening Star Rehearses Jackson County's Murder Record.*"* Hughes' death is also discussed in, "Awaiting Their Doom. The Batch of Murderers Confined in the Independence Jail," *Kansas City (Mo.) Star*, 6 Aug. 1886, 1. "The Penalty Paid. Edward Calhoun Sneed Hanged at Independence Soon after Noonday His Last Day," *Kansas City* (Mo.) *Star,* 24 June 1887, 1.

[14] "In Kansas City Forty Years Ago," *Kansas City* (Mo.) *Star,* 4 Mar. 1918, 12.

[15] Ibid., 12 Oct. 1918, 14.

[16] *Jackson County Historical Society JOURNAL*, 1968 (Summer), XI: 2, 2.

[17] *A History of Jackson County*, 640.

[18] Jackson County Historical Society Archives, Document ID L32F12. Prisoners and jail inmates at this time may have had the opportunity to meet with Mother Mary Jerome Shubrick, whose story is reviewed in a later "Jailbreak" section of this book.

CELL

6

WHEN BOTH SHERIFF & MARSHAL PROTECTED JACKSON COUNTY (1871-1924)

A burgeoning post-war reconstruction boom saw Kansas City grow and take over Independence's role as the majority in Jackson County. The increase in population and activity necessitated larger quarters for the proper functioning of Jackson County government.

It was at this time that separate quarters for Jackson County government was instituted in Kansas City (though the Jackson County Courthouse on Independence Square remained and is still today (2009) the County Seat).

A COUNTY JAIL IN KANSAS CITY

In 1870, the Jackson County Court purchased the partially-completed Nelson House Hotel on the northeast corner of 2nd and Main Streets in Kansas City. The Nelson House Hotel was designed by noted Kansas City architect, Asa Beebe Cross, whom you may recall, also designed the 1859 Jackson County Jail in Independence.

The foundations the Nelson House Hotel had been laid in 1869, and were "finished up" by action of the County Court in 1871.[1] The first use of this building as a jail was in 1871. The first prisoner, "was a red handed man from Independence, and John Farrell was the jailor who locked him up."[2]

The modern Jackson County Jail in Kansas City gradually became the holding space for hard cases, dangerous criminals, and the bulk of county prisoners, especially as the rise of municipal police forces evolved. This jail, used between 1871 and 1892, was also the location of one of two *legal* hangings (or, judicial executions) during this period. (See Appendix B: *Legal Hangings in Jackson County, 1839-June 1933*).[3]

The 1859 Jackson County Jail in Independence was alleviated of overcrowded conditions, and led to its use as overflow from Kansas City for misdemeanor crimes (excepting Frank James), including:

Horseracing on public streets	Firing guns in town
Operating a gaming house	Assault and battery
Riots and routs	Creating of noise by drunks or minors
Indecency	Disturbing a religious gathering; and,
Building a privy "not over a pit."	

A MARSHAL FOR JACKSON COUNTY

Jackson County became unique in Missouri when the legislature on February 1, 1871, established the office of Marshal of Jackson County…an elected post that was to be filled *in addition to* the traditional Sheriff of Jackson County. According to the act:

> *"The Marshal of Jackson County shall be elected by the qualified voters of said county on the first Tuesday after the first Monday in March 1871, and thereafter on the day for holding general elections of Sheriff of Jackson County, and such elections shall be governed by the law governing elections of sheriff.*
>
> *"He shall hold his office for two years and until his successor is elected and qualified….*
>
> *"If any vacancy occur in the office of marshal, it shall be filled as vacancies in the office of sheriff are filled…..*
>
> *"The marshal may appoint one or more deputies with the approbation of the judge of the criminal court of Jackson County, and every such appointment shall be in writing, and with the oath of office endorsed thereon shall be filed in the office of the clerk of said court and recorded in the office of the recorder of deeds.*
>
> *"Every deputy so appointed shall possess all the powers and may perform any of the duties prescribed by law to be performed by the marshal.*
>
> *"The marshal shall be a conservator of the peace within his county, and shall have all the powers in criminal cases that are or may be law conferred on sheriffs.*
>
> *"The marshal shall attend all sittings of the criminal court of Jackson County, and all process issued by the criminal court or the judge or clerk thereof shall be directed to and served by said marshal.*
>
> *"During the continuance of any vacancy in the office of marshal, or when the marshal shall be a party, or when it shall appear to the court out of which the process shall issue, or to the clerk thereof in vacation, that the marshal is related to any party thereto, the sheriff of Jackson County shall execute process issuing from the criminal court of said county.*

"The marshal shall have the same power, be subject to like proceedings, and incur the same liabilities on all process placed in his hands as the sheriff of said county has or is subject to in similar cases.

"He shall be allowed the same compensation for service as is now or may be allowed to sheriffs for similar services.

"The marshal shall be ex-officio jailor of Jackson County, and shall in all respects be governed by the laws now or hereafter in force in relation to jails and jailors."[4]

After the Marshal's post was created, the Sheriff was responsible for civil affairs. The Marshal pursued, apprehended, and jailed alleged criminals.[5] What about the jailors? They were specialized "Deputy County Marshals" who staffed the jail. The Jailors and their families occupied the home adjacent to the 1859 Jackson County Jail.

Jesse Woodson James

When the marshal's position was abolished 53 years later in 1924 a long time employee at the Courthouse, Dell Womack said, ***As I recollect the chief reason Jackson County was given a marshal was*** [the sole purpose of catching] ***Jesse James***."[6]

The first Jackson County Marshal to fill the newly created position was Major Granville Dyson Page, who served after the March 1871 election through the end of 1872. And, at the November 1872 elections, Page was re-elected and resumed his post for a full, two-year term, between 1873 and 1874.[7]

Page had not yet migrated to Jackson County when the 1850 U. S. Census was taken. He was listed on September 9, 1850, in Front Royal, Warren County, Virginia, a 19-year-old clerk in a store. This would make Page having been born about 1831 or 1832.[8]

From records discovered thus far, it appears that Granville D. Page married 21-year-old Martha C. Ashby about 1853.[9] A son, Henry C., was born in 1854 or 1855. Martha died on March 14, 1855, and was buried in the Oakwood Farm Cemetery in Delaplane, Fauquier County, Virginia.[10] Presumably, Page married Martha's sister, Nattelen (or Natildia) Ashby, and a daughter, Serena "Rena" Page, was born in August 1857.[11]

By May 1860, Granville D. Page was recorded having purchased the defunct 1841 Jackson County Jail (on Lot Number 2), as discussed earlier in this compendium.

The following month, on June 8, 1860, Page, a 28-year-old "negro trader," was listed in the U.S. Census with children: Henry C., age 6; and, Serena, 3; and, the children's 50-year-old grandmother, Alcinda Ashby (all born in Virginia). Mrs. Granville Page had

Major Granville Dyson Page

died. The Missouri Slave Schedules for Independence, Jackson County, Missouri, list Page, a negro trader, with a 12-year-old-female-mulatto under the census heading "Fugitive from State." Alcinda Ashby was listed with three mulatto slaves: a 22-year-old female, and two males, aged 10 and six.[12] [Note: A Granville R. Page, 43-years-old in 1860, was listed in Lafayette County, Missouri. Though clearly related, this prominent farmer and slave owner should not be confused with Granville D. Page of Jackson County.][13]

On December 31, 1860, Page married Miss Venitia Mary (nicknamed "Nish") Colcord in Jackson County, Missouri. Between 1860 and 1867, the Pages lived in the early Gothic Revival home that remains today as the historic "Overfelt-Campbell-Johnston House," also known as the "Cammie Johnston House," at 305 South Pleasant, in Independence, Missouri (see below). There, Page kept a journal, a copy of which is in the Jackson County Historical Society Archives.[14] In 1863, Mrs. Page was confined in the Union prison in Kansas City. The note her sister, Mrs. Jacob Hall, delivered to her while in prison, is also archived.[15] The jail collapsed after Mrs. Page's release. According to the structure's National Register of Historic Places nomination form, "Courtney Campbell bought the house *at auction on the county courthouse steps*" in 1867. This would indicate that Page may have lost the home for whatever reason. It was

likely as a result of the Civil War. Page volunteered to serve the Confederacy during the Civil War as Assistant Quarter Master in Joseph Orville "Jo" Shelby's *Iron Brigade of the West*, which is likely where he attained the rank, or at least attribute of "Major."[16]

In the 1870 U.S. Census for Fort Osage Township, Jackson County, Missouri, 38-year-old Page, is listed with a 30-year-old wife, Venetia, a Kentucky native, and children: Henry, 15 and Minnie (Serena in the 1860 Census), 13 (both from Page's previous marriages)(born in Virginia); and, Charles [Lafayette], 9; John [Jonathan Colcord], 5; and [Mary] Ida, 2 (all of whom were born in Missouri). A. Ashford (note variance in her surname from 1860), age 60, continued to live with the family. There is also a 17-year-old black male named Ellick Page (farm laborer, born in Arkansas), and a 23-year-old black female named Edna Page (house servant born in Virginia) living in their household.

Major Granville Dyson Page died in May 1874. One source said he was killed in a gun battle with outlaws while he was Jackson County Marshal.[17]

His son, Henry C. died the day after Christmas the previous year. They are buried in Woodlawn Cemetery in Independence (Obelisk on left).[18]

Minnie Serena "Rena" Page married Thomas C. Sawyer in Jackson County on October 31, 1877. They resided in Lafayette County, Missouri.[19]

Alcinda Ashby, by the way, was living with the Aaron F. and Sallie (Woodson) Sawyer (ages 30 and 27 respectively) family in Independence when the 1880 U.S. Census was listed; she was said to be 75-years-old.

NEW COUNTY COURTHOUSE IN KANSAS CITY

On March 22, 1873, the General Assembly of the State of Missouri, approved "an act to provide for a branch of the recorder's office in Jackson County, Missouri" and proclaimed "the recorder of deeds for Jackson County, Missouri, shall open an office at Kansas City, in which shall be recorded all deeds of trust, mortgages and other instruments affecting real and personal estates situated in range thirty-three in said county, as well as all personal property."[20]

On March 14, 1885, the General Assembly of the State of Missouri, approved an act "providing for the erection of court houses and jails in places *other than county seats*." It stipulated that "any county…in which terms of the circuit court, or courts of common pleas having circuit court jurisdiction, are by law held at a place other than the county seat, the county court of such county may cause the erection of a good and sufficient courthouse and jail at such place other than the county seat where such courts are held, and for such purpose shall have and possess all the powers conferred on it for the erection of court houses and jails at the county seat."[21] The following year, newspaper articles covered the on-going discussion for the proper site for a new courthouse.[22]

A cyclone destroyed the Jackson County Courthouse in Kansas City on May 11, 1886.[23] The upper floor of the jail building was blown off.[24]

The Jackson County Court, again, enlisted the expertise of architect Asa Beebe Cross to design a new courthouse that was constructed at 5th and Oak in Kansas City in 1887.[25] To this day, all land transactions involving the range along the Missouri-Kansas border are transacted at the Jackson County Courthouse in downtown Kansas City. All other land transactions are handled through the Jackson County Courthouse at the County Seat in Independence.

A second jail facility at 219 East Missouri Avenue replaced the Second Street lock down, and was used between 1893 and 1935. The County Courthouse and Jail were Cross' last extensive works before his death in 1894.[26] All legal hangings (or judicial executions) in Kansas City took place at this jail (See Appendix B: *Legal Hangings in Jackson County, 1839-June 1933*).[27]

[1] Birdsall, 490. "Major A. B. Cross Dead," *Kansas City* (Mo.) *Star*, 18 Aug. 1894, 1.

[2] "Jail Prisoners to be Moved," *Kansas City* (Mo.) *Star*, 25 Mar. 1892, 6.

[3] At the time of this publication (2009) the site is occupied by a law firm (it was once utilized by the Kansas City Water Department). Frazier, Harriet C. *Death Sentences in Missouri, 1803-2005.* (Jefferson, Nc.: McFarland & Co., Inc., Publishers, 2006), 102.

[4] *Laws of the State of Missouri*, 1871, 26th General Assembly, Regular Session, 87-88.

[5] Harry S Truman Library. *Oral History Interview with Henry P. Chiles* by J. R. Fuchs, November 1, 1961, 73-74.

[6] "Marshal's Star on Shelf," Kansas City (Mo.) Star, 6 Jan. 1925, p. 5, c.1. *Laws of Missouri*, 1921, 51st General Assembly, Regular Session, 220-222, approved March 11, 1921. Also, Harry S Truman Library. *Oral History Interview with Henry P. Chiles* by J. R. Fuchs, November 1, 1961, pages 73-74:

> FUCHS: *Mr. Truman supported John Miles for county marshal in 1920. Now is that a job that died out?*
> CHILES: *Yes, it's been abolished. It used to be in Jackson County — there used to be a sheriff who took care of the civil affairs of the sheriff's office and this marshal, the criminal. He had the jail and he patrolled and arrested; he was like police. But, the marshal handled the criminal end of the thing. Johnny Miles ran and Johnny was a very popular. Republican. Nearly all of these veteran soldiers backed him. I had a nephew who went out and worked for him, and I give him the dickens and he just worked the same. I understood Truman backed Miles.*
> FUCHS: *Later on, I believe by 1924, Miles was serving as sheriff and I wondered about the two jobs.*
> CHILES: *Miles was marshal; was he ever sheriff?*
> FUCHS: *Yes, he later on served as sheriff and I wondered if as you say, if the sheriff later on took the job that the marshal did in those days?*
> CHILES: *They did combine the two, but I think that was after Mile's time in office. The sheriff's job was entirely civil and the marshal had the jail and the prisoners and did the patrolling and the arresting; but Miles, he won by a big, big majority. All these veterans were for him, everyone of them. You couldn't get a one of them to vote against him. I had a nephew that I thought I could have some influence over, and he wouldn't listen to me.*

[7] "Marshal's Star on Shelf," *Kansas City* (Mo.) *Star*, 6 Jan. 1925, p. 5, c. 1. The first notation found in Jackson County Court minutes was 12 June 1871.

[8] National Archives and Records Administration, M432, Roll 980, sheet 57A. He was listed beside fellow store clerk, 28-year-old Robert S. Norris.

[9] Martha C. Ashby, age 18, was listed in the 1850 U.S. Census for Ashby's District, Fauquier County, Virginia, with her younger sister, Nattelen H., age 14, and their mother, Alsinda/Alcinda Ashby, age 38. They lived on a farm of 70-yer-old Mary Grigsby, and her grown children still living at home.

[10] Baird, Nancy, Carol Jordan and Joseph Scherer. Fauquier County (Va.) Tombstone Inscriptions. Volume 2. (Bowie, Md.: Heritage Books, Inc. 2000), 153. Martha's tombstone also reveals that she was born 12 Jan. 1821. The cemetery is located on the north side of Route 724, one mile west of Route 17. There is a ball tombstone in the yard against a meat house, and other stones in a plot behind a house and garden. At the time the tombstones were transcribed in September 1993, it was apparent that there had been an iron fence and evidence of a number of graves.

[11] *Portrait and Biographical Record of Lafayette and Saline Counties, Missouri.* (Chicago: Chapman Bros., 1893), 429-430; explains that Rena's mother was "Natildia Ashby…a lady of refinement and culture, born and educated in Virginia." Her birth date is from the 1900 U.S. Census enumeration of Rena and her husband, Thomas C. Sawyer, and family, in Lafayette County, Missouri.

[12] Missouri Slave Schedules. Eighth Census, National Archives and Records Administration, M653, Roll 662 (Dallas thru Lafayette Counties). Granville D. Page's 12-year-old slave "might" be 23-year-old Edna Page listed with the family 10 years later. And, the 6-year-old male slave "might" be 17-year-old Ellick Page from the 1870 Census.

[13] Granville R. Page's parents were Axel H. and Sarah (Ennis) Page, both native Virginians, as were his paternal and maternal grandparents. Sarah's father was John Ennis and Axtel's father was Joseph Page. Axel H. Page made his home in Warren County, Kentucky, where Granville R. was born in January, 1817. In 1827, Axtel Page and family moved to Lafayette County, Missouri. *Portrait and Biographical Record of Lafayette and Saline Counties, Missouri.* (Chicago: Chapman Bros., 1893), 429-430.

[14] Jackson County Historical Society Archives, Document ID 61F2.

[15] Jackson County Historical Society Archives, Document ID 2F16. See also Document ID 79F10.

[16] Shelby was appointed Captain of Cavalry under Sterling Price in 1861, was Colonel in June 1862, and Brigadier General from December 15, 1863. Shelby was regarded as the best cavalry leader in the Trans-Mississippi theater.

At the end of the Civil War, rather than surrender, Shelby led his Brigade into Mexico to support Maximilian in June, 1865. After Maximilian was shot in 1867, Shelby returned to Missouri and resumed farming.

[17] Jackson County Historical Society Archives, Document ID 79F10. See also Document ID L4F10-18.

[18] Page's tombstone (Lot 6, Block 43, Location A) indicates he died on May 9; his intestate estate file indicates May 11. His tombstone is also the only instance found thus far that attributes Page as "Major." Henry C. Page's tombstone also provides his birth date as 7 Mar. 1854. Page's survivors included: his widow; H. Page (although Henry C. died the previous year); Rena (Serena) Page; Charles Page; John Page, and, Ida Page. Meador, Victor. *Wills and Administrations.* (Independence, Mo.: Jackson County Genealogical Society).

[19] *Portrait and Biographical Record of Lafayette and Saline Counties, Missouri.* (Chicago: Chapman Bros., 1893), 429-430.

[20] *Laws of the State of Missouri*, 1873. This act was amended slightly on May 6, 1879. Interestingly, the authors found a mention in the Jackson County Court minutes of an election at the "Courthouse in the City of Kansas," in September 1864 (12:307:100867). Another pre-1871 reference to a "Court House in Kansas City," dates to November 16, 1869, when "members of a committee appointed by the citizens of the Kansas City School District, at a public meeting held at the Court House in Kansas City on the 12th day of Nov. 1869…." See, Baxter-Campbell-Keogh Collection of Charles Dougherty Papers, 1865-1870; Sheriff's Papers, 1869, in the Jackson County Historical Society Archives, Document ID L8F28. At the time of this printing (2009) the originals of these papers are maintained by Dougherty's great granddaughter, Barbara A. (Campbell) Magerl [granddaughter of George and Annie (O'Connell) Dougherty; daughter of William J. and Caroline I. (Dougherty) Campbell].

[21] *Laws of the State of Missouri*, 1885. This replaced a repealed act previously approved March 16, 1883.

[22] Untitled articles, *Kansas City* (Mo.) *Star*, 23 June and 28 Aug. 1886; "The New Court House," *Kansas City* (Mo.) *Star*, 15 Nov., 22 Dec., and 23 Dec. 1886.

[23] "Fatal Storm: Kansas City Visited by Fatal Cloudburst," *Kansas City* (Mo.) *Star,* 11 May 1886, 1. "Fifty Years Ago Kansas City Suffered Its Worst Storm," *Kansas City* (Mo.) *Star*, 10 May 1936.

[24] "Jail Prisoners to be Moved," *Kansas City* (Mo.) *Star*, 25 Mar. 1892, 6.

[25] *A History of the 16th Judicial Circuit* (Circuit Court of Jackson County, Missouri, 1986), 2-5.

[26] "Major A. B. Cross Dead," *Kansas City* (Mo.) *Star*, 18 Aug. 1894, 1.

[27] At the time of this publication (2009), a Kansas City Fire Department station is on the site at the southeast corner of East Missouri Avenue and Oak Street. Frazier, Harriet C. *Death Sentences in Missouri, 1803-2005.* (Jefferson, Nc.: McFarland & Co., Inc., Publishers, 2006), 102.

JAIL BREAK:
FAMOUS OUTLAWS RIDE INTO INFAMY

Decades after the War Between the States ended, the citizens of Jackson County felt the lingering bitterness and uncertainty of that great conflict.

Independence was a dangerous place, and it was a dangerous duty to even try and arrest the criminal as they were often related to the old elite, and slowly regained power and influence. Law and order had to walk a fine line between competing sympathies.

Out of these tumultuous times and fueling animosities from the outrages of the War, rode Missouri's most notorious outlaws: Jesse James and his brother Frank; Cole Younger and his band of followers; and, other bandits put Missouri on the map as the "Outlaw State" into the 20th century through prohibition and the formation of the FBI.

For nearly twenty years, these "Robbing Hoods" remained one-step ahead of the law…for the most part.

Jesse Woodson James

A James gang member, Bill Ryan, was held for trial in the 1859 Jackson County Jail. William H. Wallace, prosecuting attorney of Jackson County, had Deputy County Marshal Keshlear go to Nashville to identify Ryan, and bring him back to put in jail in Independence.[1] "Wallace gathered about him as hard-bitten a group of fighting men as the country ever saw. In that group were: Captain Maurice Moulson Langhorne, one of the hardest fighting officers in General Jo Shelby's famed cavalry brigade; H. H. Craig, a Kentuckian; [Captain] Cornelius ["Con"] Murphy, a Virginian; Colonel J. E. Payne, a Confederate regimental commander; [William G.] Whig Keshlear, whose brother was killed fighting in the Confederate army; Colonel Upton Hays and his brother Amazon Hays…. These men could shoot as hard and straight as the bandits…and for once the bandits backed off."[2]

Then, in the spring of 1882, Jesse James was murdered in St. Joseph, Missouri. *"Trained by William Clarke Quantrill, "Bloody" Bill Anderson, and other border ruffians, and cloaked in Southern sympathies, the James boys continued their crime spree and eluded capture for nearly 20 years. This caused great embarrassment to Missouri Governor Thomas T[heodore]*

Thomas Crittenden

Crittenden and his U.S. Senatorial aspirations. Under pressure from railroad and bank lobbying forces, Crittenden [in 1881] issued an extremely controversial and virtually unprecedented $50,000 bounty on the James Gang (worth millions in today's dollars). This was comparable only to the reward issued for John Wilkes Booth, the assassin of President Abraham Lincoln. In cahoots with the Governor and with dollar signs dancing in his head, a member of the James Gang, Bob Ford, put a bullet in the back of Jesse's head." "It is often inaccurately stated that this was a 'dead or alive' reward. To the contrary, the money was to be paid only upon arrest and conviction of Frank or Jesse James."[3]

FRANK JAMES SURRENDERS TO THE LAW

Frank James

Died at Kc... Feb. 18- 1915

Frank at age 23 *James Taken 1866*

Alexander Franklin "Frank" James, fearing a similar fate to that of his younger brother, Jesse, began—with the aid of John Newman Edwards— negotiations with the Missouri governor to surrender. A trial was set for June 3, 1883, but was continued to August 21, 1883. He faced charges of robbery and the murders of Conductor William Westfall and stonemason Frank McMillan during an 1881 train robbery at Winston, Missouri, and also the murder of Captain John Sheets in an 1869 bank robbery in Gallatin, Missouri. The indictment against Frank James on the Sheets murder was dropped; a conviction was sought on the train robbery and murder charges only.

"Following his surrender, James was taken [on October 6, 1882] by rail to the City of Independence, Missouri. Crowds lined the tracks as the train traveled from Jefferson City to Independence. On the night of Frank's arrival in Independence" where Frank was met by his mother, wife, son, Robert, and the [Jackson County] Sheriff [, whereupon he was taken to "a reception in his honor at the Merchants Hall in which the wealthiest and most popular men were in attendance, including the Governor [Crittenden] and his wife."*[4]

"I am tired of an outlaw's life. I have been hunted for 21 years. I have literally lived in the saddle. I have never known a day of perfect peace. It was one, long, anxious, inexorable, eternal vigil. When I slept it was literally in the midst of an arsenal. If I heard dogs bark more fiercely than usual, or the feet of horses in a greater volume of sound than usual, I stood to my arms. Have you any idea of what a man must endure who leads such a life? No one can. No one can unless he lives it for himself." These words spoken by Frank James to a reporter for the *Sedalia Dispatch* reflect the feelings of the notorious outlaw after his surrender to Governor Crittenden.[5]

ACCOMMODATIONS FOR FRANK JAMES AT THE 1859 JAIL

Frank James was delivered to the 1859 Jackson County Jail in October 1882.

Upon the 100th anniversary of this historical event, the Jackson County Historical Society researched, restored, and interpreted the cell where James stayed. There has been much speculation and various accounts as to which of the cells was occupied for 112 days by James. The earliest reference to the cell appeared in the late edition of the *Kansas City Evening Star*, which stated, "Frank James is confined in the roomiest cell in the jail and has been given orders to admit no one." The largest cells in the complex are the last two cells on the east end of the first and second stories, measuring 8' x 9'. If this account is correct, it would seem that one of these four would have been the cell used. On Thursday, October 12, the *Evening Star* made another reference to Frank James and his accommodations: "His cell is now on the upper story and neat and clean. The door is unlocked and in the corridor a rocking chair has been placed for his accommodation. He is at liberty to walk downstairs when he desires, and indeed, there is nothing to prevent his walking out altogether should he be so disposed."

Other pieces of information fill out this picture. The *Saint Louis Republican* stated on October 9 that several hundred people had been in the area of the jail that day and that James was seated in the east end of the lower hallway where he greeted visitors. This would have been the east end of the hall in the cell block, the only hallway in the complex oriented from east to west. At this end also was the wood stove, the only heat in the cold stone structure. Also, a wooden and iron stairway was located at this end to the second tier of cells. This is now removed, but at the time, James could have left his cell on the second story, walked down the stairs and received his admiring crowds. For security reasons, the second floor cell also seemed to make good sense.

Oral tradition maintains that he was moved downstairs later on…possibly well founded since the jail block was a cold place in the winter. The upper cell windows consist only of iron lattice grill work, subjecting these cells to rain and snow. The lower cell windows, while without glass, were triple louvered iron shutters affording more protection from the elements. The eastern most cell on the downstairs north would have been the best access to the wood stove…and heat.

If oral tradition is correct, it is possible that James was originally jailed on the second level; but, as the crowds increased and the season wore on and the temperature decreased, he was moved to the first floor. Another possibility is the cell on the first floor at the east end on the south, which presently houses displays relating to the jail and its history; however, nothing in the primary source materials or in oral tradition specifies this cell.

In any event, Frank James was treated more like a guest than a prisoner, and was comfortably fixed as possible for his stay in Independence through the winter of 1882-83. The *Kansas City Evening Star* reported, "Now that the hand shaking is over, his

friends are beginning to have a care for his bodily comfort and are converting his cell into a cozy little home. Bob Ricketts, who visited James the other day marked on the absence of a carpet in his cell and to day he purchased a fine Brussels, paying $20 for the pattern. The carpet was sent to the repentant outlaw this morning, and is probably property tacked down by this time."[6]

By October 30, the *Kansas City Journal of Commerce* added, "A Brussels carpet has been sent to Frank James with which to make his cell comfortable; delicacies have been sent to him by many people and, it is said, he has had a concentrated, double distilled banquet, combined with an ovation ever since he has been behind bars."

The *Independence Sentinel* reported that, "From what we can learn Frank James is living about as comfortable now as any feller in the state. His cell at Independence is furnished with an elegant Brussels carpet, the walls are decorated with pictures and such furniture as he has room for is said to be of the best sort." Sporadic accounts refer to flowers and other gifts.[7]

One account said, "He sits for hours at a time conversing with his friends and giving them a history of "Life in the Saddle."[8]

The jail ledger kept at that time, which has survived and is conserved in the Jackson County Historical Society Archives, shows that James was held 112 days (from October 6 to December 31, 1882 at a cost of $.45/day; and, from January 1 to January 25, 1883, at $.35/day). His entire jail stay cost the County $47.90, which could have been more, but his meals had been furnished by his wife or friends; he did not eat "prison fare."[9]

Legend states that Frank James could even leave the Jail, with proper escort, to buy tobacco or walk on the Square. Hinton H. Noland delivered him to the Circuit Court.[10]

Jailor George Hezekiah Holland escorted James to the Independence Opera House on one occasion to see, "Sullivan's View of Ireland." Holland was reportedly dismissed for that action.

ARRAIGNMENT & TRIALS

William H. Wallace

On Sunday, November 26, 1882, a *Kansas City Evening Star* reporter accompanied Deputy County Marshal William G. "Whig" Keshlear from Kansas City to Independence. They would return the following day with Frank James who faced arraignment. In the parlor of the Marshal's Home, "Mr. Evening Star," was introduced to Mrs. Frank (Ann Ralston) James, "the wife of the redoubtable and famous bandit." Mr. James acknowledged the introduction. "The *Evening Star* took a good look as he bowed, and looked again and again as he was conversing with the "better half" of Frank James." He recounted the evening in great detail. Later, around 9 p.m., when the reporter "sought to see Frank James," Jailor George Hezekiah Holland replied, "He is not well and bade his wife good-bye earlier than usual tonight, and has gone to bed. You can see him tomorrow."[11]

James remained in the Independence jail, until William H. Wallace, prosecuting attorney, determined that there was not sufficient evidence to convict James on that murder charge. However, James was then transferred to Daviess County on February 10, 1883, to stand trial [for the Winston Train Robbery that had occurred on July 15, 1881].[12] Frank James was acquitted after a trial that lasted 12 days that summer.[13] James worked at various legal trades in the years that followed. He died at age 72 in 1915. His cremains were kept in a Kansas City bank vault and were scattered in 1944 after his wife Ann died at age 91; they rest in Hill Park Cemetery in Independence, Missouri.

[1] Wellman, Paul I. *A Dynasty of Western Outlaws* (Lincoln, Ne.: University of Nebraska Press, 1961), 114.

[2] Ibid., 118.

[3] Monaco, Ralph, Hon., compiler. Frank James Re-Enactments and Historical Documentation. Manuscript material in the Jackson County Historical Society Archives, Document ID 13F23, 24.

[4] Monaco.

[5] "Research Guides Restoration of Frank James Cell," *Jackson County Historical Society JOURNAL* 1982 (July-September), 24:3, 4,5.

[6] "For Comfort," *Kansas City* (Mo.) *Evening Star*, 28 Oct. 1882, 1.

[7] "Research Guides Restoration of Frank James Cell," *Jackson County Historical Society JOURNAL* 1982 (July-September), 24:3, 4,5. The committee assembled period furnishings and accessories for the cell including a period carpet loaned by Roger T. Sermon. When complete, the cell will include a cot, appropriate bed linens, rocking chair, side table, toilet accessories, and other special memorabilia interpreting Frank James days as a guest of the citizens of Jackson County.

[8] Rock Port *Sun*, 22 Nov. 1882.

[9] *Kansas City* (Mo.) *Evening Star,* 27 Nov. 1882.

[10] findagrave.com (viewed on 21 Oct. 2009; Hinton H. Noland born 22 Oct. 1847 – died 11 July 1932).

[11] *Ibid.*

[12] Monaco.

[13] "The Governor then pardoned the murderer of Jesse James, saying the country was well rid of him. This created a great stir, and the railroads which had contributed $50,000 for the rewards began to regret their act. One history states that the Governor and the railroad managers were in a conciliatory mood toward the James boys' "public," and joined in a plan to enable Frank James to surrender quietly on terms as favorable to him as possible. A purse of $5,000 was raised in Frank's behalf to pay lawyers and for quieting charges against him in other states. Frank surrendered at Jefferson City and was brought to Independence and impounded.... This was the only time either of the James boys ever entered a jail." Stewart, 4-5.

CELL

7

OUR GANGS,
IN TURN OF THE CENTURY CHAINS
(1880-1919)

Frank James' surrender and trial was the end of an era in Jackson County, and the 1859 Jail reflected this shift.

Cornelius "Con" Murphy was the Jackson County Marshal when on April 12, 1881, he transported "a flock of jail birds sentenced [by the Criminal Court in Independence] to the penitentiary" in Jefferson City.[1] He was also on duty when several suspected train robbers from the Blue Cut, or Glendale train robberies, were held downtown for grand jury and/or trial proceedings.[2]

The detention of Frank James at the 1859 Jackson County Jail took place on Murphy's watch (see *JAIL BREAK: Famous Outlaws Ride into Infamy*).

In November 1884, William A. "Jutt" Phillips was elected Jackson County Marshal.[3] Four years previously, Phillips, then 40 years old, had been listed in the U.S. Census for Lone Jack, Jackson County, Missouri, with his wife, Mary S., two sons and two daughters.

In November 1886, Hugh J. McGowan, who was a 21-year-old Kansas City policeman when the 1880 U.S. Census for Jackson County was taken, assumed the duties of Jackson County Marshal, and held that position for two terms through 1890.[4]

During McGowan's term, the third legal hanging, or judicial execution, in Jackson County took place in June 1887. The crime for which Edward Calhoun Sneed was executed was for the unprovoked murder of Orlean Harrison Loomis on July 26, 1884. The two men had become intoxicated in saloons in the vicinity of 23rd and Dripps Streets, whereupon Sneed tried to steal Loomis' considerable money, eventually by deadly force. Sneed narrowly escaped being lynched. Sneed's first trial and conviction was reversed, and he was granted a new trial by the Missouri Supreme Court.[5]

The instrument of death stood in an enclosure 30' x 40' just outside of the Jail in Independence. A board fence about 20' high shut out all view of it. The gallows was of pine timber, the platform containing the trap door being 10' above the ground and 10' x 12' in dimensions. Ten feet above the trap which occupied the center of the platform, was the cross-beam to which the rope was attached. The lever, which caused the trap door to drop, was at the east end of the platform and was worked from above. On the north side of the Jail, a covered approach to the gallows had been constructed of pine boards.

Marshal McGowan and his assistants tested the gallows for the last time before the execution. In the trial of the instrument, a bag of sand weighing 173 lbs. was adjusted to the rope which hung from the cross-beam and rested on the trap. Then the lever was pulled and the bag dropped the required distance with a thud.[6]

By January 1887, James Bruce Ross, served as Jailor (aka. Deputy County Marshal).[7] Ross, a former Tennessee farmer, had unsuccessfully tried striking it rich in gold or silver out West. Along his journey home he met and married Ella S. Thomas in Independence, Missouri. After Mrs. Ross, a college graduate who taught piano lessons, refused to move to Tennessee, her husband entered the criminal justice system in Jackson County. "J.B.," Ella, their son Charles G., and Ella's recently widowed mother, Rebecca Frances "Fannie" (Rogers) Thomas, moved into the residence portion of the 1859 Jackson County Jail.[8]

Helen and Louise Ross

Over the next 10 years, the Ross family kept the peace at the jail facility. Daughter Ella T. was born in the Marshal's family home in November 1887. Twins Helen and Louise Ross were born there in March 1890. The "jail birds" (as they were affectionately called by their brother, Charles) returned years later and shared childhood recollections of daily life as youthful residents in the Marshal's Home. Among other stories, they told how they, as young girls, were forbidden to wander along the north side of the site where farmers would hitch their horses and wagons before patronizing merchants on Independence Square. The danger wasn't so much the teams of animals, but the likelihood that that they would overhear unbecoming language from prisoners taunting from the barred windows of the Jail. A prisoner once gave their older brother, Charlie, a carved bone knife in return for Charlie having passed some tobacco to him.[9]

Henry P. Stewart succeeded McGowan as Marshal in 1891; he held the position through 1894. He actually held the title a bit longer because after William M. Sloan defeated Deputy County Marshal Joseph B. Keshlear in November 1894, a quarrel over the results ensued. Even after a recount in March 1895, the matter was taken to the Missouri Supreme Court. After all the ballot box stuffing, burning of ballots, and substitution of ballots, intimidating of voters and other election crimes, Sloan was found to have been elected by a narrow majority of 18 votes. Still, Keshlear was the beneficiary of the forgeries of election returns and was commissioned formally that summer.[10]

Henry P. Stewart

Keshlear was defeated at the end of 1896 by Samuel H. Chiles, but Keshlear stubbornly fought and won the right to hold onto the post until January 1897, rather than November 24, the date established by custom.[11] Sam Chiles had served under General Joseph "Jo" Shelby's company, and had followed him to Mexico rather than surrender. But, after the War had worked back into society preceding his election to Jackson County Marshal.[12] Chiles won a second term in November 1898.[13]

Under Chiles' authority, Deputy County Marshal Joel B. Mayes—who, in the next decade would later serve as Jackson County Marshal—had charge of the 1859 Jackson County Jail at Independence in January 1899. Mayes immediately, "*made some much needed improvements in and about the building. For one thing, he has put a large bath tub in the jail and arranged to supply it with hot and cold water. The jail has not heretofore had a bath, though the need of one was keenly felt. In addition to this improvement there have been others made. That part of the jail used by the jailer as a residence has been replastered and repapered and thoroughly renovated throughout. There are at present about twenty prisoners confined in the jail, and as part of them are tramps the bathing apparatus will answer a good purpose.*"[14] At one point in time, it was noted that "trustees who worked in the jail during the day boiled the blankets for the beds every two weeks, washed the cement floors daily, and cooked…prisoners. The trustees bathed twice a week while those on the chain gang bathed daily.[15]

At this time, there were several publicized attempted jail breaks between 1898 and 1907.[16] This *Jackson Examiner* newspaper ran a story about officials finding forbidden accoutrement for potential jail breaks:

"Every little while those in charge of the Kansas City and Independence jails make a thorough search of the cells and always find forbidden things such as fine saws, manufactured saws and all sorts of curious things which are smuggled in some way….

"A search at Kansas City some time ago brought to light with other things a four pound hammer. The tool had been hidden under the bath tub and it was never known by which prisoner. One night as the jailer in charge was about to lock the cells he heard something suspicious. The cells are locked simultaneously by the throwing of a big lever which throws the bolts in the doors of each cell. As he threw the big lever the deputy heard a noise and then he opened the lever and threw it a second time. He again heard the noise and at once a search was ordered and the big hammer found under the bath tub. A prisoner had used the hammer to break off one of the steel bars across an opening and when the big lever was closed he would strike the bar with all his force depending on the noise of the slipping bolts into their sockets to conceal his work. The bars being chilled steel, he figured, would break under the blow and would be easy to pull out. But, the hammer was not heavy enough and the deputy heard the sound of the blow.

"Sometimes prisoners are found with a set of very fine small saws fit to cut through anything. But the favorite saw is made from a case knife. The best silver plated case knives have a fine steel blade and the blade is of the same general thickness. With two of these placed edge to edge and a quick blow, teeth are made and when properly used these saws will easily cut through heavy bars.

"There have been cases of breaking jail in Independence and Kansas City and ingenuity is developed which if applied to honest labor would bring success to the criminal."[17]

Jackson County Marshal John P. Maxwell, a Grain Valley farmer, won in November 1900.

In November 1902, the man who would later become famous as Kansas City's "Boss" of politics, Thomas J. "Tom" Pendergast, was elected to the office of Jackson County Marshal.[18] Previously, Pendergast had held the position of Superintendent of Streets in Kansas City. Even then, "Alderman Pendergast," was dubbed, "the North End Political Boss."[19] Beyond his brief tenure as Jackson County Marshal, Pendergast's sensational career as a "goat" boss is widely known, and well documented.

Albert "Al" Heslip won as Jackson County Marshal in the November 1904 and 1906 elections. A *Kansas City Star* article titled, "The Promised Jail Reform," reported, "*Mr. Heslip now realizes more than ever the responsibilities of his office—that his duty to the public and to the prisoners under his charge cannot be fulfilled without an intelligent study of the question of prison regulation and the application of the most approved methods.*"[20]

Heslip asked for an open-air exercise yard and additional cell room. Eventually, cell room was added; but, prisoners were soon afforded all the open-air exercise they could stand.

INITIATION OF THE CHAIN GANGS

In the late 1800s, the Jackson County Jail population began to grow along with that of the County. All that labor going to waste in the jail weighted heavily on the minds of public officials and the institution of the "chain gang" was introduced, which had already proved successful in other communities. Such labor built and improved many Jackson County roads, sewers and other public facilities.[21] Prisoners were kept at the County Poor Farm (Truman Medical Center today) while working on roads in that vicinity.[22] In July 1892, residents in Fort Osage Township, signed a petition at Buckner, Mo., pledged to construct "barracks at Buckner…for the occupancy when not at work of part of the chain gang…while at work on the county roads in Fort Osage Township…." Shares of the "Buckner Hill Jail Company" were transferred to Chase Henthorn in December 1893. [23]

Mel Hulse

A turn of the century report that, "For the first time in the recollection of old timers there is not a prisoner in the Independence jail, the doors are open and unguarded. Thursday afternoon under the orders of Marshall Maxwell, deputies Melville "Mel" Hulse and Curren (sic) took the remaining prisoners to Kansas City…. [The jail] will be thoroughly cleaned and fumigated from top to bottom and all the doors, windows and walls will be gone over and repaired and made stronger. It is understood that during the summer the County Court will organize a chain gang at the Independence jail so it is not likely to remain empty very long."[24]

There was some early dissention in the ranks with this situation. Chain gangs tried to stop work in 1903, for instance. In July, Jailor Nicholas H. Phelps, deputy Twyman, and Chain Gang Superintendant Sam Yankee drew their revolvers to squelch a rebellion.[25] And, in October, three prisoners held up guards on the chain gang, took a revolver and keys and escaped to the woods at the rock quarry three miles south of Independence near the Chicago and Alton cut on Lee's Summit Road; only one was recaptured.[26] In November 1909, Ed C. Hughes, superintendent of the chain gang, ordered new locks for the shackles after two men escaped the previous week.[27]

John Van Buren Martin, jailor, recorded that his jailhouse prisoners kept him rather busy during 1906. Many 'guests' were brought to Independence from Kansas City. These imports brought along dope and razors which they managed to smuggle into the jail quarters. Trouble arose with the new prisoners along with their contraband. In August 1907 Marshal Hulse prevented an attempted escape when he discovered two keys fashioned from an aluminum comb.[28]

Back in those days friends and relatives of the prisoners brought baskets of food and other delicacies to provide a variation in the prison fare. These were stored in the jail refrigerator. Martin related in his record that he was troubled with thieves who broke into the jail and rifled the ice box of its stored food.

On June 15, 1906, prisoners of the Jackson County Jail went on a hunger strike. The strikers complained that they did not get enough to eat while they worked the roads. Jailer Martin stoutly defended his meals, saying, "We take hot prepared meals to the chain gang every Noon hour." Ann Crowder served as a cook at the 1859 Jackson County Jail from 1902-1908.[29]

Another source said Martin sends a pound of meat for each man at Noon.[30] Several months before that, a newspaper report said, "Jailor Martin every day sends a wagon load of dinner to the chain gang.... For each of the 35 prisoners he sends a quart dipper full of beans, one half pound of meat, and one half pound of bread and one pint of strong coffee. The food is well wrapped and arrives steaming hot."[31] A 1919 report noted that, "meals brought to the men were mainly baked beans, boiled potatoes and boiled meat."[32]

The Jackson County Court decided to increase the chain gang in numbers from 40 to 60 workers. Although there were instances when an initiative to abolish the chain gain was raised, the workforce remained so "employed" until 1919.[33]

One source indicated the work of the chain gangs was slow because the prisoners started late and quit early and weren't motivated or stimulated by any burning desire for accomplishment.[34] However, these additional able bodied prisoners were provided the opportunity to work off a reduced sentence by building all the roads near Independence in chain gangs.[35] A 1913 newspaper report announced, "*Of the entire bunch, five were taken in iron shackles, the rest are free from any bonds whatever and work practically on parole.*"[36] The next month reported, "*Mr. Parr has eight men under him and they work hard, and do 100 feet of rocking every day.*"[37]

Ben Turoff recalled that as a boy, "*I used to watch the chain gang being taken from the county jail…in the morning and returned each evening. They wore heavy shackled chains around each ankle with barely enough room to walk. They were taken to and from their work on county roads in wagons [two rows of prisoners faced out and seated back to back]*[38]*, drawn by a team of horses. The wagons were of a box type of 2 by 8's atop each side, around the rim of the wagon bed for them to sit. A box with steps was used to get them on and off the wagons. Each wagon had an armed guard along. At noon the jail cook would send their noon meal in 5 gallon milk cans.*"[39]

Chain gangs left their quarters six days a week at sunrise and returned at sunset.[40] The clanking of the chains and ribald songs of the prisoners as they were transported over the city streets was a signal for all mothers within earshot to collect the coming generation until the dreadful wagons had passed. Occasionally, mothers didn't get there in time and those are the times recalled.

At the turn of the 19th Century, Sam Yankee was one of the men in charge of the County prisoners on the chain gangs, with George Soehle as superintendent of the road building. Another team found in local sources were superintendent Ed C. Hughes and "Babe" Parr. And, yet another source listed George W. Shaw as "Special Road Overseer" in charge of the chain gang.[41] The "County Chain Gang" as reported in the *Jackson County Democrat*, March 25, 1909, listed: Superintendent, James Shepard; Clerk, Forest Allen; Powder Man and Guard, Ray Self; and Guards, John Berry; George Binger; W. S. Craddock; James Stults; and John N. Bethel.

Major John L. Miles, who served as the last Jackson County Marshal, recalled that at one point they were having much trouble with escaping prisoners. He said that the County Court allowed him $150 to purchase two good blood hounds to track down escaped prisoners and they were used to good advantage.[42]

Chain gangs were in use at least until the 1859 Jackson County Jail was decommissioned in 1933.[43]

KANGAROO COURT

Every class of prisoner charged with nearly every kind of crime that did not call for a penitentiary term or a death sentence was represented in the county jail. Mexican- Italian- Native- African-Americans, and nearly every other race was represented.[44]

In March 1905, a kangaroo court came into existence in the County Jail. It is said to have enjoyed the formal supervision of a judge, clerk, and Marshal, all duly elected by the prisoners themselves. In fact, two courts were active, one for the white prisoners, and one for the black prison population.

When a new prisoner was escorted into the cellblock, the cry of "Fresh fish, Fresh fish" rang out in the corridors. If he was a former resident, he understood and expected the next call of the clerk. "Oh, Yes, Oh Yes, the honorable kangaroo court of Jackson County is now in session."

The new man was duly arrested by the "Marshal" in perfect order and solemnity, the officials, imitating the judicial tones of then judge Swofford [sic.] and clerk McClanahan. The charges levied by the kangaroo court were usually, "Breaking into jail without permission of the inmates."

The court was usually fully informed as to the financial position of the new resident and he was invariably found guilty and fined in accordance with his ability to pay. This money was used by the other prisoners to buy things that they wanted. With the payment of the fine the new member was declared "In" and prepared to initiate the next unfortunate.

Sometimes the new prisoner resists, refuses to plead guilty and when fined refuses order for his money. Then, the edict of the Kangaroo Court is that the prisoner be stripped and held and lashed with a strap. No matter what the resistance, no matter how much strength it requires, the new man is overpowered and whipped. A few applications of the lash usually bring the necessary order for the money.

The jailors do not interfere with the Kangaroo Court, except to see that the undue severity is not used. The prisoners carry on their own matters to the certain point and the jailors say that instead of being detriment, it is a help in the management of the Jail.[45]

While the Jail proper was strong enough for all ordinary purposes, it became very much behind the times with regard to keeping the building maintained, reasonably clean and sanitary. The 1859 Jackson County Jail, as late as January 1901, was not connected with the public sewer. The private sewer built by the County drained into an open run which drains into the Spring Branch.[46]

All classes were huddled closely together. When one became ill or was injured, there was no other place to keep them. Jailor John Van Buren Martin admitted that on more than one occasion when an operation had to be performed on a prisoner, the family's dining table had to be used. Nor was there any other place for women prisoners; for several years leading up to this time, women prisoners were sent to Kansas City.[47]

In 1907, there were 37 prisoners at the 1859 Jackson County Jail. More prisoners meant the need for expanded quarters.

Jackson County Marshal Albert "Al" Heslip was on duty in 1907 when the Jackson County Court let the contract for an addition to the jail building at the cost of $8179.47.[48] The new, two-story, brick-clad, concrete structure was added against the back, or east-facing wall of the 1859 limestone cellblock, continuing the long axis orientation (east-west) of the stone jail. The exterior brick walls are laid in common bond with Flemish variation, on a formed concrete foundation.[49]

North and south walls have 9 bays. The north and south windows are double-hung with 2 over 2 lights, and exterior iron bars. Sills and lintels are limestone. The primary exterior entrance door is at the west end of the south wall, and recessed two steps down from the level of the rear courtyard east of the kitchen wing. There is a partial basement under the annex.

Access doorways were carved out of the limestone walls on each floor of the 1859 structure, opening up to 14 steel cages per floor in the new addition. Barred windows allowed for light and ventilation.[50] During the day, prisoners roamed around the center "foyer" when they weren't working on roads. The cells were set against each wall, seven to each side on two floors (28 double cells in all).

A new steam heat furnace was installed in September. In November, it "was used for the first time…. While during these first few days, the sensation of having more heat than they had formerly with stoves, is very pleasant, the new paint on the radiators made the atmosphere in the rooms smell pretty musty. The residence of the jailor is also equipped with the steam heat.[51]

This expansion served for nearly a quarter of a century.

Joel B. Mayes of Blue Springs was elected Jackson County Marshal in November 1908 and took office on January 1, 1909. Joel and Emily Mayes temporarily lived with their son, dentist Claude Mayes, at 912 South Main. They purchased their own lot on South Main where they built their own home.[52] Mayes was re-elected in November 1910. Meanwhile, Nicholas H. Phelps, his wife Emma C. and their 14-year-old son William J. Phelps, lived in the residence portion of the 1859 Jackson County Jail—the year the lock down turned 50-years-old.

Events in one prominent Independence family's mansion between October and December 1909 had an impact on the community and eventually involved Jackson County's peace officers. Colonel Thomas Hunton Swope (at the left), who had made a fortune in Kansas City real estate, donated for the benefit of

future Kansas Citians thousands of acres for "Swope Park." In the last few months of his life, the 82-year-old bachelor with an estimated net worth of $3.5 million ($86.2 million in 2009) 'retired' to his widowed sister-in-law's home in Independence, where several of his nieces and nephews lived.

On October 2, Swope was given a "digestive pill," by Dr. Bennett Clark Hyde, the husband of Swope's niece, Frances. Swope became violently ill and he

died the next day. Swope's beloved cousin, Colonel Moss Hunton, had died in the Swope mansion two days before from similar circumstances. Hyde said that the cause of death was "apoplexy," but the nurses became suspicious. Hyde stayed in the Swope mansion looking after other family members after a mysterious epidemic of typhoid fever befell the household (there were no other cases of the fever in Independence). Nine people came down with typhoid fever, and one son, Chrisman Swope, died after being treated by Hyde. By this time, there were five nurses in the Swope mansion, and they later testified that they became afraid that Hyde was trying to kill off the entire Swope clan to collect the family fortune. After autopsies on the bodies of Colonel Swope and Chrisman Swope revealed traces of strychnine and cyanide, Dr. Hyde was indicted on two murder charges, one count of manslaughter and eight counts of poisoning.

James A. Reed, former Prosecuting Attorney of Jackson County and later U.S. Senator from Missouri, was hired by the Swope family as a Special Prosecutor and the famous Kansas City Defense Attorney, Frank P. Walsh, represented Dr. Hyde. The trial lasted six weeks and included 69 witnesses. A key prosecution witness, Dr. George T. Twyman, died just before the trial was to begin. Hyde's wife stood by him throughout the trial. Hyde was convicted of murder; but, upon appeal the case was remanded by the Missouri Supreme Court for retrial. A second trial ended when a juror disappeared or absconded. A third trial ended with a hung jury, and charges were eventually dropped.

State of Missouri vs. B. Clark Hyde trial was a monument to the power of money in the criminal justice system. Hyde's wealthy wife hired the best attorneys available to defend him. The circumstantial evidence was significant, combined with a possible motive; but, whether the proof reached the threshold of reasonable doubt is questionable.[53]

Frank P. Walsh   Bennett Clark Hyde   James A. Reed

Dr. Hyde awaited trial in the Jackson County Jail at Kansas City, where, according to deputy Hoffman, Hyde received special privileges.[54] It is a wonder if living conditions there were like those at the 1859 Jackson County Jail. There "*the beds are unsanitary and would suggest new mattresses and blankets. Soap and towels are provided but there is not sufficient cups and spoons to serve all prisoners. Evidence shows there were not more than four dogs in the jail at one time and that they were there for catching rats. We find no evidence of black jacks being harshly used. Bread was served on more than one occasion wherein it was rat eaten.*"[55]

Then, too, you must imagine the sanitary provisions, for they are not generally a matter of public record. Prisoners were responsible for cleaning out the cells. On humid days, as is often the case during the summer in Missouri, the cells undoubtedly gave off an odor that must have been overpowering. Though there is no formal record, there was *at least* one out-house (or, privy) at the rear of the lot that predated "sanitary sewers."

In March 1911, Marshal Mayes placed W. H. Montgomery in charge of the Jail in place of Nicholas H. Phelps.

Martin J. Crowe succeeded Mayes in the November 1912 and 1914 elections. Harvey C. "Harry" Hoffman continued as Deputy Chief Marshal, and Jesse "Jess" Allen became Jailor. Allen, who had previously been a bartender in a saloon, moved into the 1859 Jackson County Jail with his family. He died there from a cerebral hemorrhage on April 28, 1918.[56]

Mrs. Rudolph Etzenhouser headed a group of members from the Church of Jesus Christ of Latter Day Saints in 1915 to establish a prison library. It was the purpose of the group to give each prisoner a copy of the Holy Bible to have while imprisoned and to take with him when released. The group also wanted to provide a permanent library of books.[57]

During the Great War, Harry C. Hoffman—who had served as Deputy Chief Marshal in 1915—was elected as Jackson County Marshal, from 1916-1921. Hoffman lived with his family at 3208 E. 30th Street, in Kansas City, Missouri.[58] During this time of conflict and crisis, Hoffman created a large reserve deputies force that stood ready to act in emergency capacity at the call of the marshal. More than 250 were enlisted from Kansas City alone.[59]

Hoffman served during the devastating Spanish Influenza epidemic that ravaged populations worldwide in 1918.[60] Jackson Countians were not without great loss. Then, too, was the threat of an outbreak of smallpox. The warden at the Missouri State Penitentiary, for instance, required a certificate of vaccination for all prisoners being transferred. W. C. Dunn, Chief Deputy Marshal, answered one particular directive by saying that all prisoners in Jackson County had already been vaccinated.[61]

---

[1] Murphy was elected in 1880 and again in 1882.

[2] "The Blue Cut Robbery," and "Train Robbers," *Kansas City* (Mo.) *Star*, 3 Oct. 1881, 1, and 27 Mar. 1882 respectively.

[3] "The County Election Returns from the County Court," *Kansas City* (Mo.) *Star*, 8 Nov. 1884. Also, Marshall and Morrison, 83.

[4] "When They Take Office," *Kansas City* (Mo.) *Star*, 10 Nov. 1886, 1. "McGowan on the Board: The Ex-County Marshal A State's World's Fair Commissioner." 16 Jul. 1891, 1. Also, Marshall and Morrison, 83.

[5] "Hanged," *Kansas City* (Mo.) *Star*, 24 June 1887, 1.

[6] "The Penalty Paid. Edward Calhoun Sneed Hanged at Independence Soon after Noonday His Last Day," *Kansas City* (Mo.) *Star,* 24 June 1887, 1. An August 6, 1886, *Star* article, *"Awaiting Their Doom. The Batch of Murderers Confined in the Independence Jail."* gave the name as Richard Loomis

[7] "Taylor Taken Away Guarded by Fifteen Armed Men." Kansas City (Mo.) Star, 28 Apr. 1896, 1.

[8] Alderman, 6, 28, 82, 116. Charles Ross grew up to win the Pulitzer prize before going to Washington, D.C., and serving as press secretary to his childhood friend, Harry S Truman.

[9] Holmquist, Mrs. Helen (Ross) and Miss Louise Ross. "Born in Marshal's Home: Twins Celebrate 75th Birthday," *Jackson County Historical Society JOURNAL* 1965 (Mar.), 12. Ross, Miss Helen. "Ross Twins, Born in Marshal's House Recall Independence Square of Mid-90's," *Jackson County Historical Society JOURNAL* 1969 (Summer), 8, 9. And, "Marshal's Daughters Visit the Old Jail," *Jackson County Historical Society JOURNAL* 1969 (Spring), 7, which highlights James Bruce Ross' two other daughters, Mrs. Frances (Ross) Leake and Mrs. Virginia (Ross) Weston, who were born after the Ross family had moved the Jail. The recollection and assignation of Ross as "Marshal" in these recollections is not entirely accurate; rather, Ross was "Jailor" would have been a "Deputy County Marshal."

[10] "No Justice for Sloan: Keshlear Beneficiary of Election Forgers." Kansas City (Mo.) Star, 12 July 1895. According to Marshall and Morrison, however, Stewart was elected in 1894. Neither Sloan or Keshlear's names appear in their roster of Jackson County Marshals, 83.

[11] Again, Keshlear's name does not appear in Marshall and Morrison's listing of Jackson County Marshals. In fact, they don't list a Marshal between Henry P. Stewart (1894) and S. H. Chiles (1898), 83. By the 1900 U.S. Census for Jackson County, Keshlear was listed with his family at 1629 Jefferson, Kansas City, Missouri. He was a 44-year-old

detective. The Keshlear's shared the home with the Edward "Plug" O'Flaherty family. 24-year-old Matt O'Flaherty was a County Deputy Sheriff.

[12] Joseph Orville "Jo" Shelby, cavalry General who never officially surrendered, led his troops to Mexico. Later, he became a Federal Marshal in Kansas City.

[13] "Democrats Are All Swept In." Kansas City (Mo.) Star, 9 Nov. 1898, 1.

[14] According to the *Lee's Summit Journal*, 27 Jan. 1899, as reprinted in the *Jackson County Historical Society JOURNAL* 1996-97 (Winter), which incorrectly identifies it as 1889.

[15] Alderman, 50.

[16] "Almost a Jail Delivery," *Kansas City* (Mo.) *Star*, 21 Apr. 1898, 10. "Cut Their Way Out of Jail," *Kansas City (Mo.) Star*, 16 May 1898, 2. The *Jackson* (Independence, Mo.) *Examiner* reported on 27 Oct. 1899, 1:5, that nine prisoners who were being kept in the corridor of the insane ward at the County Farm escaped; six were recaptured. Also, "Thomas Hill," *Jackson* (Independence, Mo.) *Examiner*, 27 Oct. 1899, 1:3. Hill had escaped and captured by Jailor Mayes south of Independence. Hill refused to surrender until slightly wounded by a bullet from Mayes' pistol. *The Oak Grove* (Mo.) *Banner*, 1 Feb. 1901, reported "Saws Found in the Jail," and that there were 44 prisoners in the Jail, all of whom "would have soon gained their liberty if the plot had not been discovered." Jail breaks from the Jackson County Jail in Kansas City were also reported.

[17] *Jackson* (Independence, Mo.) *Examiner,* 10 June 1899, 4, 3. The Oak Grove (Mo.) Banner reported on 1 Feb. 1901 in an article titled, "Saws Found in the Jail," that the forbidden item was found in a prisoner's mattress. Other related articles from the *Jackson* (Mo.) *Examiner* ran on 6 Apr. 1906, 9:1, describing the discovery of a home-made morphine/opium pipe; and, on 2 Aug 1907, 1:4, describing an aluminum key made by one of the prisoners from a comb passed to him by his mother.

[18] "County Marshal's Deputies." Kansas City (Mo.) Star, 20 Dec. 1902, 1.

[19] "Tom Pendergast's Successor." Kansas City (Mo.) Star, 22 Dec. 1902, 1.

[20] "The Promised Reform." *Kansas City* (Mo.) *Star*, 2 Aug. 1905. Heslip appears as a 56-year-old farmer at 1128 West 70th Street, with his wife and son in the 1910 U.S. Census for Kansas City, Jackson County, Missouri. Belview Precinct, ED 99. Ward 5. Line 89.

[21] Clemenson, 8. Also, "They Must Work There," *Kansas City* (Mo.) *Star,* 1 Aug. 1905, 1.

[22] "Thomas Hill," *Jackson* (Independence, Mo.) *Examiner*, 27 Oct. 1899, 1:3. Hill had escaped and captured by Jailor Mayes south of Independence. Hill refused to surrender until slightly wounded by a bullet from Mayes' pistol.

[23] Jackson County Historical Society Archives, Donald G. Stubbs Collection of Isaac G. "Ike" Chiles Family Papers, Document ID L32F22. In this petition, 44 subscribers provided their signature and amount of their individual pledge which ranged from $2.00 to $25.00. "It is to understood and agreed, that said subscription is to be of the character of stock in the erection and property of said structure of not less than five dollars each and that when the purposes for which it was erected is consummated, then to be disposed of to the best advantage and each subscriber to receive his pro-rate of the nett (sic.) proceeds of such sale." William G. Childs was selected to carry out the erection and sale of the structure. The barracks that eventually became known as the "Buckner Hill Jail" building was constructed; a "Paid" or "Pd" notation is next to most every name on the July 25, 1892 petition. The total collected was $417.00 (although "387" appears to be penciled in as a total). On June 12, 1894, Chase Henthorn assigned his rights, title and interest in the Buckner Jail Building to C. G. Hamilton. On October 25, 1894, Hamilton conveyed the rights, title and interest in the Buckner Jail to W. G. Childs consisting of 29 shares of stock in the Company.

[24] *Come and Spit on the Floor*. Volume 2 referencing *Jackson* (Independence, Mo.) *Examiner*, 28 June 1901, 8, 1.

[25] *Ibid.,* 3 Jul. 1903, 9:1. The 21 Aug. 1903, 7:1, edition reported the chain gang numbered 27, counting 'Jubilee,' who is a small sized negro."

[26] *Ibid.,* 2 Oct. 1903, 3:1. Also Hale and Beck, 25. George Soehle was superintendent of the road building. The men, Charles Caldwell (Hottentot), Ed Bright, George Wood and about 17 others from the chain gain were working in a rock quarry three miles south of Independence. Hottentot got a gun from one of the guards and turned upon him. Of the three, only Ed Bright was re-captured. Other revolts/escapes were reported in the 8 Mar., 29 Mar., and 3 May 1907 editions.

[27] *Come and Spit on the Floor*. Volume 2 referencing *Jackson* (Independence, Mo.) *Examiner*, 29 Nov. 1909, 8, 3.

[28] "Escape Attempt Prevented," *Jackson* (Independence, Mo.) *Examiner*, 2 Aug. 1907, 1:4.

[29] *Ibid.,* Volume 4:87 referencing *Jackson* (Independence, Mo.) *Examiner*, 31 Jan. 1908, 5:2.

[30] Chain Gang Struck," *Independence* (Mo.) *Examiner*, 13 June 1906.

[31] *Jackson Examiner* (Independence, Mo.) 9 Feb. 1906, 7:2.

[32] *Come Spit on the Floor*, Volume 8:155, referencing *Jackson* (Independence, Mo.) *Examiner*, 11 Jul. 1919, 2:5.

[33] Wilcox, Pearl. "Housing for Unruly Citizens," *Independence Daily News*, undated news clipping in the Jackson County Historical Society Archives. Also, *Come Spit on the Floor*, Volume 5:62, referencing *Jackson* (Independence, Mo.) *Examiner*, 6 Sept. 1912, 1:5; and, Volume 8:157, referencing *Jackson* (Independence, Mo.) *Examiner*, 20 Jul. 1922, 2:7.

[34] Wilcox, Pearl. "Housing for Unruly Citizens," *Independence Daily News*, undated news clipping in the Jackson County Historical Society Archives.

[35] *Independence (Mo.) Examiner*, 24 July 1907.

[36] "Work Without Shackles," *Independence* (Mo.) *Examiner*, 19 Sept. 1913.

[37] *Come Spit on the Floor*, Volume 6:81, referencing *Jackson* (Independence, Mo.) *Examiner*, 3 Oct. 1913, 1:5.

[38] Wilcox, Pearl. "Housing for Unruly Citizens," *Independence Daily News*, undated news clipping in the Jackson County Historical Society Archives.

[39] Turoff, Ben. "I Remember…" *Jackson County Historical Society JOURNAL* (March) 1964, V:3:9. Also, Turoff's deposition in the Jackson County Historical Society Archives manuscript collection, Document ID 113F8. Two accounts referring to the jail by Milton Perry may also be found in the Society's collections: a written history (Document ID 192F11) and an oral history transcript (Document ID 252F1). Turoff's parents were Samuel and Annie Turoff, Polish Russians who emigrated to the Unites States in 1882. The family lived at and operated a dry goods store at 101 West Lexington Avenue, Independence, Missouri. Ben had a younger brother, Sidney.

[40] Working on the chain gang was, no doubt, laborious. One inmate, Cy Proctor, opted for it though. He objected to a year in jail because the hot weather was approaching. He promised to be good and to work so Judge Anderson gave him two months on the chain gang with a provisional warning that the other ten months would be added if he appeared in court again. Proctor stole a calf from Henry Warren south of town and sold the calf. He needed the $3.50 which he got for the calf. *Jackson* (Independence, Mo.) *Examiner*, 21 June 1907.

[41] "Chain Gang at Work," *Independence* (Mo.) *Examiner*, 19 June 1923. Jackson County Court minutes list these employees, but the records must be read day-by-day, page-by-page to discover them. This insurmountable task awaits a willing volunteer.

[42] Gentry, Sue. "Major Miles Recalls Last Use of the Old County Jail Here," undated, unsourced newspaper clipping in the Jackson County Historical Society Archives.

[43] *Independence* (Mo.) *Examiner*, 1 Mar. 1933.

[44] *Come Spit on the Floor*, Volume 8:157, referencing *Jackson* (Independence, Mo.) *Examiner*, 10 Feb. 1922.

[45] *Jackson Examiner* (Independence, Mo.) 3 Mar. 1905. Also, "For One Cigarette, $1,000," *Kansas City* (Mo.) *Star*, 8 Sep. 1922, 1.

[46] Hale and Beck, 25-26, referencing an 18 Jan. 1901 *Jackson* (Independence, Mo.) *Examiner* article.

[47] "County Jail Inspected," *Independence* (Mo.) *Examiner*, 30 May 1906.

[48] *Come and Spit on the Floor* (4:87) referencing *Jackson* (Independence, Mo.) *Examiner*, 5 Apr. 1907, 5:3. Also, "Increase Jail Room: County Court Asks Estimates on Plan—For Larger Chain Gang," *Jackson* (Independence, Mo.) *Examiner*, 1 Feb. 1907. And, "Independence Jail Too Small," *Kansas City* (Mo.) *Star*, 8 Mar. 1907.

[49] Flemish bond, also known as Dutch bond, has historically always been considered the most decorative bond, and for this reason was used extensively for dwellings until the adoption of the cavity wall. It is created by alternately laying headers and stretchers in a single course. The next course is laid so that a header lies in the middle of the stretcher in the course below. Again, this bond is one brick thick. It is quite difficult to lay Flemish bond properly, since for best effect all the perpendiculars (vertical mortar joints) need to be vertically aligned. If only one face of a Flemish bond wall is exposed, one third of the bricks are not visible, and hence may be of low visual quality. www.absoluteastronomy.com/topics/Brickwork (viewed 12 Feb 2009).

[50] *"Jail," Independence (Mo.) Examiner, 20 June 1907.*

[51] "Jail Improvements," *Independence* (Mo.) *Examiner,* 13 Nov. 1907.

[52] "Starting the Year in Jail." Kansas City (Mo.) Times, 1 Jan. 1909, 1. Also, the U.S. Census for Independence, Jackson County, Missouri. ED 11; SHEET 8B; LINE 55.

[53] The mystery and intrigue associated with the unfortunate turn of events that transpired in Independence in Autumn 1909—while stirring imaginations and prompting regular inquiries to the Jackson County Historical Society Archives—has never yet been compiled and published…until now. In time for the centennial observation, former *Kansas City Star* newspaper editor, Giles Fowler, releases *Deaths on Pleasant Street* (Kirkville, Mo.: Truman University Press) in Autumn 2009.

[54] "Dr. B. Clark Hyde's Jailers Found Him a Conceited, Scornful Man: Harry C. Hoffman, Now a River Worker, Recalls the Troubles with the Accused Physician, His Curses, Demands, and Self-Centered Attitude While He Was Under Charges*, Kansas City* (Mo.) *Star*, 28 Aug. 1934.

[55] *Come Spit on the Floor*, Volume 5:61-62, referencing *Jackson* (Independence, Mo.) *Examiner*, 28 Oct. 1910, 5:1. See also the *Independence* (Mo.) *Examiner*, 9-15 Oct. 1910, for an article about the treatment of prisoners being investigated by a committee appointed by the Jackson County Court. Some of the charges were the dogs being allowed to sleep on the beds of prisoners; six spoons to 35 prisoners; one towel for the same 35 men to dry their faces; one man doing without supper three times; and, roaches being found frequently in the gravy. A year earlier an inspection by six members of a grand jury revealed some shocking and nauseating living conditions, "A Jail of the Dark Ages," *Kansas City* (Mo.) *Star*, 30 May 1906, 1.

[56] Stewart, 3. According to Allen's son-in-law, Mr. Orville Campbell. U.S. Census for Independence, Jackson County, Missouri (Jesse Allen in 1910; ED 10; PAGE 8A; LINE 39) (Anna Allen in 1920; ED 8; PAGE 4B; LINE 69). Also, Allen's 1918 death certificate, copies of which are on file in the Jackson County Historical Society's Archives.

[57] Wilcox, Pearl. "Housing for Unruly Citizens," *Independence Daily News*, undated news clipping in the Jackson County Historical Society Archives. Also, Hale and Beck, 31. In an effort to raise funds for the purchase of books the group sponsored several entertainments and programs of various natures during the year. One in particular was held at the Lewis Out-Door Theater, located on the ground later occupied by the Granada Theater. A silver offering was taken. There is no record of how much was collected but the general admission to the theater was five cents. Several young people who took active part in the promotion were Misses Grace Koehler, Edith Orick, Mabel Briggs, Mrs. Vena Etzenhouser Tipton, Mrs. James Bunt, Mr. Clyde Jones, Orlando Nace and Gomer Watson. Record of the success of the venture was not located.

[58] 1920 U.S. Federal Census, Jackson County, Missouri. 10th -15th Precinct, ED 166, SH 10B, Line 62. See also 14 May 1959 letter from Harry C. Hoffman to Donald R. Hale in the Jackson County Historical Society Archives.

[59] "Flock to Marshal's Reserve," *Kansas City* (Mo.) *Star*, 22 Jan. 1918.

[60] Interestingly, "there [were] fewer prisoners in the Jackson County Jail than at any other period in the last ten years…. Usually at this time of the year the number of prisoners averages around two hundred. Today only seventy-five persons are in jail. The decrease is attributed to the war." "Few Prisoners in Jail," *Kansas City* (Mo.) *Star*, 19 Oct. 1918.

[61] "Prisoners Must Be Vaccinated," *Kansas City* (Mo.) *Star*, 17 Nov. 1921, 1.

CELL

8

PROHIBITION NEARLY DRIED UP NEED FOR 1859 JAIL (1919-1933)

Carry [Carrie] A. Nation's wish was posthumously granted when Prohibition became the law of the land.[1] (Nation died in 1911 and is buried south of Kansas City, in the Belton Cemetery, Cass County, Missouri.)

When U.S. Census enumerator Ambrose W. Searcy visited the County Jail at Independence early in 1920, details were provided for 19 prisoners, in addition to "Chief Jailor" Harden T. Hall, his wife, Katherine May, and their son Harden T., Jr.[2]

However, on March 3, 1920, Jackson County Criminal Court Judge Ralph S. Latshaw announced the closing of the Jackson County's Jail in

Independence. Abolition of chain gangs, shortage in County funds, and lack of prisoners because of Prohibition's closure of saloons justified the move.[3]

95

After nearly a year, however, Major John L. Miles, elected as Jackson County Marshal in November 1920 for a term which he began on January 21, 1921, asserted that the Marshal was required to keep a jail in operation at the county seat. So, Miles recommended to the Jackson County Court on February 11, 1921, that the jail be kept in operation. The Jail was re-opened for quartering of about 30 short-term prisoners.[4] Twelve prisoners were transferred from the County Jail in Kansas City on March 14, 1921, and were put to work cleaning up the "Old Jail." All the bunks were provided with new mattresses; a number of new cots were purchased and placed in the halls upstairs. Up to 30 prisoners in total were anticipated to be transferred, where they were soon put to work on the chain gang.[5]

Lawmen in Jackson County had their hands full during Prohibition. On one instance in August 1921, Marshal Miles, with deputies and two federal inspectors, raided a boat house on the Missouri River at Cement City that was said to be owned by a man named, "John the Greek." Two dozen bottles of home brew were found on the boat. Concealed on the river bank under vines was 100 gallons of mash. In a nearby garage owned by "John the Greek," was found a home brew outfit and 30 gallons of liquor. "John the Greek" was not at home when the officers called; he was reported to be in Kansas City. A man and woman on the house boat escaped while the search of liquor was under way.[6]

The following May, one of Miles' liquor raids on two area chicken dinner farms that specialized in "jazz and booze" "hip pocket" parties brought the arrest of 14 men (women arrested in the raids were released without sufficient evidence to charge them). Among the establishments named were: White City Gardens (87th and Topping); Edgewood Farm (90th and Prospect, south of Dodson).[7] In other reports, Oakhurst dinner farm; The Castle dinner farm (operated by Mrs. Fay Fullbright opposite Mount Washington Cemetery on Van Horn Road...present-day Truman Road) in the Washington Park (present-day Mount Washington) area; Castle Cranny Crow (83rd and Prospect); and Brookside Gardens (15th Street, one mile east of the then Kansas City city limits) were brought to task. Miles said he would continue to raid the road houses until evidence of liquor sales was obtained.[8]

Tom Pendergast

While there were obviously raids in the countryside (that is, unincorporated Jackson County), thanks to Tom Pendergast, prohibition simply "never existed in Kansas City." Pendergast kept the bars open and the liquor flowing, and Kansas City's federal prosecutor (who was on Pendergast's payroll) never brought a single felony prosecution under the Volstead Act.[9] In other words, the Pendergast machine allowed the local liquor interests to continue unabated in supplying citizens with illegal alcohol.

Jail breaks, or attempted ones, added to the intrigue of this time. On more than one instance, soap on smuggled saws quieted the noise; blankets were tied together to make scaling ropes.[10]

At the end of Miles' tenure on December 31, 1924, the long standing office of Jackson County Marshal was abolished by a law enacted by the Missouri General Assembly on March 11, 1921. The law was structured to take effect at the end of the term in which he currently served. By the new act, "the sheriff's office will take over the work of the marshal's office…. Jackson County will be without a marshal, but the marshal's office will be conducted by deputy marshals. Additional deputy sheriffs will be appointed later…which would bring his list [from 31] to sixty appointees."[11]

And, in the fall election of 1924, Miles, a popular figure, was elected Jackson County Sheriff. He served from January 1925 through 1928.

In 1929, Miles was appointed chief of police of Kansas City, and retired in April 1939.[12]

The residence's living quarters were renovated and overhauled for the new County Jailer, George McPherson, and his family, who moved in on or just after March 1, 1929. At the time, the *Independence Examiner* reported "a surprising roominess in the living quarters…three rooms on the first floor and three rooms and the bath on the second floor. All the rooms are being decorated and hardwood floors will be laid in the rooms not already provided with them."[13]

The 1859 Jail served Jackson County for another decade during the 1920s before remodeling and expansion of the Jackson County Courthouse on Independence Square included the addition of modern jail cells.

In spring 1933, the Jackson County Court cut 20 men from the list of deputies in the Sheriff's office. So, the Sheriff, trying to adjust the work of his office to the reduced number of men and not give up his ideas of patrolling the county, closed the jail and removed the prisoners to Kansas City. This also stopped the chain gang. When, at a critical time in the severely downturned economy of the Great Depression, the County Court unceremoniously decommissioned its relict 1859 lock down in June 1933.[14]

---

[1] Official records and family Bible spell her maiden name as "Carry Amelia Moore," and it is this spelling that she used most of her life. Carry A. Nation fought for a number of reforms from hygiene to world peace to women's suffrage and even prison reform. However, it was the hatchet she raised—literally and figuratively—against alcohol and gambling that gained her notoriety. Standing six feet tall and weighing almost 180 pounds, Nation began in 1890 leading hymn-singing women into saloons, where they would smash the liquor stock with stones, hatchets, and canes.

[2] Additional details about the Harden family are provided as footnotes in *Appendix A: Lawmen Serving Jackson County in Independence, Missouri: 1827-1933.* U.S. Census for Blue Township, Independence, Jackson County, Missouri, ED9, SH11A; the address then was 219 North Main.

[3] "No Booze Jail is Closed," *Kansas City* (Mo.) *Star,* 4 Mar. 1920.

[4] Hale and Beck, 31-32. Also, Gentry, Sue. "Major Miles Recalls Last Use of the Old County Jail Here," undated, unsourced newspaper clipping in the Jackson County Historical Society Archives.

[5] "Re-Open the Jail Monday," and, "Cleaning Up Old Jail," *Independence* (Mo.) *Examiner,* 9 and 15 Mar. 1921, 1. Also, "Reopen Independence Jail," *Kansas City* (Mo.) *Star,* 10 Mar. 1921, which indicated that 30 of the 200 prisoners in Kansas City were being taken to Independence.

[6] "Marshal Raids a Houseboat," *Kansas City* (Mo.) *Star,* 27 Aug. 1921. It was a busy time, as just a few days earlier there had been a jail break of 13 prisoners, "Two of Fugitives Captured," *Kansas City* (Mo.) *Star,* 22 Aug. 1921, 1.

[7] "Cases of Fourteen up Friday," *Kansas City* (Mo.) *Star,* 22 May 1922, 2.

[8] "Chicken Farms Not All in Same Class," *Kansas City* (Mo.) *Star,* 14 Dec. 1921, 2; "Light Fine on Booze Sale," *Kansas City* (Mo.) *Star,* 17 Dec. 1921; "Dinner Farms Rouse Ire," *Kansas City* (Mo.) *Star,* 31 May 1922, 1; "Chicken Dinner Farmer Held," *Kansas City* (Mo.) *Star,* 20 June 1922.

[9] Burns, Ken. "Kansas City: A Wide Open Town." *JAZZ.* Public Broadcasting System Documentary, 1997.

[10] On 22 Aug, 1919, prisoners sawed bars of the rear (east) windows on the second floor of the jail addition and managed to squeeze through a 9" x 11" opening. When a third prisoner injured his leg in the fall to freedom, his plight prevented an additional 20 from escaping. On 20 June 1920, a suspicious jailor caught six attempting to escape from the second floor. In July 1921, Jesse Curran and Garret Malon escaped and were later caught. Steel bars were replaced. And, in August 1921, 13 prisoners escaped after cutting bars prompting new bars of the hardest steel. A jail break was foiled on June 19, 1922.

[11] "Sheriff and Deputies Sworn," *Kansas City* (Mo.) *Star,* 2 Jan. 1925, 4.

[12] Gentry, Sue. "Major Miles Recalls Last Use of the Old County Jail Here," undated, unsourced newspaper clipping in the Jackson County Historical Society Archives. Marshal's Star on Shelf," *Kansas City* (Mo.) *Star,* 6 Jan. 1925, p. 5, c. 1. Miles was the last elected County Marshal in Jackson County before the post was abolished by Missouri State Law (*Laws of the State of Missouri,* 1921, 51st General Assembly, Regular Session, 220-222). See also, Harry S Truman Library *Oral History Interview with Henry P. Chiles* by J. R. Fuchs, November 1, 1961, pages 73-74:

FUCHS: Mr. Truman supported John Miles for county marshal in 1920. Now is that a job that died out?

CHILES: Yes, it's been abolished. It used to be in Jackson County — there used to be a sheriff who took care of the civil affairs of the sheriff's office and this marshal, the criminal. He had the jail and he patrolled and arrested; he was like police. But, the marshal handled the criminal end of the thing. Johnny Miles ran and Johnny was a very popular. Republican. Nearly all of these veteran soldiers backed him. I had a nephew who went out and worked for him, and I give him the dickens and he just worked the same. I understood Truman backed Miles.

FUCHS: Later on, I believe by 1924, Miles was serving as sheriff and I wondered about the two jobs.

CHILES: Miles was marshal; was he ever sheriff?

FUCHS: Yes, he later on served as sheriff and I wondered if as you say, if the sheriff later on took the job that the marshal did in those days?

CHILES: They did combine the two, but I think that was after Mile's time in office. The sheriff's job was entirely civil and the marshal had the jail and the prisoners and did the patrolling and the arresting; but Miles, he won by a big, big majority. All these veterans were for him, everyone of them. You couldn't get a one of them to vote against him. I had a nephew that I thought I could have some influence over, and he wouldn't listen to me.

[13] "Remodel of Old Jailer's Home," *Independence* (Mo.) *Examiner,* 9 Feb. 1929, 1.

[14] "Independence Jail May Open," *Lee's Summit* (Mo.) *Democrat,* 23 May 1933, 1.

JAIL BREAK: QUIET HELPMATES: WOMEN WHO HELPED JACKSON COUNTY'S LAWMEN

We've explored the lawmen who strove to keep justice and order in check in the Jackson County Jail. Now, consider the many strongwomen who literally gave their lives in service to their husbands who had chosen an elected position forcing his family to lead an unglamorous and often dangerous lifestyle.

One account of a Jackson County Jail inspection provides an indirect example of the accommodations the lawman's wife had to endure: *"There is almost no provision made for the treatment of the sick or injured. For example, there is no operating table.... On more than one occasion when an operation had to be performed on a prisoner, use had to be made of the dining table."*[1]

The duties of the wife of the county official who occupied the home at any one time—

besides being a homemaker and raising children—was that of Jail Matron. The Marshal (or more likely, Jailor) and his family were offered the residence as partial compensation for maintaining law and order in the district. In addition, he received monthly wages. The Jail Matron added to the family income by preparing the prisoner's meals (and sometimes for jurors and visiting lawmen who may have stayed at the Marshal's Home), for which she received a few dollars a month.

As B. J. Alderman notes in the introduction to her book, *The Secret Life of the Lawman's Wife*, "County jails were designed to provide an atmosphere of home: families moved in, family members cooked for the prisoners, cared for their needs, and kept them from escaping." Often, prisoners assisted with daily chores of operating the home…and prison. "Pets roamed freely between jail and house. Children helped around the place, and many befriended the inmates."

Alderman's study examines and puts into context—through authentic stories of women and children—a unique family lifestyle rarely contemplated. In the Marshal's home, children had the responsibility of bringing in wood, starting the fire, taking out ashes, cleaning kerosene lamp globes, filling kerosene lamps, or beating rugs. Traditionally, the youngest child was responsible for emptying the bedside chamber pots (or, 'thunder mugs') each morning.

Specific stories of several of the women who faithfully served the myriad aspects of tending to prisoners at one time or another in the 1859 Jackson County Jail in Independence, Missouri, are also a part of Alderman's work, including:

Mrs. James Bruce (Ella S. [Thomas])Ross;
Mrs. Joseph W. (Lydia) Potts;
Mrs. Jesse "Jess" (Anna J.) Allen;
Mrs. Jesse E. "Jess" (Jennie S.) Curran;
Mrs. Melville "Mel" (Alice "Mama") Hulse; and,
Mrs. Henry (Mary [Brady]) Bugler—who was the first

wife/mother/matron to live in the residence adjoining the 1859 Jackson County Jail—endured, perhaps, more loss and hardship during her tenure than any other woman to live here. The Buglers unhappy story is discussed elsewhere in this history.

Another interesting event we've uncovered describes an evening of entertaining by **Mrs. Nicholas H. (Emma C.) Phelps** during the holiday festivities of 1909:

"There was a sound of revelry by night...it came from the dining room of the county jail building. The occasion was the first annual possum dinner of the Independence Possum Club. It was not in the jail strictly speaking, but in the residence portion of the building occupied by N. H. Phelps, county jailor and his family. The people who went on the hunt and a large number of invited guests were present, the number being 69. From under the skillful hand of the colored cook at the jail came the possum to the table. Then there was the indispensable sweet potato on each plate. There was celery and olives and salads and pumpkin pie and coffee and beer for those that like it. Mrs. Phelps and Miss Mattie Willey, assisted by Mr. Phelps and others, served the dinner. Perhaps a majority of those present had never eaten any possum and a large number entered upon the meal with misgivings for they had heard a lot of yarns. By the curfew whistle blew, the last morsel of possum had been eaten and the little pile of bones picked clean spoke eloquently of the appreciation of the guests. Nearly everyone declared that possum meat was much better than he had expected. Then came the speech making without no dinner is complete. Mayor Llewellyn Jones presided and acted as toastmaster. Nearly everyone who went on the hunt related his experiences and several invited guests regretted that they had not been among the hunters.... A rising vote of thanks was tendered to Mrs. N. H. Phelps who entertained the dinner party.... And to Mrs. George St. Clair, wife of George St. Clair, superintendent of the county farm, who served refreshments to the hunters at midnight last Friday night."[2]

"DUPONT HEIRESS BECOMES "PRISONER'S FRIEND" MOTHER MARY JEROME SHUBRICK (1830-1894)

Not all the quiet helpmates were relatives or employees of the elected lawmen. Mother Mary Jerome Shubrick spent her final years (1884-1894) in Independence after establishing the Sisters of Mercy motherhouse at St. Mary's Academy. She visited the jail and became well known for her acts of kindness to the prisoners. She brought them food and reading matter, as well as writing and mailing letters for them. She heralded reform, higher standards of professionalism in management and administration for prisons in Missouri.[3]

Shubrick, whose mother was of the illustrious DuPont family, worked at the Jackson County Jail where she was given her own key. It is on permanent exhibit at the 1859 Jail, Marshal's Home and Museum. Her efforts earned her the name— which appears on her grave marker—"The Prisoner's Friend."

Reform came, but none too quickly; it would take another 20 years to see results. The call for complete classification and separation of prisoners and upgraded facilities was the foundation of one sociological study performed by the University of Missouri in 1904.[4] These refinements necessitated additional staff quota…and their formal training. By the turn of the 20th Century, county jails began to assume added functions of punishment and reform.

[1] "County Jail Inspected," *Independence* (Mo.) *Examiner*, 30 May 1906.

[2] *Come and Spit on the Floor* (3:90-91) referencing *Jackson* (Independence, Mo.) *Examiner*, 3 Dec. 1909, 3:3. This cuisine must have become popular at the jail by this time because in 1903 Phelps had fed 35prisoners a possum Thanksgiving feast, which they popularly voted for over turkey (they also provided turkey to those who did not like possum), "'Possums for Prisoners," Kansas City (Mo.) Star, 24 Nov. 1903, 6.

[3] McKim, Judy. "DuPont Heiress Becomes 'The Prisoner's Friend.'" *Jackson County Historical Society JOURNAL* 1995 (Summer) 35:2, 5. Mother Mary Jerome Shubrick (1830-1894) lived her life dedicated to teaching and helping the poor and imprisoned. The richness of her life should not be measured by the wealth of her belongings, but rather by her social ministry, remembered in her simple epitaph, "The Prisoner's Friend."

Mother Jerome's final years were spent in Independence, Missouri, after having established the Sisters of Mercy mother house at St. Mary's Academy. Her work at the Jackson County Jail was so important that she was given her own key, which is now on exhibit at the 1859 Jail, Marshal's Home and Museum.

Mother Mary Jerome Shubrick was born Alicia Shubrick in 1830, the daughter of Irvine and Julia Sophie (DuPont) Shubrick. Her ancestry was especially distinguished: her father was a commander in the U.S. Navy and hero in the War of 1812 and her mother was a member of the illustrious DuPont family of Wilmington, Delaware. Alicia's early life was one of luxury at a family estate on the Brandywine in Delaware.

Her mother was a devout Catholic all her life. Her husband was an inspirational influence on their daughter, and a close bond of affection existed between them. Tragedy struck the family when three deaths occurred within the short space of time from 1847 and 1849. Alicia's oldest brother, Thomas, was killed in the Mexican War; her father died; and still another brother, Francis, perished in a West Coast fire.

It is likely that these traumatic experiences had a profound effect on the beautiful young Alicia, motivating her to a life dedicated to works of mercy and service to others. Family correspondence, preserved among the DuPont's historical papers, indicates that in the early 1850s young Alicia was studying various Catholic religious congregations, learning the "social service" type of work being done by the Sisters of Mercy, then newly established in America.

On March 1, 1853, Alicia entered the Convent of the Sisters of Mercy at the age of 23 years. She received the religious garb of a Sister of Mercy and the name Sister Mary Jerome. Two years later, she made a profession of vows. When a branch of the Mercy Institute was opened in St. Louis in 1856, she was a member of the initial group sent there, serving as mother assistant until 1858. Because of a temporary decline in health she returned to the New York community in 1860.

Four years later, Mother Mary Jerome Shubrick headed a group of sisters sent to Worcester, Massachusetts, where she remained for over 16 years, establishing schools, a hospital, and an orphanage. In 1880, she and two others departed for the Midwest. By 1884, she and her sisters were permanently established in Independence, Missouri, with a motherhouse, novitiate, and an academy.

Locally, Mother Jerome became well known for her personal visits and ministrations to prisoners and jail inmates. Besides supplying them with food and reading materials, she and her sisters often wrote letters for the prisoners to their families and friends, and assisted in preparing the condemned to meet their fate. In Independence, she had her own key to the County Jail and stood with the chaplain at some hangings in the town Square. There is reliable testimony that Mother Jerome had the unclaimed body of one murderer, who was hanged for his crimes, buried in a corner of the sisters' plot in Woodlawn Cemetery. Since the fellow had died deeply repentant, Mother Jerome thought his remains deserved better than the potters' field.

At the age of 64, Mother Mary Jerome died on February 5, 1894, in Independence, at St. Mary's Convent, which was razed in 1959. Her remains rest in Woodlawn Cemetery where her simple grave marker bears an inscription, "The Prisoner's Friend."

[4] Ellwood, Charles A., Ph.D. *A Bulletin on the Condition of the County Jails of Missouri*. (Columbia, Mo.: University of Missouri Department of Sociology, July 1904), 1-20.

CELL

9

ADAPTIVE RE-USE DURING DEPRESSION ERA (1933-1945)

Sheriff Thomas "Tom" Bash turned over the keys of the "Old Jail" to Charles Tucker, president of the Jackson County Community Welfare League, and Mrs. J. H. Ryan, executive secretary.

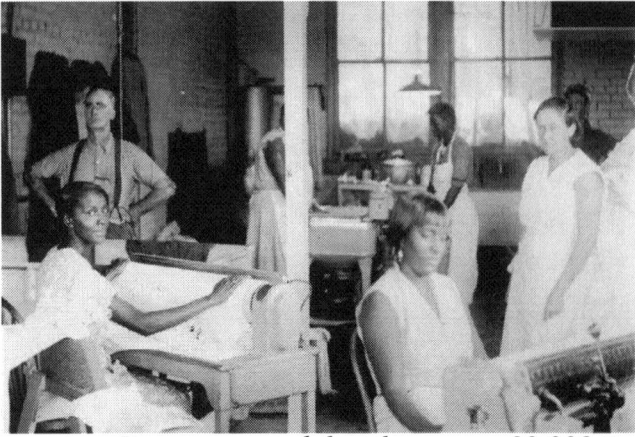

"Mrs. Ryan planned to use the Jail kitchen for canning fruits and vegetables and the balance of rooms for storing provisions. During 1934 great improvements were made to the Jail at a cost of $10,00 after the League received a Federal allocation of $7,000. The Jail kitchen was remodeled with the latest equipment. The old cell blocks on the first floor became storage bins. An extension was built adjoining the kitchen at the rear for the preparation of vegetables for canning. It was reported that there were 92,000 tin cans on hand for the canning season."

Additionally, improvements were made to the heating, wiring, and plumbing of the building. The first floor of the former Marshal's home became the office of the government Free Employment Office. The second floor was used for women's sewing projects.

Four beds were placed in the building to care for transients. The executive secretary of the League stated, *"This is the realization of a social center for the county."*[1]

The Rural Resettlement Administration and Farm Security Administration also used the former Jail facility throughout the Great Depression years.

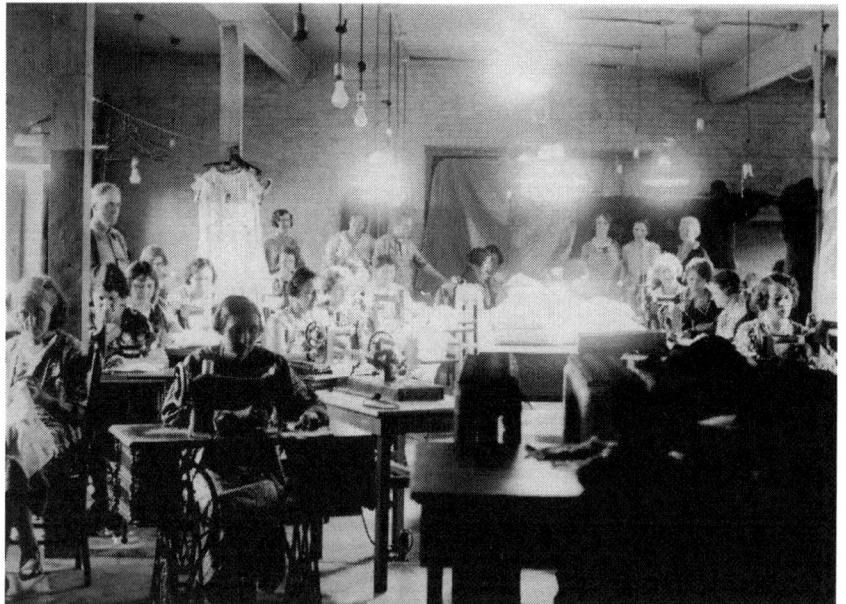

Ivan S. Slaughter worked in the "Old Jail" facility as a head loan officer for the Farm Security Administration from about 1937-38 to 1942-43, before leaving to work along with his wife, Jo Dorothy, at the Pratt & Whitney munitions plant during World War II.[2]

In June 1937, eight steel cells in the 1907 addition were removed to make spacious workrooms for the regional relief services of the Works Progress Administration (WPA). They were cut with acetylene torches and removed to Ikey Lieberman's junkyard.[3]

As mentioned above, sewing, canning and other useful public work programs operated at the "Old Jail" that helped give people viable work at a great time of need in our country's history. Fortunately, the heavy-duty iron doors and window grates in the two-story, 1859 cell block escaped the scrap drives of World War II, and are therefore, original throughout.[4]

---

[1] This served charitable causes for several years , until a canning factory was opened at 1450 West Lexington Avenue. "Remodel Jail at Cost of $10,000," *Independence (Mo.) Examiner*, 27 April 1934. Also, Hale and Beck, 33-34.
[2] Slaugher, Ivan S., Jr. *Seems Like Old Times* (Ivan Slaughter, 2005), 242, 256.
[3] "City Jail's Old Steel Cells Relegate to the Junk Yards," *Independence* (Mo.) *Examiner*, 19 June 1937, 1.
[4] Adams, W. Howard. "How to Turn a Jail Into a Historical Museum." *Museum News*. (December 1961), 40:4, 28-31.

CELL

10

MID-CENTURY PROGRESS THREATENED A PARKING LOT (1945-1958)

After the WPA ceased, and other organizations re-located, the Jackson County Court between May and September 1945 decided to deed its interest in the "Old Jail" to the City of Independence.

The City of Independence, which had already owned 12 feet of this parcel (Lot 2) since 1881, then, deeded the entire property on October 23, 1945, to the Tiery J. Ford Post Number 21 of the American Legion in consideration of $100.[1]

The Legion used the building as their headquarters for a couple of years. Architects Weatherford and DeFoe drafted the specifications for a remodeling project; but, bids far exceeded the building fund, and minimal work was done.[2]

In 1949, the Legion moved to the old telephone building at 318 West Maple; but, retained ownership of the Old Jail.[3] Jackson County's defunct 1859 Jail would remain vacant for nearly a decade.[4]

By 1953, "mutually agreeable plans for preservation of the old Jackson County Jail" were being sought.[5]

To the rescue of Jail—This delegation of historically and promotionally minded citizens inspected the Jackson County Jail building this morning to see what might be done about saving the historic landmark which the Legion owners have announced they will raze.

However, the *Independence Examiner* newspaper reported on August 13, 1956, that the Legion announced plans to tear down the building because of its unsafe condition. In hasty conferences with Rufus Burrus, attorney for the Legion, and Mayor Robert P. Weatherford, a committee was formed to study an engineering, survey, title, and financing project.[6] Members of the delegation are pictured at the left.

Milton F. Perry, formerly at Williamsburg, Virginia, and later a member of the museum staff at West Point, who came to Independence as a member of the museum staff of the Truman Library, made the preliminary study of the building. A committee of professional advisors included: Dr. William J. Murtagh, then of the National Trust for Historic Preservation, and later, Keeper of the National Register of Historic Places; Charles Van Ravensway, then director of the Missouri Historical Society, St. Louis, and later, director of the Henry Francis DuPont Winterthur Museum, Wilmington, Delaware; Robert Stewart, Consultant to the St. Louis County Park Commission; and, Ross Taggart of the Nelson Gallery of Art, Kansas City. Independence Mayor William H. Sermon responded by establishing a committee with American Legion representatives to devise a plan for the building's restoration. "*I know everybody is happy that the old jail building will be preserved. It has been a problem worrying historical-minded citizens for a good many years,*" he said.[7]

---

[1] The property was originally part of the 160 acres ceded by the United States to Jackson County for county seat purposes. The county commissioners reserved the public square for a courthouse and then divided the 160 acres into large lots, cut streets through the heavy timber and held an auction sale of the lots. The purchaser of the lot on which the 1859 Jackson County Jail stands today sold to Jacob Gregg, who later became Jackson County Sheriff. The 50 feet on Main Street eventually came into the ownership of Peter Gastell who deeded it to Jackson County for the 1859 Jackson County Jail, on December 22, 1850, for $1,200. "Old County Jail Building is to Serve Charity," *Independence* (Mo.) *Examiner*, 29 June 1933. Also, $730 bill of sale for Lot 2, Old Town, from Jackson County to City of Independence, April 1881; Jackson County Court minutes (21:99); "Jackson County Historical Society and How it Grew," *Jackson County Historical Society JOURNAL* (Winter 1986) 28:1, 28. Hale and Beck, 34.

[2] *Independence (Mo.) Examiner*, 17 May 1946.

[3] "Old Jail Back to City for Museum Use." *Independence (Mo.) Examiner*, 30 July 1958.

[4] Hale and Beck, 34.

[5] Stewart, 7. And, Jackson County Historical Society Archives, Document ID L50F2-8.

[6] Rufus Burrus is presumed to be a descendant of former Jackson County Sheriff, Major John W. Burrus, who served from 1859 until his death in office in May 1861.

[7] "Old Jail Back to City for Museum Use." *Independence (Mo.) Examiner*, 30 July 1958.

CELL

11

HISTORICAL SOCIETY, PRESIDENT HARRY S TRUMAN'S CALL TO ACTION (1958-2008)

The initial preservation sentiment from 1956 faded. In 1958, American Legion Post President Everett Fessler, and several Post officers met over supper at the Holiday Inn on the northwest corner of 40 Highway and Noland Road to discuss their options regarding the "Old Jail," as the City of Independence was pressuring them to either repair or remove the building. A man at an adjoining table overheard their conversation, introduced himself and his demolition business, and offered to raze the building in exchange for being allowed to keep the salvaged materials. They each agreed this was the best possible solution. Fortunately, other nearby diners overheard the exchange and immediately phoned W. Howard Adams, the first President of the Jackson County Historical Society. Mr. Fessler then got a late night call and the two gentlemen worked out a plan that mutually benefited the Legion Post and positioned the Society to save a unique, irreplaceable relict of County heritage. By the next morning, the two organizations had secured a 'stay of execution' for the then 100-year-old building.[1] The current (2009) frontage of the land on Main Street is 53.84 feet (south 20.34 feet of Lot 2, and north 33.50 feet of Lot 3, Independence Old Town), and the depth extends to Lynn Avenue on the east.[2]

Transferring title of the Old Jail. Seated, left to right: W. Howard Adams; Mayor William H. Sermon. Standing: Roy Layland, JCHS ; Edgar G. Hinde, Sr., and Warren Gray, representing the American Legion.

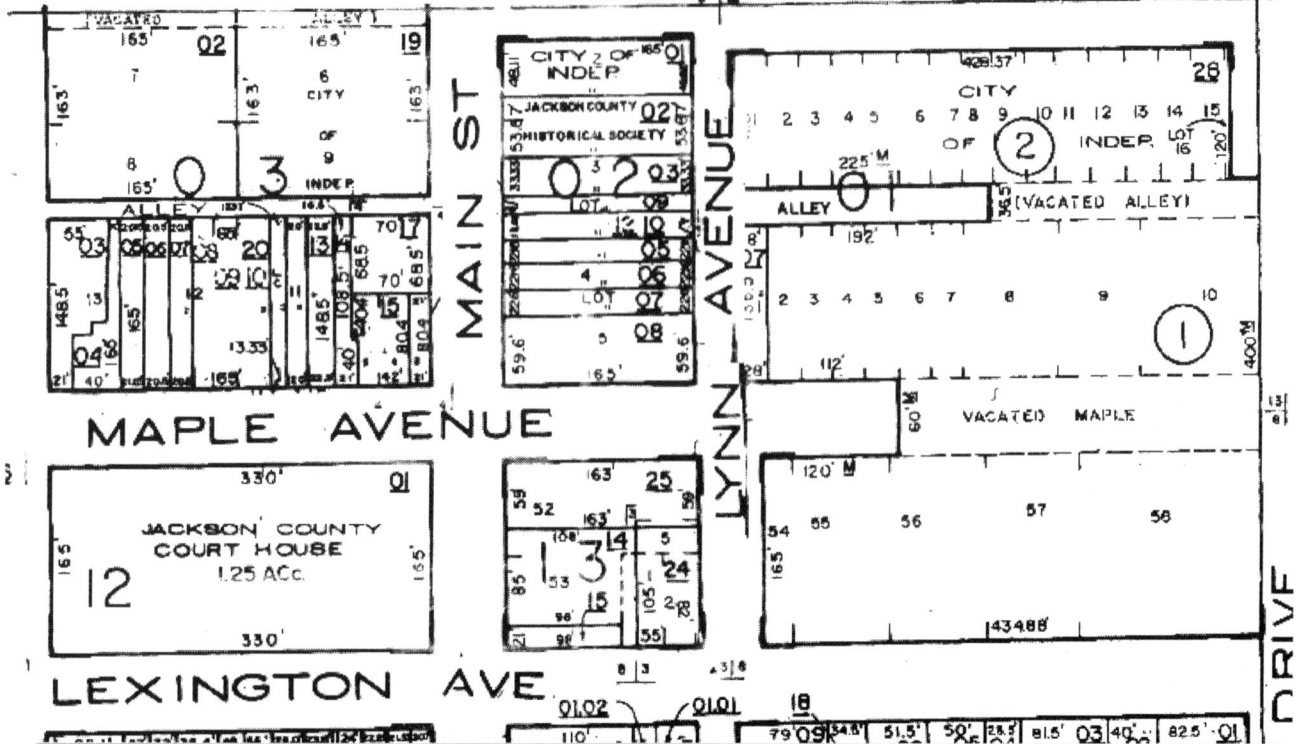

Jackson County Assessment Department Map, as of 2009.

Those who had wanted the building torn down easily secured estimates of $60-75,000 as the minimum amounts necessary to begin restoration of the building.

On the other hand, there were those whose dedication so blinded them to realities that they thought $5-10,000 would do the job.

A clearer estimate by disinterested persons with construction experience felt that $20-30,000 would put things in good order.[3]

A fervent capital campaign ensued under the leadership of the Jackson County Historical Society's first President, William Howard Adams.

To raise funds for the restoration of "The Old Jail" and convert the Jackson County Jail and adjoining Marshal's Home into the Jackson County Museum, former United States President Harry S Truman made the first capital campaign call. Truman, a Missouri Democrat, solicited his friend, a Republican, Mr. Joyce C. "J.C." Hall, founder of Hallmark Cards, Inc., who pledged the first $1,000 to the cause.

Individuals and civic organizations rallied to contribute more than $30,000 for the restoration.[4] They also rallied to W. Howard Adams' call for donations of authentic furnishings for the reconstruction of period rooms in the residence portion of the "Old Jail," an for historical artifacts for museum exhibition. This is a tradition that continues today.

It was estimated that 4,770 people visited the 1859 Jail, Museum Home and Museum in the first seven-month period from opening day on Sunday, June 28, 1959, through January 30, 1960.[5]

111

HOWARD FAMILY ONE-ROOM SCHOOL HOUSE

The only major change introduced to this site is a one-room schoolhouse, 12' x 16' that was relocated intact to the museum complex, restored and dedicated on June 19, 1960.

William Bullitt Howard was born in 1821 on his father's farm in Jefferson County, Kentucky, about nine miles from the present city of Louisville. After his marriage to Maria Duncan Strother (1825-1865) in 1844, he came with her to Jackson County. He purchased 1,000 acres, mostly in Blue Township, and six years later he added 883 acres.

Soon afterward, Mr. Howard added another 400 acres to his holdings, to the south in Prairie Township. On this property he built the Howard home in 1854—an excellent Missouri example of Greek Revival architecture.

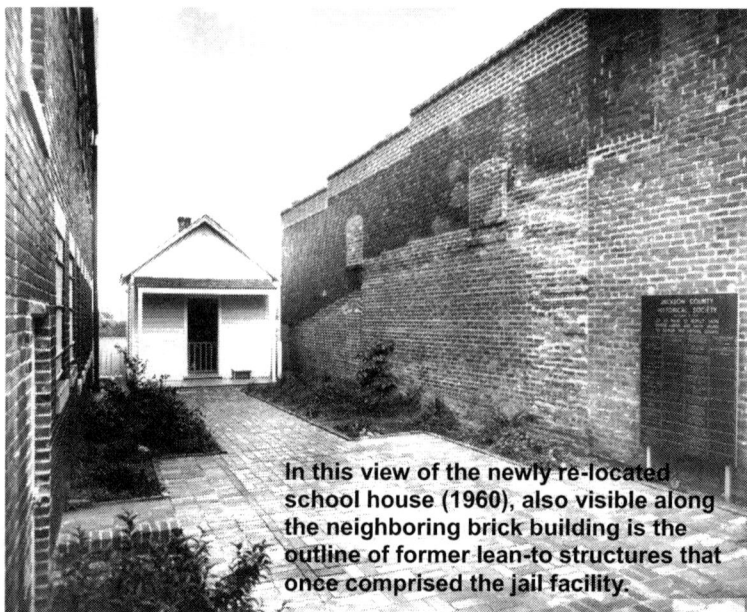

In this view of the newly re-located school house (1960), also visible along the neighboring brick building is the outline of former lean-to structures that once comprised the jail facility.

At the time of the Civil War, William Buillitt Howard, a known Southern sympathizer, was arrested by Colonel William Ridgeway Penick, a Federal officer in command of Independence.[6] Howard, with his brother-in-law, spent one month in the Jackson County Jail just yards away from where the school house now resides. He was released on $25,000 bond and the condition that he, his wife and three children would leave the State for the duration of the War. The Howard home was one of those ordered to be burned under Order No. 11. The story was— and it has never been disproved—that Cole Younger and his brothers saved the home from burning. Maria Howard died in October 1865 while the family was in exile in Kentucky. Howard returned to Jackson County, re-claimed his property, and buried his wife in a family cemetery on his land next to two of their children who had died while young.[7]

Howard then set aside 70-acres of farmland, and filed a plat in October 1865 with the Jackson County Record of Deeds for the town of Strother (after his wife's maiden surname), where present-day downtown Lee's Summit is situated.[8]

In 1867, William Howard, age 46, married 21-year-old Mary Catherine Jones, a school teacher from Waverly, Missouri. They built the school house near the Howard family home in 1870. Of the six Howard children—Marie, Robert, May, and Thomas—were the only students who ever attended school in the little building (Florence and William Jr. attended school in Lee's Summit after the family moved into town in 1879). The Howard children's two teachers were Miss Joy Leonard, and later Miss "Scottie" Buchanan, both of Independence. In those days, part of the teacher's salary was room and board, so the teachers lived with the Howard family.[9]

William Howard died in 1896 and was buried beside his first wife in the Howard family cemetery. Mrs. Mary Howard desired to be buried in the Lee's Summit Cemetery that Howard had contributed to the City; she died in 1908.

Thanks to a generous donation by local historian, Donald R. Hale, the Jackson County Historical Society maintains an invaluable collection of original papers from the William Bullitt Howard family.

Independence educator Mary Childers utilizes the Howard School House each year when she and her students attend a week-long session, in period clothes, re-enacting what it was like to be educated in a one room school house on the American frontier.

Draft of statement for campaign to restore the old County Jail:

I commend the Jackson County Historical Society for its effort to develop a museum to display historic treasures of the past. The old jail building is one of our few standing mementos of early days in this area, and well worth preserving. I am glad that it is a County-wide movement, as all the people of the County share the heritage of great events and lives that have made our history.

Harry S. Truman

The completion of the 1859 Jail, Marshal's Home and Museum restoration was dedicated was on May 3, 1964. Here, former President, Harry S Truman, presides at the Jail's dedication ceremonies.

Three episodes of the Civil War-era made-for-television movie, "Friendly Persuasion," were filmed at the 1859 Jail, Marshal's Home and Museum in March 1975. The 18-hour-day began at 8 a.m. when city trucks spread loads of dirt to cover the brick walks. Simulated jail bars covered the front shuttered windows of the Marshal's Home. The TV crew art director carefully measured the window space and the bars were wedged in without using a screw or nail. Then, the sign, "City Jail Cincinnati," was placed over the Marshal's office door. Filming for the movie about a Quaker family involved in helping runaway slaves escape to Canada during the Civil War got under way late in the day, around 4:30 p.m. [10]

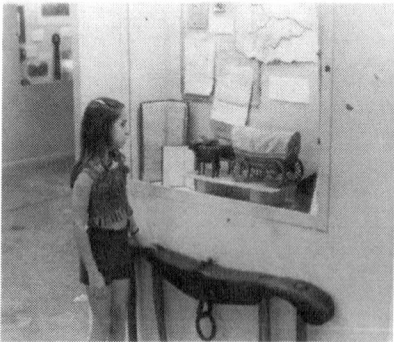

Over the years, countless residents and tourists have toured the site. School children who toured the museum when it first opened have grown up, and now their children are taking in the experience for themselves.

The goal of this museum, as with most, is to provide an unobstructed view of "those old times" so that they "cease to be old times and would become part of the present, not only as if they had happened yesterday but as if they were still happening, the men who walked through them, actually walking in breath and air and casting an actual shadow on the earth they had not quitted." [11]

By the early 1990s, roof, flashing, masonry and paint were in need of attention. The buildings enjoyed a "facelift" with $9,009 in Community Development Block Grant (CDBG) funds, through the City of Independence, which provided masonry work, painting and roof work between 1992 and 1995. In spring 1995, insurance monies from a hail damage claim ($2,280) and Friends of the Jail funds ($1,358) replaced hail-damaged roofing on the Marshal's Home and Jail. An additional $8,933 in CDBG funds provided for the painting of windows, trim and gate, and replacement of rotted gate posts. After two years absence (as the masonry work continued), the shutters on the Marshal's Home were re-hung. Period hardware from the 1850s was purchased through a source in Cooperstown, New York.

In June 1995, employees of the U.S. Department of Agriculture helped at the Museum by repairing the porch of the Howard Schoolhouse, painting and repairing the benches in the courtyard and installing a window unit air conditioner in the upstairs office among other general clean up tasks. Their much appreciated volunteer efforts were provided through the United Way, CFC and Points of Light Foundation Day of Caring.

In 1993, the Jail Museum received a Conservation Assessment Project (CAP) grant from the National Institute for the Conservation of Cultural Property. The recommendations from this assessment placed a high priority on proper climate control. Electronic dataloggers which record the humidity and temperature levels in different areas of the Museum and Marshal's Home were installed and the information analyzed through a Conservation Project Support matching grant of $1,685 from the Institute of Museum Services.

The analysis prepared the way for the purchase and installation of a new HVAC system which created a more consistent and appropriate environment for the buildings and the collection. Additional matching funds of $25,000 were secured to aid in the $60,000 project.[12]

New paint, shutters and signage made the jail façade attractive once again. As the needs of the exterior were met, attention shifted to improving accessibility, lighting and visitor comforts.

In addition to maintaining regular hours throughout the tourism season, the Museum continues to participate in the annual Santa-Cali-Gon festival; conducts occasional candlelight tours; decorates the Marshal's Home and hosts special Christmastime tours; and in 2007 began an annual Ghost Tours event in October, which became instantly popular. The foresight of one Independence resident, Roger "T." Sermon, Jr., has greatly assisted the Museum with its continued operations by establishing a dedicated revenue stream through the Roger T. Sermon Fund, a component fund at the Truman Heartland Community Foundation.

In 2004, the Jackson County Historical Society celebrated its 45th anniversary having operated 1859 Jail, Marshal's Home and Museum, a site that was listed on the National Register of Historic Places on June 15, 1970.[13]

Roger "T." Sermon, Jr.

Scenes for the 2006 made-for-television movie, "Bad Blood," produced by Kansas City Public Television, were filmed in the parlor of the Marshal's Home of the 1859 Jackson County Jail.

And, in 2008 the Jackson County Historical Society celebrated its 50th Golden Anniversary of incorporation. The following year, another historic anniversary was commemorated.

JACKSON COUNTY HISTORICAL SOCIETY

Celebrating 50 Years

1958-2008

[1] Recollection of Everett Fessler. Stewart, 7.

[2] "Old Jail Transferred to American Legion," *Independence* (Mo.) *Examiner*, 23 Oct. 1945. "Old Jail Back to City for Museum Use." *Independence (Mo.) Examiner*, 30 July 1958. The map pictured is the current (2009) Assessment Map of Jackson County, Missouri (Map Number 26-230), which shows the Jackson County Historical Society's frontage to be 53.67 feet. However, the Assessment Department's Property Account Summary lists the legal description as stated in the text, which accounts for 53.84 feet.

[3] Adams, 31.

[4] Stewart, 7.

[5] Brooks, Dr. Philip C. "Dr. Brooks Reports on Museum Operations." Vol. 3, No. 1 (March 1960) *Jackson County Historical Society JOURNAL*, 2. The *Kansas City* (Mo.) *Times* article, "History's Lamp Lit in Old County Jail," 9 July 1959, records the opening date as June 27, where more than 1,000 visitors were attracted.

[6] Colonel William Ridgeway Penick, commander of the Fifth Missouri State Militia stationed in Independence, was a radical Unionist, stating that the guerrilla problem could be wiped out "if hemp, fire, and gunpowder were freely used." Penick routinely assassinated suspected guerrilla sympathizers. "The Hounds of Old Pennock," *Blue and Grey Chronicle:* Vol. 5, No. 6, p. 1. "List of Prisoners at Independence [1863]", Also, *Blue and Grey Chronicle:* Vol. 4, No. 4, p. 10. Also, quantrillsguerrillas.com/xoops/modules/news (viewed on 28 Nov. 2009). His official biography from the 1881 *History of Buchanan County, Missouri*, states: "Most of the active military service he performed was…contending with guerrillas, commanded by Todd, Quantrell and other desperate commanders, of the same kind."

[7] The home burned in 1967. The walled cemetery survives, though it is in the middle of a strip-store parking lot at Lakeview off of M-291 Highway.

[8] *Jackson County Historical Society JOURNAL*, September 1960, 7. Howard's grandson, William T. Howard, of Lee's Summit, inherited the family home and 320 acres of the original 2,000-acre farm. In 1868, the name of the town of Strother was changed to Lee's Summit, and incorporated to honor Dr. Pleasant Lea (the "Summit" because of the Missouri Pacific Railroad line between St. Louis and Omaha) (the "Lea" was misspelled on the first depot, and never corrected).

[9] Marie, Robert, May and Thomas Howard.

[10] Gentry, Sue. "Movie Crew Takes Care of Old Jail," *Independence* (Mo.) *Examiner*, 29 Mar. 1975.

[11] Faulkner, William. Intruder in the Dust. (New York: Random House, 1948).

[12] Clemenson, Gay and Jane Pickett Sharon. "Because of Grants, Volunteers: Jail & Museum Get New Exterior." *Jackson County Historical Society JOURNAL* 1995 (Fall) 35:3, 3.

[13] U.S. Department of the Interior, National Park Service, National Register of Historic Places Inventory, Nomination Form, prepared by M. Patricia Holmes, Research and Architectural Historian, Missouri State Park Board, State Historical Survey and Planning Office, April 10, 1970.

CELL

12

THE NEXT HALF CENTURY
OF YOUR JACKSON COUNTY MUSEUM
(2009-2059)

In 2009, the Jackson County Historical Society recognized the 1859 Jackson County Jail as having survived and been a part of 150 years of incredible Jackson County, history.

2009 also marked the 50 anniversary of the Jackson County Historical Society's ownership and operation of the "1859 Jail, Marshal's Home and Museum" historic site. A comprehensive overview of the restoration and first 50 years is published separately in the Spring 2009 edition of the *Jackson County Historical Society JOURNAL*.

In June 2009, the Jackson County Historical Society recognized the 150th Anniversary of the 1859 Jackson County Jail with a weekend-long celebration. A living history event re-captured several of the most prominent events that transpired at this historic site. Special lectures focused on "Frontier Justice" and "Social Outlaws" offered an overview of how this historic site's heritage is intertwined with local—and indeed—American history.

An exclusive Society member's dinner hosted by Ophelia's restaurant on Independence Square served up a unique social gathering for people who love and support local history…and its preservation. And, rekindling "Opening Day" from 1959, visitors attending the Jail Museum's Open House on Sunday, June 7, 2009, enjoyed free museum admission. This commemorative souvenir publication was also produced as part of this prestigious occasion.

The nonprofit Jackson County Historical Society, supported by memberships, donations and bequests, continues a half century tradition of presenting engaging, educational programs; raising awareness of historic preservation; encouraging scholarly research into local history; staging historically accurate re-enactments; and, installing entertaining, interpretive museum exhibits about Jackson County's illustrious heritage.

One of the favorite acts of chance in the game Monopoly™ directs players to: *"Go to Jail. Go Directly to Jail. Do Not Collect $200."* We would rather invite you to turn over your "bail" to the Jackson County Historical Society's endowments so we may continue to serve the public into the next half century!

We appreciate your dedication, and welcome your support.

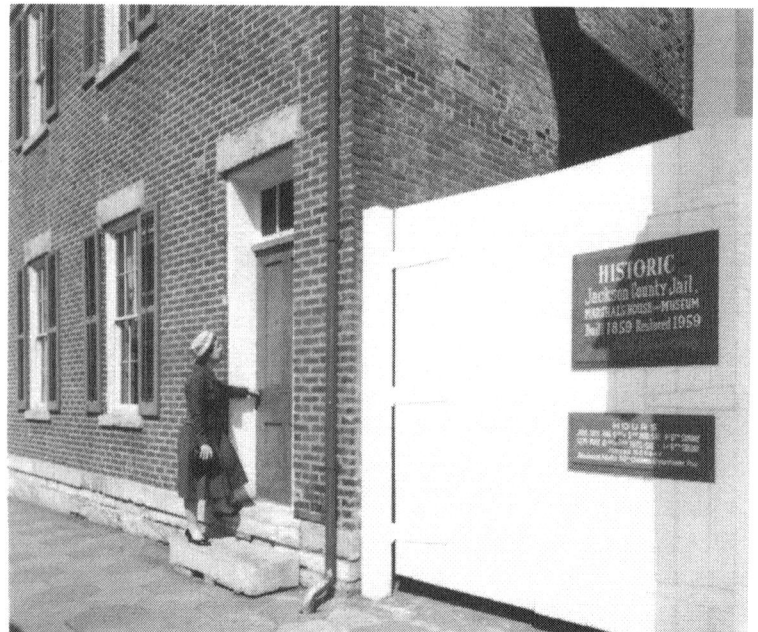

APPENDIX

A

LAWMEN SERVING JACKSON COUNTY IN INDEPENDENCE, MISSOURI: 1827-1933

Jackson County became unique in Missouri when the legislature on February 1, 1871, established the office of Marshal of Jackson County…an elected post that was to be filled ***in addition to*** the traditional Sheriff of Jackson County. When the position was abolished 53 years later in 1924, a long time employee at the Courthouse, Dell Womack said, "*As I recollect the chief reason Jackson County was given a marshal was [the sole purpose of catching] Jesse James.*"[1]

After the Marshal's post was created, the County Sheriff was *responsible for civil affairs.*

The County Marshal *pursued, apprehended, and jailed alleged criminals.*[2]

What about the jailors? They were specialized "deputies" who staffed and were *responsible for guarding the jail.* The jailors and their families occupied the home adjacent to the 1859 Jackson County Jail.[3]

There are references in Jackson County Court minutes that indicate that posts changed hands in the early days as early as July or August; later they appear to transfer power after November elections (and commissions approved by the Missouri Governor, in the case of the County Sheriff). And, at other times, newly elected officials appear to have assumed their charge on January 1. Unless otherwise specified, the dates outlined below are those *full-year terms* (January-December) for which the officials were elected to serve, even though they *may* have technically held the post in the months preceding.

Though admittedly incomplete, this is the first and most comprehensive list to date (2009) of lawmen who served Jackson County <u>in Independence</u>. A more comprehensive study of lawmen, including a compendium of officials in Kansas City and environs is a task available to any interested party desiring to embark upon a project that would take years of concentrated research.

This enumeration is a "working roster" assembled by David W. Jackson from a variety of sources located in or available through the Jackson County Historical Society Archives.[4]

We recognize the occasional difficultly ascertaining if "the Marshal" being referred to in certain sources was the "County Marshal," <u>or</u> the "City Marshal" (aka. Chief of Police) for Independence <u>or</u> Kansas City; and, if "the jail" referred to the County Jail in Independence <u>or</u> Kansas City. The author made every attempt to ensure accuracy and cite references. Sources and citations for the early sheriffs are noted previously in their respective biographies.

An asterisk (*) indicates those documented as having lived in the 1859 Jail residence.

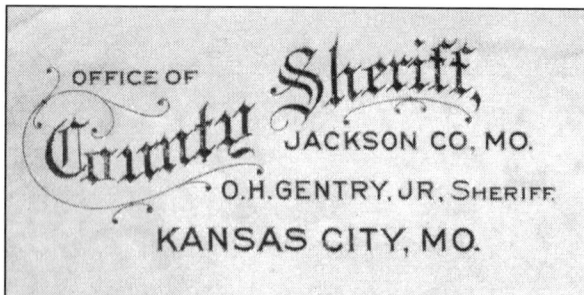

Left: Business card of O. H. Gentry, Jr., Sheriff of Jackson County, Missouri. Gift of Mary Shaw "Shawsie" Branton.

Below: Prisoners being taken to Jefferson City by Missouri River boat, "The Chester," when Harvey C. "Harry" Hoffman was Jackson County Marshal.

SHERIFF	MARSHAL	JAILOR

1827-1830 Captain Joseph "Joe" Reddeford Walker
     Jacob Gregg, Deputy

1831-1832 Joseph Brown

1833-1836 Jacob Gregg   Lewis Franklin[5]

1837-1840 John King
Joseph H. "Joe" Reynolds, Deputy

1841-1844 Joseph H. "Joe" Reynolds

1845-1846 Colonel Thomas Pitcher   Davy D. Harrell (Harrell)[6]

1847-1848 Benjamin Franklin Thomson

1849-1852 George W. Buchanan

1853-1854 Benjamin Franklin Thomson

1855-1858 William Botts   Henry Bugler[7]
   John Brady[8]
                                            A. Chandler[9]
                                       James A. Steel[10]

1859-May 1861 Major John W. Burrus   **1859 Jackson County Jail Completed**   *Henry & Mary (Brady) Bugler[11]
                                  February-March 1860   John Brady[12]

May 1861 William B. Rogers (appointed acting)[13]   *Henry & Mary (Brady) Bugler

May 1861-Oct. 1861 Oliver P. W. Bailey[14]   **First Civil War Battle of Independence** *Henry & Mary (Brady) Bugler
                                    August 11, 1862

Oct. 1861-Oct. 1862 Tandy Westmoreland[15]   *Henry & Mary (Brady) Bugler[16]

Oct. 1862 Beverly W. Todd (appointed elisor)[17]   *Henry & Mary (Brady) Bugler[18]

Nov. 1862 Henry Bugler (appointed elisor)[19]   *Henry & Mary (Brady) Bugler[20]

Dec. 1862 William C. Miles (appointed elisor)[21]

1863-13 Jul 1865 John G. Hayden[22]   ***Order No. 11* issued August 25, 1863** *Henry & Mary (Brady) Bugler[23]
                            Civil offices declared vacant   John Brady[24]
          Second Civil War Battle of Independence James Colburn[25]
                                October 21 & 22, 1864   James Culbertson[26]
                                                    Thomas Fox[27]

SHERIFF	MARSHAL	JAILOR
13 Jul 1865-1866 Henry Hudson "Harry" Williams[28] C. W. Carr (Sheriff Proper)[29] Gabriel Smith (Sheriff Proper)[30]		*Henry & Mary (Brady) Bugler (Killed at the Jail 13 June 1866) *Mrs. Henry (Mary Brady) Bugler (Continued as matron at the jail from after her husband was killed, and her 4-year-old son was shot) James Culbertson (night watch)[31] Dennis Dillon[32]
1867-1870 Charles Dougherty[33] John Farrell, Jailor@KC (1868-1880)[34]		*Mrs. Mary (Brady) Bugler (Continued through August 1867)[35] *Richard Ryan[36] John Brady[37] C. R. Brown[38] Timothy Conroy[39] A. J. Liddil[40] Dennis McCarty[41]
1871-Jul 1872 James L. Gray[42] John Farrell, Jailor@KC (1868-1880)[44] July-Dec. 1872 appointment unknown	Major Granville Dyson Page (12 Jun. 1871-1872)[45]	Redmond Dee Silvers[43]
1873-1874 C. B. L. Booth(e)[46] 	Major Granville Dyson Page[47]	Redmond Dee Silvers
1875-1876 C. B. L. Booth(e)[48] John Farrell, Jailor@KC (1868-1880)[50]	Patrick Connor(s)[49]	Redmond Dee Silvers

Four Year Terms

SHERIFF	MARSHAL	JAILOR
1877-1880 Oliver P. W. Bailey[51] John Farrell, Jailor@KC (1868-1880)[54]	James W. Liggett (1877-1880)[52] Frank Butterick, Deputy[55] R. Y. "Bud" Freeman, Deputy[56] Anderson/Amasa/Amazon Hays, Deputy[57] Henry H. Hughes, Deputy (-Feb 1877)[58] William G. "Whig" Keshlear, Deputy[59]	Captain Maurice M. Langhorne[53]
1881-1884 John C. Hope[60] Thomas William Gleason, Deputy[63] Edmund R. Lee, Jailor@KC[65]	Captain Cornelius "Con" Murphy, Sr.[61] D. Gregg, Deputy[64] Anderson/Amasa/Amazon Hays, Deputy[66] William G. "Whig" Keshlear, Deputy[67] John T. Murphy, Deputy[68] Hinton H. Noland[69]	George Hezekiah Holland[62]

Two Year Terms

SHERIFF	MARSHAL	JAILOR
1885-1886 W. T. Hickman	William A. "Jutt" Phillips[70] Melville "Mel" Hulse, Deputy[72] ? Liggett, Deputy[73]	Redmond Dee Silvers[71]

SHERIFF	MARSHAL	JAILOR
1887-1888 W. T. Hickman[74] William S. Sitlington, Deputy, KC William H. Winslip, Deputy, KC D. C. Greenwood, Deputy, KC Robert R. Kreeger, Deputy, Indep.	Hugh J. McGowan[75] Colonel George W. Belt, Deputy[77] Frank Fitzpatrick, Deputy[78] John Flemming, Deputy[79] R. Y. Freeman, Deputy[80] Melville "Mel" Hulse, Deputy[81] Joseph B. Keshlear, Deputy[82] ? Liggett, Deputy[83] Cy Near, Deputy[84]	*James Bruce & Ella S. (Thomas) Ross[76]
1889-1890 William S. Sitlington[85]	Hugh J. McGowan[86] Joseph B. Keshlear, Deputy[87] Robert S. Stone, Deputy[88]	* James Bruce & Ella S. (Thomas) Ross
1891-1892 William S. Sitlington[89]	Henry P. Stewart[90] John Halpin, Deputy[92] Thomas W. Herson, Deputy[93] Robert S. Stone, Deputy[94]	* James Bruce & Ella S. (Thomas) Ross[91]
1893-1894 John P. O'Neil[95]	Henry P. Stewart[96] Thomas W. Herson, Chief Deputy[98] Holly Jarboe, Deputy[100] Joseph B. Keshlear, Deputy[101] James B. McGowan, Deputy[102] Jacob Newhouse, Deputy[103] Joseph T. Stewart, Deputy[104] Robert S. Stone, Chief Deputy[105]	* James Bruce & Ella S. (Thomas) Ross[97] C. C. "Kit" Lattimer, Night Jailor[99]
1895-1896 John P. O'Neil[106]	Henry P. Stewart (-July 1895)[107] Clark Brown, Deputy[109] Michael Casey, Deputy[111] John Halpin, Deputy[113] Thomas W. Herson, Deputy[114] Holly Jarboe, Deputy[115] Joseph B. Keshlear (July 1895-1896)[116] William G. "Whig" Keshlear, Chief Deputy[117] Donald Latshaw, Deputy[118] C. C. "Kit" Lattimer, Deputy[119] John T. Murphy, Deputy[120] Jacob Newhouse, Deputy[121] Edward "Plug" O'Flaherty, Deputy[122] Joseph T. Stewart, Deputy[123] Samuel A. Wilson, Deputy[124]	* James Bruce and Ella S. (Thomas) Ross[108] Jerome B. Estes, Night Jailor[110] Mrs. Kate Grogan, Matron[112]
1897-1898 Robert S. Stone[125]	Samuel Hamilton Chiles[126] Clark Brown, Deputy[128] H. W. Chiles, Chief Deputy[130] J. J. Dunn, Deputy[132] James Gallagher, Deputy[133] Joseph Gentry, Deputy[134] Matt S. Kenney, Deputy[135] F. L. Leahey, Deputy[136] Joel B. Mayes, Deputy[137]	*Joseph W. and Lydia Potts[127] Jerome B. Estes, Night Jailor[129] Mrs. Kate Grogan, Matron[131]

Thomas J. "Tom" Pendergast, Deputy[138]
Stephen C. Reagan, Deputy[139]
Captain H. J. Taylor, Deputy[140]
Robert S. Turner, Deputy[141]
Cassimer J. "Casper" Welch, Deputy[142]
Samuel A. "Lum" Wilson[143]

1899-1900 Robert S. Stone[144]   Samuel Hamilton Chiles[145]   *Joel B. and Emma C. Mayes[146]
                                        Henry Clay "Bruz" Chiles, Deputy[147]   Samuel A. "Lum" Wilson[148]
                                        Charles Clark, Deputy[149]
                                        Tom Leahy, Deputy[150]
                                        Matt O'Flaherty, Deputy[151]
                                        Thomas J. "Tom" Pendergast, Deputy[152]
                                        Henry Shrank, Deputy[153]

1901-1902 Winfred S. Pontius[154]   John Patton Maxwell[155]   *David H. Curran[156]
N. E. Moore, Deputy[157]   Melville "Mel" Hulse, Deputy[158]   Ann Crowder, Cook[159]
A. A. Stewart, Deputy[160]   J. C. Morris, office work[161]
                                        Henry Rummell, outside work[162]

1903-1904 John P. Gilday[163]   Thomas J. "Tom" Pendergast[164]   *Nicholas H. & Emma C. Phelps[165]
                                        J. G. Chestnut, Deputy[166]   *Melville "Mel" & Alice Hulse
                                        Jerry Fitzgerald, Deputy[167]   George Soehle, Chain Gang Super.[168]
                                        James Gallagher, Deputy[169]   W. W. Twyman[170]
                                        Joseph Ghent, Deputy[171]   Sam Yankee[172]
                                        B. Johnson, Deputy[173]   Ann Crowder, Cook
                                        William J. Leahy, Deputy
                                        Joseph T. Stewart, Deputy[174]
                                        Joel B. Mayes, Deputy[175]
                                        Claud Monday, Deputy[176]
                                        John O'Brien, Deputy[177]
                                        C. M. J. J. Welch, Deputy[178]
                                        A. Well, Deputy[179]

1905-1906 Charles P. Baldwin[180]   Albert "Al" Heslip[181]   *John Van Buren Martin[182]
William H. Gregg, Deputy[183]   Vernon Downing, Deputy[184]   *Melville "Mel" and Alice Hulse[185]
                                        Elmer E. Kethcart, Deputy[186]   Ann Crowder, Cook
                                        W. L. Lawrence, Deputy[187]
                                        James Moran, Deputy[188]
                                        L. H. Naumann, Deputy[189]
                                        N. B. Olson, Deputy[190]
                                        C. A. Shauver, Deputy[191]
                                        Joseph T. Stewart, Deputy[192]
                                        B. Swigart, Deputy[193]
                                        Isaac N. Wagner, Deputy[194]
                                        H. E. Weisflog, Chief Deputy[195]
                                        Clarence C. Whaley, Deputy[196]
                                        W. I. Winn, Deputy[197]
                                        Charles W. Yocum, Deputy[198]
                                        G. G. Young, Deputy[199]

1907 (Jan-Sep) Charles P. Baldwin[200] Albert "Al" Heslip (1907-1908)[201] *John Van Buren Martin[202]
1907 Sep-1908 W. J. Campbell[203]   James V. McNamara, Deputy[204]   Ann Crowder, Cook
29 Deputies[205]

SHERIFF	MARSHAL	JAILOR

1909-1910 John M. Rood[206]

Joel B. Mayes[207]
James Gilwee, Chief Deputy
William E. Bridges, Deputy[210]
Harvey C. "Harry" Hoffman, Deputy[212]
Frank Jasper, Deputy[213]
Robert Lee Nivens, Deputy[215]
Joseph T. Stewart, Deputy[217]
Joseph Strauss, Deputy[219]
Henry Tralle, Deputy[221]
Morgan Williams, Deputy[223]

*Nicholas H. and Emma C. Phelps[208]
W. W. Twyman, Custodian[209]
Ed C. Hughes[211]

James Shepard, Chain Gang Super.[214]
Forest Allen, Clerk[216]
Ray Self, Power Man & Guard[218]
John N. Bethel, Guard[220]
John Berry, Guard[222]
George Binger, Guard[224]
S. Craddock, Guard[225]
James Stults, Guard[226]

1911-1912 John M. Rood[227]

Joel B. Mayes[228]
Homer Cook, Deputy[230]
E. S. Dudley, Deputy[232]
Thomas Holloway, Deputy[233]
Charles Kemper, Deputy[234]
Thomas Malone, Deputy[235]
James J. McCormick, Special Deputy[236]
Joseph McGuire, Deputy[237]
Robert Lee Nivens, Deputy[238]
Joseph Strauss, Deputy[239]
Jerry Sullivan, Deputy[240]
Morgan Williams, Deputy[241]

William H. Montgomery (1911-[229]
L. S. Tudor, Night Jailor[231]

1913-1914 Edward Winstanley[242]
John Riley Jones, Deputy[245]

Martin J. Crowe[243]
Harvey C. "Harry" Hoffman, Chief Deputy[246]
Robert Lee Nivens, Chief Deputy[247]
Homer Cook, Deputy[248]
E. S. Dudley, Deputy[249]
Thomas Holloway, Deputy[250]
Thomas Jones, Deputy[251]
Charles Kemper, Deputy[252]
Thomas Kerns, Deputy[253]
William J. Leahy, Deputy[254]
Herbert Lewis, Deputy[255]
Thomas Malone, Deputy[256]
Joseph McGuire, Deputy[257]
George Parent, Deputy[258]
J. W. Scoville, Deputy[259]
John Stokes, Deputy[260]
Joseph Strauss, Deputy[261]
Jerry Sullivan, Deputy[262]
Thomas Teefy, Deputy[263]
Morgan Williams, Deputy[264]

*Jesse "Jess" and Anna J. Allen[244]

Deputy Sheriff shield of John Riley Jones

1915-1916 Edward Winstanley[265]
John Riley Jones, Deputy[267]

Martin J. Crowe[266]
25 Deputies, some from 1914 list[268]
Harvey C. "Harry" Hoffman, Chief Deputy[270]
Thomas Carroll, Deputy[272]
Robert Lee Nivens, Deputy[273]
John Klingbell, Deputy[274]
Clarence Skinner, Deputy[275]

*Jesse "Jess" and Anna J. Allen
Fred Brew, Chain Gang Guard[269]
John Cockrill, Chain Gang Guard[271]

SHERIFF	MARSHAL	JAILOR

1917-1918 Overton H. Gentry, Jr.[276]   Harvey C. "Harry" Hoffman[277]   *Jesse "Jess" & Anna J. Allen[278]
      Joseph H. Gentry, Deputy[279]   *Melvin "Mel" Allen[280]
      Robert Lee Nivens, Deputy[281]   Mrs. Mary Troutman, Matron[282]

1919-1920 Overton H. Gentry, Jr.[283]   Harvey C. "Harry" Hoffman[284]   *Harden T. "Dutch" Hall[285]
      Wade Brownfield, Deputy[286]   26 Deputies[287]   Mrs. Mary Troutman, Matron[288]
                                    John W. Hayward, Deputy[289]
                                    Robert Lee Nivens, Deputy[290]
                                    John Stokes, Deputy[291]

1921-1922 Fred A. Richardson[292]   Major John L. Miles[293]   *Jesse E. "Jess" & Jennie S. Curran[294]
38 Deputies[295]   Robert Lee Nivens, Chief Deputy[296]   J. J. Metcalf[297]
    Charles M. Blackman, License Inspector[298]   Robert C. Phipps[299]
    Arthur J. Brown, Deputy[300]   Mrs. Mary Troutman, Matron[301]
    Edwin S. Carroll, Deputy[302]
    W. C. Dunn, Deputy[303]
    John W. Gibson, Deputy[304]
    John E. Gresham, Deputy[305]
    N. B. Hatch, Deputy[306]
    M. L. Hines (African-American), Deputy[307]
    Jack M. Kasoi, Deputy[308]
    J. L. Masters, Deputy[309]
    George McGinnis, Deputy[310]
    George W. Miles, Deputy[311]
    Harry Mills, Deputy[312]
    B. B. Morris, Deputy[313]
    J. B. O'Day, Deputy[314]
    Ben D. Pugh, Deputy[315]
    Russell Reeves, Deputy[316]
    Walter L. Saymon, Deputy[317]
    Simon Stoll, Deputy[318]
    Clarence C. Whaley, Deputy[319]

1923-1924 Fred A. Richardson[320]   Major John L. Miles[321]   John W. Gibson[322]

County Marshal position abolished
December 31, 1924

SHERIFF	JAILOR

1925-1926 Major John L. Miles[323]
31 Deputies[325]

John W. Gibson[324]

1927-1928 Major John L. Miles[326]

1929-1930 Jefferson H. Smedley[327]

*Harry W. Gallagher[328]
George McPherson[329]

1931-1932 Jefferson H. Smedley[330]

Kenneth Kabrick[331]

---

[1] "Marshal's Star on Shelf," Kansas City (Mo.) Star, 6 Jan. 1925, p. 5, c.1. *Laws of Missouri*, 1921, 51st General Assembly, Regular Session, 220-222, approved March 11, 1921. Also, Harry S Truman Library. *Oral History Interview with Henry P. Chiles* by J. R. Fuchs, November 1, 1961, pages 73-74:

FUCHS: Mr. Truman supported John Miles for county marshal in 1920. Now is that a job that died out?

CHILES: Yes, it's been abolished. It used to be in Jackson County — there used to be a sheriff who took care of the civil affairs of the sheriff's office and this marshal, the criminal. He had the jail and he patrolled and arrested; he was like police. But, the marshal handled the criminal end of the thing. Johnny Miles ran and Johnny was a very popular. Republican. Nearly all of these veteran soldiers backed him. I had a nephew who went out and worked for him, and I give him the dickens and he just worked the same. I understood Truman backed Miles.

FUCHS: Later on, I believe by 1924, Miles was serving as sheriff and I wondered about the two jobs.

CHILES: Miles was marshal; was he ever sheriff?

FUCHS: Yes, he later on served as sheriff and I wondered if as you say, if the sheriff later on took the job that the marshal did in those days?

CHILES: They did combine the two, but I think that was after Mile's time in office. The sheriff's job was entirely civil and the marshal had the jail and the prisoners and did the patrolling and the arresting; but Miles, he won by a big, big majority. All these veterans were for him, everyone of them. You couldn't get a one of them to vote against him. I had a nephew that I thought I could have some influence over, and he wouldn't listen to me.

[2] Harry S Truman Library. *Oral History Interview with Henry P. Chiles* by J. R. Fuchs, November 1, 1961, 73-74.

[3] Stewart, 3. According to Allen's son-in-law, Mr. Orville Campbell. Campbell also stated, "that the trustys [trusties] did the cooking in the kitchen of the jail."

[4] Copies of related newspaper clippings, U.S. Census, and, Missouri Death Certificates documenting outlaws, lawmen, and their families have been assembled into the Jackson County Historical Society Administrative Records, *LOCK DOWN* Research Files (and 1859 Jackson County Jail 150th Anniversary Records, 2009).

[5] Pratt, Parley P. *History of the Late Persecution Inflicted by the State of Missouri Upon the Mormons*. (Detroit: Dawson and Bates, 1839) (boap.org/LDS/Early-Saints/PPratt-pers.html; viewed 18 Mar. 2009).

[6] Jackson County Court minutes (6:233).

[7] Prior to the completion of the 1859 Jail—when the 1841 Jail was in use—Bugler and others were being paid by the Jackson County Court for "guarding the jail." Jackson County Court minutes (11:174:98756; 11:209; etc.).

[8] Ibid. John Brady helped guard the Jackson County Jail from at least 1858-1867 (according to the range of Jackson County Court minutes studied in detail for this compendium). He and his wife, Hester, both Irish immigrants, were listed in the 1870 U.S. Census for Blue Township, Jackson County, Missouri. John, a farmer, was then 39, Hester 36 [she was probably closer to 40]. Children listed in their household were: Agnes, 8; Charles, 5; John Jr., 3; William, 4 months. Ten years later when the 1880 U.S. Census was taken, John, a farmer, was 49 and Hester was 51; their three eldest children were still living at home. John Brady died 4 Jan. 1883, age 53 years. Hester "Hettie" died 4 Jan. 1902, age 72. They are buried in St. Mary's North, a section adjoining Woodlawn Cemetery in Independence, Missouri. At least two infant sons are also buried there, Johnie (July 9, 1860-Agu. 4, 1861; they obviously named their son born about 1867 John, too) and Willie (3 Mar. 1870-6 Dec. 1872). John and Hester were affiliated with St. Mary's Church, and their names are on a stained glass window in the Church. There are two other Brady plots where other relatives are buried in St. Mary's section of Woodlawn. Daughters of the American Revolution—Independence Pioneers Chapter. *Woodlawn Cemetery Tombstone Inscriptions*.

[9] Prior to the completion of the 1859 Jail—when the 1841 Jail was in use—Bugler and others were being paid by the Jackson County Court for "guarding the jail." Jackson County Court minutes (11:174:98756; 11:209).

[10] Ibid.

[11] The 1859 Jackson County Jail was completed between February and March 1860. In June, Henry Bugler was listed as "Jailor," in the 1860 U.S. Census for Independence, Jackson County, Missouri. Although there were occasional disbursements for other individuals, there are *regular* entries in the Jackson County Court minutes documenting Bugler's payment for "jailor's fees" for "guarding the jail." Many, but not all entries were noted between the time when the 1859 Jackson County Jail opened in early 1860 through Bugler's murder in June 1866. Those noted during this Sheriff's tenure include: 11:264:99031; 11:546:99788; and, 11:623:100041.

[12] John Brady was paid to guard the Jail, January 1861. Jackson County Court minutes (11:546:99788).

[13] William B. Rogers, Jackson County Coroner, acted as Sheriff in the interim between Burrus' death and the confirmation of Bailey; Rogers was still acting as of 20 May, Jackson County Court minutes (11:626:10052; and 11:630:10065). Rogers was a slave owner and owned five in 1850 and two in 1860; it does not appear from their ages and gender that they were the same over that ten year span. A William B. Rogers (15 Jul. 1804-9 May 1863) is buried in Woodlawn Cemetery. Daughters of the American Revolution—Independence Pioneers Chapter. *Woodlawn Cemetery Tombstone Inscriptions.*

[14] Oliver P. W. Bailey resigned as Jackson County Treasurer, Jackson County Court minutes (11:624:100044). Bailey was appointed Jackson County Sheriff on 13 May 1861, Jackson County Court minutes (11:624:10047).

[15] "It appears to the satisfaction of the Jackson County Court here that there is no sheriff, coroner, or other ministerial officer in Jackson County to attend to the Court, the Court appoints Tandy Westmoreland Sheriff for the time being." Jackson County Court minutes (12:160:100247; 12:164:100272; 12:168:100292; 12:171:100310). Westmoreland (3 May 1808-1 Feb. 1880) is buried in Woodlawn Cemetery. Daughters of the American Revolution—Independence Pioneers Chapter. *Woodlawn Cemetery Tombstone Inscriptions.*

[16] Disbursement to Bugler for guarding the Jail during this Sheriff's tenure, as recorded in Jackson County Court minutes: 12:165:100280; 12:169:100302; 12:172:100316.

[17] Appointed "for the time being there being no sheriff or coroner." Jackson County Court minutes (12:176:100325). It appears that Todd, a merchant, may have been one of the larger slave owners in Jackson County, with 18 slaves in 1850, according to Missouri Slave Schedules that list "Beverly B. Todd."

[18] Disbursement to Bugler for guarding the Jail during this Sheriff's tenure, as recorded in Jackson County Court minutes, 12:177:100332.

[19] Jackson County Court minutes (12:178:100336; 12:180:100346; 12:181:100353; 12:185:100373).

[20] Disbursement to Bugler for guarding the Jail during this Sheriff's tenure, as recorded in Jackson County Court minutes, 12:178:100340.

[21] Jackson County Court minutes (12:187:100378).

[22] Ibid., (12:211:100513; 12:214:100524). Hayden was, "Kansas City Marshal" when the 1860 U.S. Census was taken. Judging from the Slave Schedules, he had four slaves in one slave house, a 30-year-old female with three young children: 4-year-old male (mulatto); 2-year-old female (mulatto); and a 4-month-old male (mulatto). Without a male slave old enough to father the children, and the fact that the children were all mulatto, or mixed race, it makes one wonder who the father might have been.

[23] Disbursements to Bugler during this Sheriff's tenure, as recorded in Jackson County Court minutes: 12:207:100494; 12:211:100509; 12:219:100544; 12:221:100556; 12:224:100568; 12:236:100629; 12:240:100648; 12:244:100681; 12:359:101137; 12:364:101172.

[24] Jackson County Court minutes (12:359:101138; 12:364:101172).

[25] Ibid., (12:359:101139).

[26] Ibid., (12:362:101156).

[27] Ibid., (12:207:100494). Jackson County Historical Society Archives Document ID 19.2F15.

[28] Ibid., (12:374:101211; 12:396:101292). Birdsall, 643. Williams was previously elected Sheriff of Miami County, Kansas, in 1857 and re-elected in 1859. In June, 1861, he entered the Third Kansas Volunteers and was elected Major of that regiment. This regiment was afterward consolidated with the Fourth Regiment and called the Tenth. Major Williams served in this capacity until the regiment was mustered out, commanding the regiment in the battles of Cane Hill, Prairie Grove, Van Buren, and Fort Wayne. He participated in the battle of Pilot Knob on the staff of Gen. Ewing. As Provost-Marshall of the District of St. Louis, he had charge of the military prisoners for several months. Being honorably mustered out of service in February, 1865, Williams returned to Kansas City, where his family had resided since 1863, and was elected Sheriff of Jackson County, Mo., serving eighteen months. In April, 1867, he returned to Osawatomie; he appeared in the 1880 U.S. Census there, a 51-year-old hardware dealer, living with his wife, Mary, 38; and their children: Minnie, 16; Walter, 14; Charles, 12; and, Fannie, 3. The eldest two had been born in Missouri. Cutler, William G. *History of the State of Kansas.* Miami County. (Chicago, Il.: A. T. Andreas, 1883), 1.

[29] Jackson County Court minutes (12:396:101292).

[30] Ibid., (12:396:101292). March 1866.

[31] Ibid., (13:354:101583; February 1866), (13:442:101933; July 1866).

[32] Ibid., (12:375:101651)

[33] Dougherty married Isabel Pool at St. Mary's in Independence, Jackson County, on 10 Jan. 1858. Pool was the daughter of Irish immigrants Henry and Anne Pool. They immigrated from County Kilkenny about 1830 with two older children; Isabel was born in Pennsylvania before the family left their home and traveled a flat bottom boat down the Allegheny and Ohio rivers, then up the Mississippi and Missouri. Henry Pool was well known and respected first Postmaster at Independence, who, in 1849, purchased 160 acres on the north side of present-day 24 Highway and Sterling Avenue, where Fairmount Park would be developed many years later.

The 1870 U.S. Census for Independence, Jackson County, Mo., listed Irish immigrant Sheriff Dougherty, age 37; his wife Isabel "Belle," 32; their children: Hugh [Henry], 11; George, 9; and, Daniel, 4. They had a 23-year-old, male Irish immigrant as a domestic servant, and a 23-year-old, male Irish immigrant as a Sheriff's clerk living with them. The Dougherty's later had a fourth child, Charles, Jr.

Dougherty, who often appeared as Jackson County Collector in Jackson County Court minutes, served as Sheriff through December 1870. Earlier that year, when the *Kansas City Times* Publishing Company (at its 5th and Main location in Kansas City) dissolved on 20 Feb. 1870, Charles Dougherty, together with John C. Moore and John N. Edwards, were the purchasers.

In the 1900 U.S. Census for Blue Township, Jackson County, Missouri, 63-year-old Isabel, is listed with her 75-year-old Irish immigrant, spinster sister, Mary Pool. The Dougherty's son, Hugh, was killed in the cyclone that hit downtown Kansas City May 11, 1886. The Dougherty home east of Noland Road on Short Street in Independence still stands. Dougherty is buried in St. Mary's section of Woodlawn Cemetery in an unmarked grave, per his request.

Jackson County Court minutes (13:37; 13:601:102563; and, 13:607:102593 Feb. 1867). Birdsall, 574, 643. "Postmaster in the Beaver Hat: Descendants of Henry Pool Cherish Family Legends of Early Citizen," by Barbara Magerl, *Jackson County Historical Society JOURNAL*, 1981 (Spring), 23:1, 6-8. "Fatal Storm: Kansas City Visited by Fatal Cloudburst," *Kansas City* (Mo.) *Star,* 11 May 1886, 1. Also, Baxter-Campbell-Keogh Collection of Charles Dougherty Papers, 1865-1870; Photocopies of Sheriff's Papers, 1869, in the Jackson County Historical Society Archives, Document ID L8F28. At the time of this printing (2009) the *originals* of these papers are maintained by Dougherty's great granddaughter, Barbara A. (Campbell) Magerl [granddaughter of George and Annie (O'Connell) Dougherty; daughter of John William and Caroline I. (Dougherty) Campbell].

[34] "Ligget's Successor," *Kansas City* (Mo.) *Times*, 20 Nov. 1880, 5:3-4; Farrell became jailor when the county building at Kansas City was erected; he served 12 years. "The Ins and Outs: Marshal Liggett Steps Down and Out and the New Marshal Steps In," *Kansas City* (Mo.) *Star*, 22 Nov. 1880, 1. Also, the 1880 U.S. Census for Jackson County.

[35] This end date was deduced from the time Mrs. Bugler seems to disappear from the minutes, and when Richard Ryan was reimbursed, as noted below in August 1867.

[36] Jackson County Court minutes (14:43:102999; May 1867). Ryan was reimbursed $12 for whitewashing the Jail, $22.80 for boarding Crazy Sal (a pauper), and $17.20 for boarding prisoners (14:118:103342; August 1867). This was the authors' justification for ascertaining his occupancy of the residence portion of the 1859 Jail.

[37] Jackson County Court minutes (13:598:102549; January 1867), (13:607:102593; February 1867), (13:634:102708; March 1867).

[38] Sheriff requested to discharge C. R. Brown and Tim Conroy from further duty as guard for the County Jail. Jackson County Court minutes (14:99:103272; July 1867).

[39] Ibid., (13:616:102638; March 1867), (14:25:102885; April 1867), (14:43:102998; May 1867), (14:66:103099; June 1867). Sheriff requested to discharge C. R. Brown and Tim Conroy from further duty as guard for the County Jail. Jackson County Court minutes (14:99:103272; July 1867).

[40] Ibid., (14:66:103098; June 1867).

[41] Ibid., (13:589:102506; January 1867), (13:608:102601; February 1867), (14:25:102886; April 1867).

[42] Birdsall, 643. Gray died in office. Jackson County Court minutes (16:639). Gray was a slave owner; he had six in 1850 and seven in 1860, but it appears from age and gender assignments that only one may have been kindred to both enumerations. Gray is buried in Woodlawn Cemetery. The tombstone inscription says he died 19 Oct. 1873 (this conflicts with County Court minutes). Daughters of the American Revolution—Independence Pioneers Chapter. *Woodlawn Cemetery Tombstone Inscriptions.*

[43] Silvers who was born in Jackson County in 1833, had walked to the California Gold Rush in 1849 and later to gold mining in the Black Hills with Independence companion, Charles Henry. The clipping describes Silvers as *"the first jailer of Independence under the first Marshall Jackson County ever had. He served several terms as jailer and again served in the positing under W. J. Phillips. He was for a number of terms City Marshall of the City of Independence."* Undated news clipping in the Jackson County Historical Society's Archives. The U.S. Census for 1860, 1870 and 1880 list Redmond's profession as a "farm hand," "hayman" and, "keeping house" respectively.

[44] "Ligget's Successor," *Kansas City* (Mo.) *Times*, 20 Nov. 1880, 5:3-4; Farrell became jailor when the county building at Kansas City was erected; he served 12 years. "The Ins and Outs: Marshal Liggett Steps Down and Out and the New Marshal Steps In," *Kansas City* (Mo.) *Star*, 22 Nov. 1880, 1. Also, the 1880 U.S. Census for Jackson County.

[45] A full description of the first Jackson County Marshal, Major Granville D. Page, appears in a previous chapter. "Marshal's Star on Shelf," *Kansas City* (Mo.) *Star*, 6 Jan. 1925, p. 5, c. 1.

[46] In the 1870 U.S. Census for Kansas City, Jackson County, Missouri, 43-year-old Virginia native Booth(e), a farmer, was listed with his 36-year-old Indiana native wife, Elizabeth, and their children: John W., 19; Abigail, 17; Ada Bell, 12; James, 9; Corinth (daughter), 7; Nancy A., 6; Fanny, 4; Sidney (son), 1. By the 1880 U.S. Census for Kansas City, Jackson County, Missouri, Booth(e) was 53, a deputy constable, listed with Elizabeth and their children: Bija, 28 (also a deputy constable); Nancy A. "Nannie," 16; Fannie, 13; Sydney, 10; Forrest, 8; Gertie, 7; and, Sena, 5. Birdsall, 643. Jackson County Court minutes (17:111).

[47] "Marshal's Star on Shelf," *Kansas City* (Mo.) *Star*, 6 Jan. 1925, p. 5, c. 1. Marshall and Morrison, erroneously list Granville D. Page as "George" D. Page. They also name **Jeremiah Dowd** as the second Jackson County Marshal in 1873 (page 83); this has not been authenticated in other sources.

[48] In the 1870 U.S. Census for Kansas City, Jackson County, Missouri, 43-year-old Virginia native Booth(e), a farmer, was listed with his 36-year-old Indiana native wife, Elizabeth, and their children: John W, 19; Abigail, 17; Ada Bell, 12; James, 9; Corinth (daughter), 7; Nancy A., 6; Fanny, 4; Sidney (son), 1. By the 1880 U.S. Census for Kansas City, Jackson County, Missouri, Booth(e) was 53, a deputy constable, listed with Elizabeth and their children: Bija, 28 (also a deputy constable); Nancy A. "Nannie," 16; Fannie, 13; Sydney, 10; Forrest, 8; Gertie, 7; and, Sena, 5. Boothe died 17 Mar. 1888; his wife, Elizabeth, died 24 Feb. 1919; they are buried in Woodlawn Cemetery. Daughters of the American Revolution—Independence Pioneers Chapter. *Woodlawn Cemetery Tombstone Inscriptions*. Birdsall, 643. Jackson County Court minutes (17:111).

[49] "Marshal's Star on Shelf," *Kansas City* (Mo.) *Star*, 6 Jan. 1925, p. 5, c. 1. In the 1870 U.S. Census for the 2nd Ward of Kansas City, Jackson County, Missouri, Patrick Connors was a 28-year-old, Irish immigrant working as a laborer. He *might* be the same 38-year-old boilermaker listed in the 1880 Census.

[50] "Ligget's Successor," *Kansas City* (Mo.) *Times*, 20 Nov. 1880, 5:3-4; Farrell became jailor when the county building at Kansas City was erected; he served 12 years. "The Ins and Outs: Marshal Liggett Steps Down and Out and the New Marshal Steps In," *Kansas City* (Mo.) *Star*, 22 Nov. 1880, 1. Also, the 1880 U.S. Census for Jackson County.

[51] In the 1880 U.S. Census for Independence, Jackson County, Missouri, Jackson County Sheriff O.P.W. Bailey, a 46-year-old Kentucky native, was listed with his 47-year-old Pennsylvania native wife, Frances, and their children: Frances, 17; Ellen H., 12; and Charles H. 7. Birdsall, 643. Confirmed through Jackson County Court minutes.

[52] "Jottings," *Kansas City* (Mo.) *Daily Journal of Commerce*, 28 Nov. 1876, 4:2; "Ligget's Successor," *Kansas City* (Mo.) *Times*, 20 Nov. 1880, 5:3-4; "The Old and the New," *Kansas City* (Mo.) *Times*, 23 Nov. 1880, 8:1; "Marshal's Star on Shelf," *Kansas City* (Mo.) *Star*, 6 Jan. 1925, p. 5, c. 1. Also, "Why Mattie Collins Shot Judge: J. M. Adams, Sr., of Buckner Recalls the Killing of [Jonathan] Dark," *Kansas City* (Mo.) *Star*, 14 July 1915, 3. This article mentions "Marshal Liggett," and the "newly installed force of county marshals," as it pertained to Collins getting Dick Liddil to turn states evidence against members of the Jesse James gang. The incidents reportedly took place between 1869-1871; but, these dates don't align with the documented tenure of the Jackson County Marshals. James W. Liggett, who was from Bath, Kentucky, married Sophia Crow Stone in Jackson County on 15 Dec. 1856. He owned one, 12-year-old female slave in 1860. The 1870 U.S. Census for Blue Township, Jackson County, Missouri, lists James and Sophia Liggets (sic.), ages 35 and 33 respectively, with their children: Alonzo, 12; William E., 10; and Leouma, 8 months. The 1880 Census for Kansas City, Jackson County, Missouri, listed James, Marshal, 45; Sophia, 44; Alonzo, 22; William, 20; Lulu, 12; and, James, 3 months. William Liggett married Maggie I. Clements in Jackson County, Missouri, on 10 Nov. 1885; a Lulu Liggett married Samuel W. Atkinson in Jackson County on 22 Dec. 1887. "The Ins and Outs: Marshal Liggett Steps Down and Out and the New Marshal Steps In," *Kansas City* (Mo.) *Star*, 22 Nov. 1880, 1. See also, Marshall and Morrison, 83.

The headline of Liggett's obituary said, "For four years he was Marshal of Jackson County;" but, in the text it read he, "held the position of CITY MARSHAL from 1878-1882." "J. W. Liggett Dead," *Kansas City* (Mo.) *Star*, 29 Mar. 1899, 5.

He was Marshal on 23 Feb. 1877 when he announced, "the docket for the season of the criminal court…will be the longest in the history of Jackson County. With three or four murder trials…." as printed in, "In Kansas City Forty Years Ago," *Kansas City* (Mo.) *Star*, 23 Feb. 1917, 14. Liggett was Marshal when Richard Green was hanged on 1 Mar. 1878: "Went Happily to His Death," *Kansas City* (Mo.) *Star*, 28 Dec. 1898. He was Marshal between Dec. 1878 and Jan. 1879, as announced "In Kansas City Forty Years Ago," *Kansas City* (Mo.) *Star*, 5 Dec. 1918, 16; and, 13 Jan. 1919, 12. He was defeated by Murphy in the November 1880 elections.

However, there continued to be a Deputy Marshal Liggett mentioned in *Kansas City Star* newspaper articles between May 1885 and Oct. 1887. "A Desperado Taken," *Kansas City* (Mo.) *Star*, 22 May 1885; and, "Herdman Coming to Kansas City," *Kansas City* (Mo.) *Star*, 25 Oct. 1887, 1.

According to her death certificate Sophia Liggett, who was born 17 Aug. 1835, died on 23 Apr. 1922. She is buried in Elmwood Cemetery in Kansas City, Missouri.

[53] Maurice (sometimes spelled Morris) Moulson Langhorne (1834-1898), son of John Wesley and Martha Nelson (Branch) Langhorne, married 23 Oct. 1859 to Anne Maria Wallace (1836-1920), daughter of Reuben and Mary Wallace. Langhorne had an exciting young adulthood crossing the plains in 1849 and returning via the Isthmus of Panama in 1851, only to drive cattle to California in 1855. In partnership with Mr. McClanahan, he opened a stationery store in Independence in 1859; their inventory was plundered by the Confederate soldiers of Sterling Price. Langhorne enlisted in the Confederate Army (Company E, 2nd Missouri Cavalry, which was detailed for escort duty to General Shelby) and was promoted to Captain in 1863. An interesting sidelight to the Battle of Independence was noted by John N. Edwards in his book, *Shelby and His Men*, *"The army camped in and around Independence, during the night of the 21st. Captain M. M. Langhorne being the first man to enter the town, and as it was his former place of residence, he can be pardoned for the pride and bravado which prompted his hot charge through the streets (XXIV, 424)."* After the War, Langhorne went with General Shelby to Mexico. Langhorne was employed as Deputy County Marshall from 4 Dec. 1876-28 Nov 1880 (another source says he was employed in 1877 and served for 6 years; then, appointed Deputy Sheriff in 1886). Birdsall, 640. Also, "Ligget's Successor," *Kansas City* (Mo.) *Times*, 20 Nov. 1880, 5:3-4; "The Ins and Outs: Marshal Liggett Steps Down and Out and the New Marshal Steps In," *Kansas City* (Mo.) *Star*, 22 Nov. 1880, 1; "The Ins and Outs: Marshal Liggett Steps Down and Out and the New Marshal Steps In," *Kansas City* (Mo.) *Star*, 22 Nov. 1880, 1; "The Old and the New," *Kansas City* (Mo.) *Times*, 23 Nov. 1880, 8:1; *Jackson* (Independence, Mo.) *Examiner*, 25 June 1898; and, Alberta Wilson Constant, "All That I Can Discover About the Life of the Late Maurice M. Langhorne," a 5-leave, unpublished manuscript in the Jackson County Historical Society Archives, Document ID 154.01F10.

[54] "Ligget's Successor," *Kansas City* (Mo.) *Times*, 20 Nov. 1880, 5:3-4; Farrell became jailor when the county building at Kansas City was erected; he served 12 years. "The Ins and Outs: Marshal Liggett Steps Down and Out and the New Marshal Steps In," *Kansas City* (Mo.) *Star*, 22 Nov. 1880, 1; "The Old and the New," *Kansas City* (Mo.) *Times*, 23 Nov. 1880, 8:1. Also, the 1880 U.S. Census for Jackson County.

[55] "In Kansas City Forty Years Ago," *Kansas City* (Mo.) *Star*, 5 Dec. 1918.

[56] "Ligget's Successor," *Kansas City* (Mo.) *Times*, 20 Nov. 1880, 5:3-4; "The Old and the New," *Kansas City* (Mo.) *Times*, 23 Nov. 1880, 8:1. "The Lee's Summit Tragedy," *Kansas City* (Mo.) *Daily Times*, 9 Sept. 1879, 5, about incarceration of Dr. R. M. McAffee for murder.

[57] "Ligget's Successor," *Kansas City* (Mo.) *Times*, 20 Nov. 1880, 5:3-4; "The Ins and Outs: Marshal Liggett Steps Down and Out and the New Marshal Steps In," *Kansas City* (Mo.) *Star*, 22 Nov. 1880, 1; "The Old and the New," *Kansas City* (Mo.) *Times*, 23 Nov. 1880, 8:1.

[58] Hughes was killed while in the line of duty in February 1877. His murderer, Richard Green, was the first public execution since 1839. "Bloody Deeds: The Evening Star Rehearses Jackson County's Murder Record," *Kansas City* (Mo.) *Evening Star*, 8 Aug. 1881. Hughes' death is also discussed in, "Awaiting Their Doom: The Batch of Murderers Confined in the Independence Jail," *Kansas City* (Mo.) *Star*, 6 Aug. 1886, 1.

[59] "Ligget's Successor," *Kansas City* (Mo.) *Times*, 20 Nov. 1880, 5:3-4; "The Old and the New," *Kansas City* (Mo.) *Times*, 23 Nov. 1880, 8:1.

[60] Birdsall, 643. Confirmed through Jackson County Court minutes. Hope (1838-1909), his wife, Mattie T. (1842-1918), and at least three of their children are buried in Woodlawn Cemetery. Daughters of the American Revolution—Independence Pioneers Chapter. *Woodlawn Cemetery Tombstone Inscriptions*.

[61] "Ligget's Successor," *Kansas City* (Mo.) *Times*, 20 Nov. 1880, 5:3-4; "Marshal's Star on Shelf," *Kansas City* (Mo.) *Star*, 6 Jan. 1925, p. 5, c. 1. "Caged Birds: Turned over to Marshal Murphy by Outgoing Marshal Liggett," *Kansas City* (Mo.) *Star*, 22 Nov. 1880, 1. In the 1900 U.S. Census for Kansas City, Jackson County, Missouri, 51-year-old Irish immigrant Cornelius Murphy, a liveryman, was listed with his wife, Mollie, 39; and their children: Cornelius, 16; Ellen, 14; Charles, 13; Mary, 11; John, 10; Daniel, 8; Cornelia, 8; and Annie, 4. Captain Cornelius "Con" Murphy, Sr., the son of Charles and Bridgett (Horgan) Murphy, was born 1 Aug. 1848 and died 28 June 1940. He is buried in Calvary Cemetery in Kansas City, Missouri. His wife, Mary A. preceded him in death. Missouri Death Certificate 21004.

[62] "Ligget's Successor," *Kansas City* (Mo.) *Times*, 20 Nov. 1880, 5:3-4; "The Ins and Outs: Marshal Liggett Steps Down and Out and the New Marshal Steps In," *Kansas City* (Mo.) *Star*, 22 Nov. 1880, 1; "The Old and the New," *Kansas City* (Mo.) *Times*, 23 Nov. 1880, 8:1.

[63] "The Ins and Outs: Marshal Liggett Steps Down and Out and the New Marshal Steps In," *Kansas City* (Mo.) *Star*, 22 Nov. 1880, 1. In 1996, Gleason's granddaughter, Anne M. (Gleason) LeCluyse donated his badge, service revolver and two photographs identifying him at and connecting him with the 1859 Jackson County Jail. See, "New Acquisitions at Jail Museum Bring More History Back Home." *Jackson County Historical Society JOURNAL* 1996 (Summer) 36:2, 3.

[64] "Ligget's Successor," *Kansas City* (Mo.) *Times*, 20 Nov. 1880, 5:3-4.

[65] "The Ins and Outs: Marshal Liggett Steps Down and Out and the New Marshal Steps In," *Kansas City* (Mo.) *Star*, 22 Nov. 1880, 1; "The Old and the New," *Kansas City* (Mo.) *Times*, 23 Nov. 1880, 8:1.

[66] "The Ins and Outs: Marshal Liggett Steps Down and Out and the New Marshal Steps In," *Kansas City* (Mo.) *Star*, 22 Nov. 1880, 1; "The Old and the New," *Kansas City* (Mo.) *Times*, 23 Nov. 1880, 8:1.

[67] Monaco. A timeline for November 27, 1882 [Monday]: "…accompanying Frank [James] was Deputy Marshal Keshlear…." The *Kansas City* (Mo.) *Evening Star*, 27 Nov. 1882, is cited and later transcribed. The article, "The Old and the New," *Kansas City* (Mo.) *Times*, 23 Nov. 1880, 8:1, states that Keshlear "went out with Mr. Ligget (sic.)."

[68] The Marshal's brother. "The Ins and Outs: Marshal Liggett Steps Down and Out and the New Marshal Steps In," *Kansas City* (Mo.) *Star*, 22 Nov. 1880, 1; "The Old and the New," *Kansas City* (Mo.) *Times*, 23 Nov. 1880, 8:1.

[69] findagrave.com (viewed on 21 October 2009; Hinton H. Noland born 22 Oct. 1847 – died 11 July 1932).

[70] "Marshal's Star on Shelf," *Kansas City* (Mo.) *Star*, 6 Jan. 1925, p. 5, c. 1. "More Arrests," *Kansas City* (Mo.) *Star*, 8 Sep. 1885. William Jutt, the son of Alanson S. and Celina (Madole) Phillips, was born 6 Sep. 1837 in New York, and died 6 July 1923. He is buried in Woodlawn Cemetery (identified as a veteran of the Union Army). His wife, Mary Susan (Tugle) Phillips died 10 years later on 23 Aug. 1933. Daughters of the American Revolution—Independence Pioneers Chapter. *Woodlawn Cemetery Tombstone Inscriptions*. Missouri Death Certificate Numbers 21417 and 26629.

[71] Undated news clipping in the Jackson County Historical Society's Archives. The clipping describes Silvers as "the first jailer of Independence under the first Marshall Jackson County ever had. He served several terms as jailer and again served in the positing under W. J. Phillips. He was for a number of terms City Marshall of the City of Independence." Also, "The VanZant Murder," *Kansas City* (Mo.) *Star*, 27 Oct. 1886.

[72] "More Arrests," *Kansas City* (Mo.) *Star*, 8 Sep. 1885.

[73] "Arrested on Warrants," *Kansas City* (Mo.) *Star*, 3 June 1885, 1.

[74] "Sheriff Hickman's Second Term," *Kansas City* (Mo.) *Star*, 24, Nov. 1886, 1.

[75] "Marshal's Star on Shelf," *Kansas City* (Mo.) *Star*, 6 Jan. 1925, p. 5, c. 1. "The New Marshal Inducted, *Kansas City* (Mo.) *Star*, 22 Nov. 1886, 1.

[76] "The New Marshal Inducted, *Kansas City* (Mo.) *Star*, 22 Nov. 1886, 1.

[77] Ibid.

[78] Ibid.

[79] Ibid.

[80] Ibid.

[81] "Murdered Their Child," *Kansas City* (Mo.) *Star*, 29 June 1887, 1. Hulse became "City Marshal" for the City of Independence after this post expired. See "Suburban Elections," *Kansas City* (Mo.) *Star*, 4 Apr. 1889; and, "Col. Crisp's Boomerang," *Kansas City* (Mo.) *Star*, 29 May 1889, 1. "Shot Down a Half Wit: Marshall Mel Hulse Kills Charles Evans in Independence," *Kansas City* (Mo.) *Star*, 7 Feb. 1897, 2. He returned as a Deputy County Marshal by 1901, and served six years in that capacity.

[82] "The New Marshal Inducted, *Kansas City* (Mo.) *Star*, 22 Nov. 1886, 1.

[83] "The Penalty Paid: Edward Calhoun Sneed Hanged at Independence Soon after Noonday His Last Day,"

Kansas City (Mo.) *Star,* 24 June 1887, 1.

[84] Ibid.

[85] "The New Sheriff," *Kansas City* (Mo.) *Star,* 24 Nov 1888, 1. His commission was signed by Missouri Governor Albert P. Morehouse on 19 Nov. 1888; the certificate is filed in the Jackson County Historical Society's Archives, Document ID L75F23.

[86] "Marshal's Star on Shelf," *Kansas City* (Mo.) *Star*, 6 Jan. 1925, p. 5, c. 1. "L. P. Garnett's Prisoners," *Kansas City* (Mo.) *Star*, 14 Oct. 1890, 2.

[87] "Banker Nichols Arrested," *Kansas City* (Mo.) *Star*, 16 Dec. 1890.

[88] Marshall and Morrison, 31.

[89] "The Officials Report," *Kansas City* (Mo.) *Star*, 6 Jul. 1891.

[90] "Marshal's Star on Shelf," *Kansas City* (Mo.) *Star*, 6 Jan. 1925, p. 5, c. 1. "The Officials Report," *Kansas City* (Mo.) *Star*, 6 Jul. 1891. Marshall and Morrison, 180-181.

[91] "Thinks He is Magnetized," *Kansas City* (Mo.) *Star*, 24 Apr. 1892, 1. Marshall and Morrison, 181.

[92] Marshall and Morrison, 177.

[93] "The Officials Report," *Kansas City* (Mo.) *Star*, 6 Jul. 1891.

[94] Marshall and Morrison, 31.

[95] *Manual of Missouri* for 1893-1894, 150.

[96] "Marshal's Star on Shelf," *Kansas City* (Mo.) *Star*, 6 Jan. 1925, p. 5, c. 1. "Henry P. Stewart is Dead," *Kansas City* (Mo.) *Star*, 3 July 1915, 3. *Manual of Missouri* for 1893-1894, 150. Marshall and Morrison, 180-181.

[97] "Two Lives for One," *Kansas City* (Mo.) *Star*, 29 June 1894, 1. "Keshlear's Deputies," *Kansas City* (Mo.) *Star* , 24 July 1895, 1.

[98] "Keshlear's Deputies," *Kansas City* (Mo.) *Star* , 24 July 1895, 1.

[99] Ibid.

[100] Ibid.

[101] "Two Lives for One," *Kansas City* (Mo.) *Star*, 29 June 1894, 1.

[102] "Naming Their Deputies," *Kansas City* (Mo.) *Star*, 17 Dec. 1894, 8.

[103] "Keshlear's Deputies," *Kansas City* (Mo.) *Star* , 24 July 1895, 1.

[104] Ibid.

[105] Marshall and Morrison, 31.

[106] *Manual of Missouri* for 1895-1896, 169.

[107] "Marshal's Star on Shelf," *Kansas City* (Mo.) *Star*, 6 Jan. 1925, p. 5, c. 1. "Keshlear is Now Marshal," *Kansas City* (Mo.) *Star,* 23 July 1895, 1. The election results were contested and a fight for the office of Marshal ensued. *Manual of Missouri* for 1895-1896, 169. "Henry P. Stewart is Dead," *Kansas City* (Mo.) *Star*, 3 July 1915, 3. Stewart went on to become Police Commissioner for Kansas City. Marshall and Morrison, 180-181.

[108] "Keshlear's Deputies," *Kansas City* (Mo.) *Star* , 24 July 1895, 1.

[109] Ibid. "New Deputy County Marshals," *Kansas City (Mo.) Star*, 29 Dec. 1896, 2.

[110] "Keshlear's Deputies," *Kansas City* (Mo.) *Star* , 24 July 1895, 1. "Marshal Chile's Force," *Kansas City (Mo.) Star*, 18 Nov. 1896, 1.

[111] "Keshlear's Deputies," *Kansas City* (Mo.) *Star* , 24 July 1895, 1.

[112] "New Deputy County Marshals," *Kansas City (Mo.) Star*, 29 Dec. 1896, 2.

[113] "Arrested at the Independence Jail Door," *Kansas City (Mo.) Star*, 26 Oct. 1896, 8; mentions William Morse (African-American) being arrested by Deputy United States Marshal C. E. Halderman, after Morse's stay in the Jail.

[114] "Keshlear's Deputies," *Kansas City* (Mo.) *Star* , 24 July 1895, 1.

[115] Ibid.

[116] "Marshal's Star on Shelf," *Kansas City* (Mo.) *Star*, 6 Jan. 1925, p. 5, c. 1. "Keshlear is Now Marshal," *Kansas City* Mo.) *Star,* 23 July 1895, 1. Keshlear was formerly Deputy Marshal, as evidenced by, "Keshlear's Unfair Fight," *Kansas City* (Mo.) *Star* , 28 Feb 1895. He was allowed 14 deputy marshals; when Marshal Chiles took office, he was allowed 11. See, "Marshal Chile's Force," *Kansas City (Mo.) Star*, 18 Nov. 1896, 1. Joseph B. Keshlear married Josephine O'Flaherty in Jackson County on 28 Oct. 1891. When the 1900 U.S. Census for Kansas City, Jackson County, Missouri, was conducted, the 47-year-old Irish immigrant was listed as a "detective" with his 28-year-old wife, a native Missourian, and their children: Zulma (sic.; daughter), 7; and Joseph Riggs, 2. Zulma married John C. Matthews in Jackson County on 4 May 1914.

[117] "Keshlear's Deputies," *Kansas City* (Mo.) *Star* , 24 July 1895, 1.

[118] Ibid..

[119] Ibid.

[120] Ibid.

[121] Ibid.

[122] Ibid.

[123] Ibid.

[124] Ibid. "New Deputy County Marshals," *Kansas City (Mo.) Star*, 29 Dec. 1896, 2.

[125] *Manual of Missouri* for 1897-1898, 192. Marshall and Morrison, 30-31.

[126] "Marshal's Star on Shelf," *Kansas City* (Mo.) *Star*, 6 Jan. 1925, p. 5, c. 1. "Marshal Chiles Force," *Kansas City (Mo.) Star*,

18 Nov. 1896, 1, initially listed these deputies, who did not end up being sworn in the following month: Joseph T. Stewart, Mr. Hagan, Charles Kelly, Thomas Hudspeth, Joe Shannon, and Frank Hughes. "New Deputy County Marshals," *Kansas City (Mo.) Star*, 29 Dec. 1896, 2. Apparently, Chiles had promised more deputyships than he could fulfill. Action was brought against him, "Not Enough to Go Around," *Kansas City (Mo.) Star*, 20 Dec. 1896. *Manual of Missouri* for 1897-1898, 192.

[127] Potts ran as the Populist nominee for Marshal against Chiles in 1896, but was induced to get off the ticket and make way for Chiles for a $1,200 deputyship. "Not Enough to Go Around," *Kansas City* (Mo.) *Star*, 20 Dec. 1896. "Almost a Jail Delivery," *Kansas City* (Mo.) *Star*, 21 Apr. 1898, 10. His name was relayed as 'Sam Potts," in "Cut Their Way Out of Jail," *Kansas City (Mo.) Star*, 16 May 1898, 2. Potts retired 31 Dec 1898. *Jackson* (Independence, Mo.) *Examiner*, 10 Dec. 1898, 3:1. The 31 Dec. 1898 edition of the *Examiner* said that the Potts family moved out of the jail, and that he had been in charge for two years. Also see, Alderman, 128, 134, 185 (1886 date incorrect). Some time later Potts accepted a position with some implement house in St. Louis. Potts was formerly in the implement business in St. Louis, "and has resumed his old place there." Undated, unattributed article in the Jackson County Historical Society's newspaper clipping files.

[128] "New Deputy County Marshals," *Kansas City (Mo.) Star*, 29 Dec. 1896, 2.

[129] "Marshal Chile's Force," *Kansas City (Mo.) Star*, 18 Nov. 1896, 1.

[130] "New Deputy County Marshals," *Kansas City (Mo.) Star*, 29 Dec. 1896, 2. "Not Enough to Go Around," *Kansas City (Mo.) Star*, 20 Dec. 1896.

[131] "New Deputy County Marshals," *Kansas City (Mo.) Star*, 29 Dec. 1896, 2.

[132] Ibid.

[133] Ibid.

[134] Ibid.

[135] Ibid.

[136] Ibid..

[137] Ibid.

[138] "New Deputy County Marshals," *Kansas City (Mo.) Star*, 29 Dec. 1896, 2. "Not Enough to Go Around," *Kansas City (Mo.) Star*, 20 Dec. 1896.

[139] "Marshal Chile's Force," *Kansas City (Mo.) Star*, 18 Nov. 1896, 1. "New Deputy County Marshals," *Kansas City (Mo.) Star*, 29 Dec. 1896, 2. "Not Enough to Go Around," *Kansas City (Mo.) Star*, 20 Dec. 1896.

[140] "New Deputy County Marshals," *Kansas City (Mo.) Star*, 29 Dec. 1896, 2.

[141] Ibid.

[142] "Marshal Chile's Force," *Kansas City (Mo.) Star*, 18 Nov. 1896, 1. "New Deputy County Marshals," *Kansas City (Mo.) Star*, 29 Dec. 1896, 2.

[143] "New Deputy County Marshals," *Kansas City (Mo.) Star*, 29 Dec. 1896, 2. "New Deputy County Marshals," *Kansas City (Mo.) Star*, 29 Dec. 1896, 2.

[144] In the 1900 U. S. Census for the 7th Ward of Kansas City, Jackson County, Missouri, Sheriff Robert S. Stone, a 42-year-old native Missourian, was listed with his 39-year-old Kentucky native wife, Mary, and their children: Shelton P., 20; Olive V., 18; Robert C., 11; Mary C., 4 months. "Their Official Majorities, *Kansas City (Mo.) Star*, 18 Nov. 1898, 2. *Manual of Missouri* for 1899-1900, 211. Robert Stone, the son of A. R. and Alpha (Shelton) Stone, was born 12 Aug. 1857 and died 8 Jul. 1922. He and his wife, Mary G. (Cooper) Stone (26 Jul 1859-16 June 1948) are buried in Woodlawn Cemetery. Daughters of the American Revolution—Independence Pioneers Chapter. *Woodlawn Cemetery Tombstone Inscriptions*. Missouri Death Certificate Numbers 21083 and 19684. Marshall and Morrison, 30-31.

[145] "Marshal's Star on Shelf," *Kansas City* (Mo.) *Star*, 6 Jan. 1925, p. 5, c. 1. "Their Official Majorities, *Kansas City (Mo.) Star*, 18 Nov. 1898, 2. *Manual of Missouri* for 1899-1900, 211. Jackson County native Samuel Hamilton Chiles, son of James and Ruth (Hamilton) Chiles, was born 12 Dec. 1844 and died 16 Sep. 1929. He and his wife, Martha S. (Hughes) Chiles (1 May 1846-9 Oct. 1932), are buried the Buckner Cemetery. Missouri Death Certificates 30686 and 32131.

[146] Started on 1 Jan 1899. *Jackson* (Independence, Mo.) *Examiner*, 10 Dec. 1898, 3:1. According to the January 27, 1899 *Lee's Summit Journal,* reprinted in the Winter 1996-97 *Jackson County Historical Society JOURNAL* (identifying it as 1889, which appears incorrect), Mayes "made some much needed improvements in and about the building," as previously relayed in the body of this text. The 1900 U.S. Census for Blue Township, Jackson County, Missouri, 45-year-old Kentucky native deputy county marshal Mayes listed with his wife, Emma C., a 41-year-old native Missourian.

[147] "Held the Deputy Blameless," *Kansas City* (Mo.) *Star*, 28 May 1900, 1. Also, *Jackson County Historical Society JOURNAL* 1968 (Summer) 11:2, 2.

[148] The 1900 U.S. Census for Kansas City, Jackson County, Missouri, listed 47-year-old deputy county marshal Wilson, a native Missourian, with his wife, Emma L., 34 from Louisiana; and, their son, George E., 13. "Polk's Wife is Dead," *Kansas City* (Mo.) *Star*, 7 Feb. 1899, 1.

[149] "Brief Bits of City News," *Kansas City* (Mo.) *Star*, 7 June 1900, 2.

[150] "Polk's Wife is Dead," *Kansas City* (Mo.) *Star*, 7 Feb. 1899, 1.

[151] 1900 U.S. Census Population Schedule.

[152] Resigned on June 7, 1900. "Brief Bits of City News," *Kansas City* (Mo.) *Star*, 7 June 1900, 2.

[153] "Held the Deputy Blameless," *Kansas City* (Mo.) *Star*, 28 May 1900, 1.

[154] *Come and Spit on the Floor* (2:86) referencing *Jackson* (Independence, Mo.) *Examiner*, 4 Jan. 1901, 1:4. *Manual of Missouri* for 1901-1902, 201. Marshall and Morrison, 24-25.

[155] "Marshal's Star on Shelf," *Kansas City* (Mo.) *Star*, 6 Jan. 1925, p. 5, c. 1. *My First Year's Record: County Marshall, by John P. Maxwell*. Jackson County Historical Society Archives, Document ID 61F20. In this pamphlet, Marshall Maxwell provides statistical data of the number and cost of prisoners between 1900 and 1901. Also, *Manual of Missouri* for 1901-1902, 201. John Patton Maxwell, son of James Q. and Julia (Cook) Maxwell, was born in Pike County, Missouri, 21 Apr. 1843, and died 19 Sep. 1916. He is buried in the Blue Springs Cemetery. His wife preceded him in death.

[156] The 1900 U.S. Census for Kansas City, Jackson County, Missouri, lists 44-year-old teamster David H. Curran, born in Ohio, with his native Missourian wife, Ada [Maxwell], 32; and children: Arthur, 17; Maud, 15; Ernest, 7; Elmer, 5; and, Edward, 2. Ada was a daughter of Jackson County Marshal John P. Maxwell (from a note in the Jackson County Historical Society Archives, Document ID 61F20). Also, *Come and Spit on the Floor* (2:86) referencing *Jackson* (Independence, Mo.) *Examiner*, 4 Jan. 1901, 1:4. Also *Jackson* (Independence, Mo.) *Examiner*, 28 June 1901, 8:1. According to a short news announcement about the donation of the William Botts Family Collection to the Jackson County Historical Society, donor Mrs. Justine Botts Selvey's "grandmother's two brothers, Jess and David Curran, were both Marshals in the Old Jail. She remembers visiting there as a child." "Family's Papers are in Archives," *Jackson County Historical Society JOURNAL,* 1967 (Spring), 10:1, 5. David was a brother of Jess, who was about 13 years his junior; see jailor for 1921-1922.

[157] *Come and Spit on the Floor* (2:86) referencing *Jackson* (Independence, Mo.) *Examiner*, 4 Jan. 1901, 1:4.

[158] *Ibid.* Hale and Beck, 29-30. Hulse had served 11 years as City Marshal for the City of Independence before resigning in April 1898, and returning as a Deputy Jackson County Marshal. Another source lists him as City Marshal 17 years from 1883 being defeated in 1900 by William Parker (See Virginia Anna (Davis) Woods "Romance" in Jackson County Historical Society Archives, Document ID 35F14.

[159] *Jackson* (Independence, Mo.) *Examiner*, 31 Jan. 1908, 5:2.

[160] "A Deputy Marshal Arrested," *Kansas City* (Mo.) *Star*, 4 Nov. 1902, 10.

[161] *Come and Spit on the Floor* (2:86) referencing *Jackson* (Independence, Mo.) *Examiner*, 4 Jan. 1901, 1:4.

[162] *Ibid.*

[163] Gilday was born in 1862 in Independence, Missouri. His family relocated to Kansas City about 1869. In 1901, Gilday was married to Mrs. Maud Wayland Dean. *Manual of Missouri* for 1903-1904, 249. Marshall and Morrison, 196-197.

[164] "Marshal's Star on Shelf," *Kansas City* (Mo.) *Star*, 6 Jan. 1925, p. 5, c. 1. "Pendergast Deputies," *Kansas City* (Mo.) *Star,* 30 Nov. 1902, 4. *Manual of Missouri* for 1903-1904, 249. Thomas J. Pendergast was born in St. Joseph, Missouri, to Irish immigrants Michael and Mary (Reidy) Pendergast, on 22 July 1872. He died 26 Jan. 1945 and is buried in Calvary Cemetery in Kansas City, Missouri. His wife, Carolyn, survived him. Missouri Death Certificate Number 1358. Marshall and Morrison, 46-47.

[165] "County Marshal's Deputies," *Kansas City* (Mo.) *Star*, 20 Dec. 1902, 1. *Come and Spit on the Floor* (2:65-66) referencing *Jackson* (Independence, Mo.) *Examiner*, 4 Apr. 1904, 6:1. *Come and Spit on the Floor* (2:61) referencing *Jackson* (Independence, Mo.) *Examiner*, 30 Dec. 1904, 1:4.

[166] "County Marshal's Deputies," *Kansas City* (Mo.) *Star*, 20 Dec. 1902, 1.

[167] Ibid.

[168] Superintendent of the chain gang road building. *Come and Spit on the Floor*. Volume 2 referencing *Jackson* (Independence, Mo.) *Examiner*, 3 Jul. 1903, 9:1. Also, Hale and Beck, 25.

[169] "Pendergast Deputies," Kansas City (Mo.) Star*, 30 Nov. 1902, 4.

[170] *Come and Spit on the Floor* (2:65-66) referencing *Jackson* (Independence, Mo.) *Examiner*, 4 Apr. 1904, 6:1.

[171] "County Marshal's Deputies," *Kansas City* (Mo.) *Star*, 20 Dec. 1902, 1.

[172] "In charge of the county prisoners." *Come and Spit on the Floor*. Volume 2 referencing *Jackson* (Independence, Mo.) *Examiner*, 3 Jul. 1903, 9:1. Also, Hale and Beck, 25.

[173] "County Marshal's Deputies," *Kansas City* (Mo.) *Star*, 20 Dec. 1902, 1.

[174] Ibid.

[175] Ibid.

[176] Ibid.

[177] Ibid.

[178] Ibid.

[179] Ibid.

[180] *Manual of Missouri* for 1905-1906, 135.

[181] "Marshal's Star on Shelf," *Kansas City* (Mo.) *Star*, 6 Jan. 1925, p. 5, c. 1. "The New Marshal's Deputies, *Kansas City* (Mo.) *Star*, 25 Dec. 1904, 8; and, "Al Heslip Sworn In," *Kansas City* (Mo.) *Star*, 29 Dec. 1904, 5. Also, "A Reprimand for Heslip," *Kansas City* (Mo.) *Star*, 5 Oct. 1906, 1. *Manual of Missouri* for 1905-1906, 135.

[182] "The New Marshal's Deputies," *Kansas City (Mo.) Star*, 25 Dec. 1904, 8; "Al Heslip Sworn In," *Kansas City* (Mo.) *Star*, 29 Dec. 1904, 5; "County Jail Inspected," *Independence* (Mo.) *Examiner,* 30 May 1906; and, "A Jail of the Dark Ages," *Kansas City* (Mo.) *Star*, 30 May 1906. Other articles from the same newspaper mentioning Martin, as extracted in *Come and Spit on the Floor* (2:66-67) include: 9 Feb. 1906, 7:2; 27 Apr. 1906, 3:1; and 14 Dec. 1906, 10:2.

[183] "Met After 43 Years," *Kansas City* (Mo.) *Star*, 17 Jul. 1906.

[184] "The New Marshal's Deputies," *Kansas City (Mo.) Star*, 25 Dec. 1904, 8; and, "Al Heslip Sworn In," *Kansas City* (Mo.) *Star*, 29 Dec. 1904, 5.

[185] Ibid. "County Jail Inspected," *Independence* (Mo.) *Examiner,* 30 May 1906. "Jail," *Independence* (Mo.) *Examiner,*

20 June 1907. The *Jackson* (Independence, Mo.) *Examiner*, 2 Aug. 1907, 1, 4, incorrectly referred to Hulse as Marshal (unless it meant "city marshal"). Melville, son of Samuel D. and Jane Hulse, was born on 15 Aug. 1843 in Oak Grove, Jackson County, Missouri. He is listed with his parents in the 1860 U.S. Census, and in the household next to them with his Pennsylvania native wife, Alice, in the 1870 U.S. Census. "After <u>serving as jailer for 10 years</u>, Mr. Hulse went to Jefferson City as yard master at the penitentiary." "Visit to Old Jail Brings Back a Flood of Memories for Her*,*" *Independence* (Mo.) *Examiner,* 22 Aug. 1956. Hulse died of typhoid fever on March 31, 1919. According to his death certificate (Number 9594), he lived at 810 West White Oak, and was Chief of Police for Sugar Creek. He had also been a gateman at the Standard Oil Refinery there. Hulse was buried in the Mecklin Cemetery near Oak Grove. Hulse's obituary said he was <u>Deputy County Marshal six years</u>, "Old Injuries Were Fatal," *Kansas City* (Mo.) *Star,* 31 Mar. 1919, 14.

[186] "The New Marshal's Deputies," *Kansas City (Mo.) Star*, 25 Dec. 1904, 8; and, "Al Heslip Sworn In," *Kansas City* (Mo.) *Star*, 29 Dec. 1904, 5. Also, "A Reprimand for Heslip," *Kansas City* (Mo.) *Star*, 5 Oct. 1906, 1; and, "One of the Deputies Out," *Kansas City* (Mo.) *Star*, 7 Oct. 1906.

[187] "The New Marshal's Deputies," *Kansas City (Mo.) Star*, 25 Dec. 1904, 8; and, "Al Heslip Sworn In," *Kansas City* (Mo.) *Star*, 29 Dec. 1904, 5. Also, "A Reprimand for Heslip," *Kansas City* (Mo.) *Star*, 5 Oct. 1906, 1.

[188] "The New Marshal's Deputies," *Kansas City (Mo.) Star*, 25 Dec. 1904, 8; and, "Al Heslip Sworn In," *Kansas City* (Mo.) *Star*, 29 Dec. 1904, 5.

[189] Ibid.

[190] Ibid.

[191] Ibid.

[192] "Shot at by Quantrell Man," *Kansas City* (Mo.) *Star*, 23 Aug. 1907, 1. Also, "The New Marshal's Deputies," *Kansas City (Mo.) Star*, 25 Dec. 1904, 8; and, "Al Heslip Sworn In," *Kansas City* (Mo.) *Star*, 29 Dec. 1904, 5.

[193] "The New Marshal's Deputies," *Kansas City (Mo.) Star*, 25 Dec. 1904, 8; and, "Al Heslip Sworn In," *Kansas City* (Mo.) *Star*, 29 Dec. 1904, 5.

[194] Ibid.

[195] Ibid.

[196] "The New Marshal's Deputies," *Kansas City (Mo.) Star*, 25 Dec. 1904, 8; and, "Al Heslip Sworn In," *Kansas City* (Mo.) *Star*, 29 Dec. 1904, 5. Also, *Come and Spit on the Floor* (2:65) referencing *Jackson* (Independence, Mo.) *Examiner*, 23 Nov. 1906, 16:2.

[197] "The New Marshal's Deputies," *Kansas City (Mo.) Star*, 25 Dec. 1904, 8; and, "Al Heslip Sworn In," *Kansas City* (Mo.) *Star*, 29 Dec. 1904, 5.

[198] Ibid. Also, Discharged of his duties September 9, 1905. "Discharged by Heslip," *Kansas City (Mo.) Star*, 10 Aug. 1905, 2.

[199] "The New Marshal's Deputies," *Kansas City (Mo.) Star*, 25 Dec. 1904, 8; and, "Al Heslip Sworn In," *Kansas City* (Mo.) *Star*, 29 Dec. 1904, 5.

[200] "Only 3 Democrats…" *Kansas City (Mo.) Star*, 7 Nov. 1906, 1. Baldwin died while in office, "Floral Tribute Impressive," *Kansas City* (Mo.) *Star*, 27 Sept. 1907, 1. Campbell was appointed by the County Court to fill Baldwin's position, "W. J. Campbell for Sheriff," *Kansas City* (Mo.) *Star*, 29 Sept. 1907, 1. Also, *Manual of Missouri* for 1907-1908, 211.

[201] "Marshal's Star on Shelf," *Kansas City* (Mo.) *Star*, 6 Jan. 1925, p. 5, c. 1. Heslip defeated Thomas Pendergast 22,099 to 18,900, or by 3,199 plurality, as reported in "Only 3 Democrats…" *Kansas City (Mo.) Star*, 7 Nov. 1906, 1. Also, "Shot at by Quantrell Man," *Kansas City* (Mo.) *Star*, 23 Aug. 1907, 1. In November, 1907, Heslip was reviewing applications for 30 special deputies to uphold a new 'Sunday Closing Law,' "Heslip to Have 50 Deputies, "*Kansas City* (Mo.) *Star*, 23 Nov. 1907. Only theaters seemed to be exempt after much protest, "A Tight Lid for Sunday, *Kansas City* (Mo.) *Star*, 17 Oct. 1907, 1. *Manual of Missouri* for 1907-1908, 211. Albert, the son of John and Jane (McShannon) Heslip, was born in Ohio on 7 June 1853, and died 25 July 1923. He is buried in Mt. Washington Cemetery. His wife, Emma, survived him. Missouri Death Certificate Number 21631.

[202] "More County Appointments," *Kansas City* (Mo.) *Star*, 7 Jan. 1907, 1. Martin died at age 86 on 24 Jan. 1919; his obituary said, "He served several years as county jailer at Independence," *Kansas City* (Mo.) *Star*, 25 Jan 1919. Missouri Death Certificate Number 1613. Martin was a Civil War veteran, enlisting in an Ohio regiment for service with the Union Army, and served for two years in the south. In 1867, he moved to Wayne City in Jackson County, before moving to Independence some years later. In the early 1900s, the *Independence* (Mo.) *Examiner* published Martin's weather prognostications each month; forecasts that were based on the position of the moon. Hickman, 405. *Independence* (Mo.) *Examiner*, 26 Feb. 1962, 13.

[203] "W. J. Campbell for Sheriff," *Kansas City* (Mo.) *Star*, 29 Sept. 1907, 1.

[204] Ibid.

[205] "All Deputies Sworn In," *Kansas City* (Mo.) *Star*, 1 Oct. 1907, 4. The deputies were not named individually.

[206] The 1910 U.S. Census for Kansas City, Jackson County, Missouri, listed 54-year-old Illinois native Sheriff Rood, with his 50-year-old wife, Sarah B., a native Missourian, with their children: Willis C. (daughter), 22; Florence, 20; Josephina, 18; and Josh A., 7. *Manual of Missouri* for 1909-1910, 229. Marshall and Morrison, 236-237.

[207] "Marshal's Star on Shelf," *Kansas City* (Mo.) *Star*, 6 Jan. 1925, p. 5, c. 1. *Manual of Missouri* for 1909-1910, 229.

[208] The 1910 U.S. Census for Blue Township, Jackson County, Missouri, lists 39-year-old Jackson County Jailor Phelps with his second wife, Emma C., 25. They were both native Missourians.

[209] *Come and Spit on the Floor* (3:89) referencing *Jackson* (Independence, Mo.) *Examiner*, 29 Jan. 1909, 1:1. The "Custodian of the Jail" was a new position responsible for being on duty all night every night at the 1859 Jackson County Jail to answer calls and keep the furnace going.

[210] "A Deputy Marshal Dead," *Kansas City* (Mo.) *Star*, 22 Feb. 1910, 4.

[211] *Come and Spit on the Floor*. Volume 2 referencing *Jackson* (Independence, Mo.) *Examiner*, 29 Nov. 1909, 8, 3. Also Beck and Hale, 25.

[212] "More County Jobs Awarded," *Kansas City* (Mo.) *Star*, 18 Dec. 1908, 1.

[213] "A Juror's Wife is Ill," *Kansas City* (Mo.) *Star*, 29 Apr. 1910.

[214] "County Court Appointments: County Chain Gang," *Jackson County* (Independence, Mo.) *Democrat*, 25 Mar. 1909.

[215] "New Marshal in Office," *Kansas City* (Mo.) *Star*, 1 Jan. 1921, 8.

[216] "County Court Appointments: County Chain Gang," *Jackson County* (Independence, Mo.) *Democrat*, 25 Mar. 1909.

[217] "Is the Confession a Ruse?" *Kansas City* (Mo.) *Star*, 18 Jan. 1910.

[218] "County Court Appointments: County Chain Gang," *Jackson County* (Independence, Mo.) *Democrat*, 25 Mar. 1909.

[219] "More County Jobs Awarded," *Kansas City* (Mo.) *Star*, 18 Dec. 1908, 1.

[220] "County Court Appointments: County Chain Gang," *Jackson County* (Independence, Mo.) *Democrat*, 25 Mar. 1909.

[221] "More County Jobs Awarded," *Kansas City* (Mo.) *Star*, 18 Dec. 1908, 1.

[222] "County Court Appointments: County Chain Gang," *Jackson County* (Independence, Mo.) *Democrat*, 25 Mar. 1909.

[223] "More County Jobs Awarded," *Kansas City* (Mo.) *Star*, 18 Dec. 1908, 1.

[224] "County Court Appointments: County Chain Gang," *Jackson County* (Independence, Mo.) *Democrat*, 25 Mar. 1909.

[225] Ibid.

[226] Ibid.

[227] "Cost to Run for Office," *Kansas City* (Mo.) *Star*, 10 Dec. 1912, 5. *Manual of Missouri* for 1911-1912, 243. Marshall and Morrison, 236-237.

[228] "Marshal's Star on Shelf," *Kansas City* (Mo.) *Star*, 6 Jan. 1925, p. 5, c. 1. *Manual of Missouri* for 1911-1912, 243. Joel B., son of Joel Mayes, was born in Kentucky on 28 Oct. 1854 and died 18 July 1931. He is buried in the Blue Springs Cemetery. His wife, Emma, survived him. Missouri Death Certificate Number 24886.

[229] "Seven Negroes Break Jail," *Kansas City* (Mo.) *Star*, 16 Apr. 1912, 1.

[230] "Crowe Makes Appointments," *Kansas City* (Mo.) *Star*, 27 Dec. 1912, 12.

[231] "Seven Negroes Break Jail," *Kansas City* (Mo.) *Star*, 16 Apr. 1912, 1.

[232] "Crowe Makes Appointments," *Kansas City* (Mo.) *Star*, 27 Dec. 1912, 12.

[233] Ibid.

[234] "Seven Negroes Break Jail," *Kansas City* (Mo.) *Star*, 16 Apr. 1912, 1. "Crowe Makes Appointments," *Kansas City* (Mo.) *Star*, 27 Dec. 1912, 12. Years later Harvey Kemper displayed a pair of handcuffs handed down in his family that had once been used at the Jackson County Jail. *Kansas City* (Mo.) *Star*, 26 Oct. 1963, 6.

[235] "Crowe Makes Appointments," *Kansas City* (Mo.) *Star*, 27 Dec. 1912, 12.

[236] Ibid.

[237] Ibid.

[238] Ibid. "New Marshal in Office," *Kansas City* (Mo.) *Star*, 1 Jan. 1921, 8.

[239] "Crowe Makes Appointments," *Kansas City* (Mo.) *Star*, 27 Dec. 1912, 12.

[240] Ibid.

[241] Ibid.

[242] *Manual of Missouri* for 1913-1914, 233.

[243] "Marshal's Star on Shelf," *Kansas City* (Mo.) *Star*, 6 Jan. 1925, p. 5, c. 1. *Manual of Missouri* for 1913-1914, 233.

[244] Allen died while in office. Stewart, 3. According to Allen's son-in-law, Mr. Orville Campbell, who also stated, "that the trustys [trustees] did the cooking in the kitchen of the jail." They fed prisoners who sat at trestle tables in the basement. Alderman, 35. U.S. Census for Independence, Jackson County, Missouri (Jesse Allen in 1910; ED 10; PAGE 8A; LINE 39) (Anna Allen in 1920; ED 8; PAGE 4B; LINE 69). Also, Allen's 1918 death certificate, copies of which are on file in the Jackson County Historical Society's Archives.

[245] Information provided by his granddaughter, Beverley (Jones) Zimmerman.

[246] "Crowe Makes Appointments," *Kansas City* (Mo.) *Star*, 27 Dec. 1912, 12. "Still 30 30 at the Jail," *Kansas City* (Mo.) *Star*, 31 Dec. 1914, 1.

[247] "Crowe Makes Appointments," *Kansas City* (Mo.) *Star*, 27 Dec. 1912, 12. "New Marshal in Office," *Kansas City* (Mo.) *Star*, 1 Jan. 1921, 8.

[248] "Crowe Makes Appointments," *Kansas City* (Mo.) *Star*, 27 Dec. 1912, 12.

[249] Ibid.

[250] Ibid.

[251] "Crowe Makes Appointments," *Kansas City* (Mo.) *Star*, 27 Dec. 1912, 12. "Still 30 30 at the Jail," *Kansas City* (Mo.) *Star*, 31 Dec. 1914, 1.

[252] Ibid. Years later Harvey Kemper displayed a pair of handcuffs that had once been used at the Jackson County Jail. *Kansas City* (Mo.) *Star*, 26 Oct. 1963, 6.

[253] "Crowe Makes Appointments," *Kansas City* (Mo.) *Star*, 27 Dec. 1912, 12.

[254] Ibid.

[255] Ibid.

[256] "Crowe Makes Appointments," *Kansas City* (Mo.) *Star*, 27 Dec. 1912, 12. "Still 30 30 at the Jail," *Kansas City* (Mo.) *Star*, 31 Dec. 1914, 1.

[257] "Crowe Makes Appointments," *Kansas City* (Mo.) *Star*, 27 Dec. 1912, 12.

[258] Ibid.

[259] Ibid.

[260] Ibid.

[261] Ibid.

[262] Ibid.

[263] Ibid.

[264] Ibid.

[265] *Manual of Missouri* for 1915-1916, 209.

[266] "Marshal's Star on Shelf," *Kansas City* (Mo.) *Star*, 6 Jan. 1925, p. 5, c. 1. *Manual of Missouri* for 1915-1916, 209. Irish immigrant Martin J., son of John and Hannah (Garrahie) Crowe, was born 14 May 1871 and died 15 Jan. 1948. He is buried in Calvary Cemetery. His wife, Lillian, survived him. Missouri Death Certificate Number 1031.

[267] Information provided by his granddaughter, Beverley (Jones) Zimmerman.

[268] The 25 deputy marshals sworn in were not all named; only the ones who were dropped and added. "Still 30 30 at the Jail," *Kansas City* (Mo.) *Star*, 31 Dec. 1914, 1.

[269] "Name More Guards for Chain Gang," *Kansas City* (Mo.) *Star*, 25 Apr. 1916.

[270] "Still 30 30 at the Jail," *Kansas City* (Mo.) *Star*, 31 Dec. 1914, 1.

[271] "Name More Guards for Chain Gang," *Kansas City* (Mo.) *Star*, 25 Apr. 1916.

[272] "Still 30 30 at the Jail," *Kansas City* (Mo.) *Star*, 31 Dec. 1914, 1.

[273] "New Marshal in Office," *Kansas City* (Mo.) *Star*, 1 Jan. 1921, 8.

[274] "Still 30 30 at the Jail," *Kansas City* (Mo.) *Star*, 31 Dec. 1914, 1.

[275] Ibid.

[276] *Manual of Missouri* for1917-1918, 199. Marshall and Morrison, 44-45.

[277] "Marshal's Star on Shelf," *Kansas City* (Mo.) *Star*, 6 Jan. 1925, p. 5, c. 1. *Manual of Missouri* for 1917-1918, 199.

[278] "A New Jailer at Independence," *Kansas City* (Mo.) *Star*, 3 Jan 1919, 3. Jesse Allen died and his son Melvin served out his unexpired term.

[279] "Funeral of a Solider Today," *Kansas City* (Mo.) *Star*, 25 Oct. 1918.

[280] "A New Jailer at Independence," *Kansas City* (Mo.) *Star*, 3 Jan 1919, 3.

[281] "New Marshal in Office," *Kansas City* (Mo.) *Star*, 1 Jan. 1921, 8.

[282] Ibid.

[283] Gentry was born in 1859 in Jackson County. He entered the pharmaceutical business at age 18 in the employ of J. C. Pendleton, of whom he became a partner by 1902. The 1920 U.S. Census for Blue Township, Jackson County, Missouri, lists 60-year-old Gentry, a drug store partner, with his 55-year-old wife, Emma [Robertson]. Marshall and Morrison, 44-45.

[284] "Marshal's Star on Shelf," *Kansas City* (Mo.) *Star*, 6 Jan. 1925, p. 5, c. 1. The 1920 U.S. Census for Kaw Township, Jackson County, Missouri, lists 46-year-old Marshal Hoffman, an Illinois native, with his 37-year-old Ohio native wife, Ida, and their children: Navhon (daughter), 17; James, 15; Harry, 13; Doris, 10; and Jean, 3. "Sues County Marshal," *Kansas City* (Mo.) *Star*, 12 Mar 1920, 2.

[285] The 1920 U.S. Census for Blue Township, Jackson County, Missouri, lists 41-year-old Missouri native "Chief Jailor" Hall at the 1859 Jackson County Jail, with his 33-year old native Missourian wife, Katherine, their son, Harden T., Jr., 16 months; and, 19 prisoners (7 white; 12 black). "A New Jailer at Independence," *Kansas City* (Mo.) *Star*, 3 Jan 1919, 3. In 1996, Hall's granddaughter donated a lock that had been used on ankle irons. A key, which had been donated the previous year by the family of another former deputy, was inserted into the ankle iron lock…and opened it. See, "New Acquisitions at Jail Museum Bring More History Back Home." *Jackson County Historical Society JOURNAL* 1996 (Summer) 36:2, 3. "Dutch" Hall was a nephew of Cole Younger (see 14 May 1959 letter of Harry C. Hoffman to Donald R. Hale in the Jackson County Historical Society Archives.

[286] Revzin, Mike. "Memories of a Prohibition Deputy." *Missouri Life* 1977 (Sept-Oct), 47-50.

[287] "More Deputy Marshals Sworn In," *Kansas City* (Mo.) *Star*, 6 Jan. 1921, 1.

[288] "New Marshal in Office," *Kansas City* (Mo.) *Star*, 1 Jan. 1921, 8.

[289] "Sues County Marshal," *Kansas City* (Mo.) *Star*, 12 Mar 1920, 2.

[290] "New Marshal in Office," *Kansas City* (Mo.) *Star*, 1 Jan. 1921, 8.

[291] "Sues County Marshal," *Kansas City* (Mo.) *Star*, 12 Mar 1920, 2.

[292] *Manual of Missouri* for 1921-1922, 187.

[293] "Marshal's Star on Shelf," *Kansas City* (Mo.) *Star*, 6 Jan. 1925, p. 5, c. 1. "Ignore Bosses on Jobs," *Kansas City* (Mo.) *Star*, 15 Dec. 1920, 1. "Marshal Names Deputies," *Kansas City* (Mo.) *Star*, 17 Dec. 1920, 15. "New Marshal in Office," *Kansas City* (Mo.) *Star*, 1 Jan. 1921, 8.

[294] In the 1920 U.S. Census for Blue Township, Jackson County, Missouri, 52-year-old Jess E. Curran, born in Ohio, was a laborer for an oil company. His wife, Jennie S., was a native Missourian of the same age. "Marshal Names Deputies," *Kansas City* (Mo.) *Star*, 17 Dec. 1920, 15. "New Marshal in Office," *Kansas City* (Mo.) *Star*, 1 Jan. 1921, 8. Cleaning Up Old Jail," *Independence* (Mo.) *Examiner,* 15 Mar. 1921, p. 1. "Two Fugitives Captured," *Kansas City* (Mo.) *Star*, 22 Aug. 1921, 1. According to a short news announcement about the donation of a collection of Botts family papers to the Jackson County Historical Society, donor Mrs. Justine Botts Selvey's "grandmother's two brothers, Jess and David Curran, were both Marshals in the Old Jail. She remembers visiting there as a child." David Curran appears to have been about 13 years older than Jess

(David H. Curran served as jailor between 1901-1902; he was about 45 at that time, which would make him about 65 in 1920). See, "Family's Papers are in Archives," *Jackson County Historical Society JOURNAL,* 1967 (Spring), 10:1, 5. Also, Alderman, 135, 138.

[295] "Ignore Bosses on Jobs," *Kansas City* (Mo.) *Star,* 15 Dec. 1920, 1.

[296] "New Marshal in Office," *Kansas City* (Mo.) *Star,* 1 Jan. 1921, 8.

[297] "Marshal Shot by a Deputy. Alleged Grafting of Sugar Creek Officer Causes Shooting in Park," *Kansas City* (Mo.) *Star,* 18 Jul. 1921, 1. "More Deputy Marshals Sworn In," *Kansas City* (Mo.) *Star,* 6 Jan. 1921, 1.

[298] "Ignore Bosses on Jobs," *Kansas City* (Mo.) *Star,* 15 Dec. 1920, 1. "Marshal Names Deputies," *Kansas City* (Mo.) *Star,* 17 Dec. 1920, 15. "New Marshal in Office," *Kansas City* (Mo.) *Star,* 1 Jan. 1921, 8.

[299] "Jailer Heard the Sawing," *Kansas City* (Mo.) *Star,* 21 June 1922, 1.

[300] "New Marshal in Office," *Kansas City* (Mo.) *Star,* 1 Jan. 1921, 8.

[301] Ibid.

[302] "Marshal Names Deputies," *Kansas City* (Mo.) *Star,* 17 Dec. 1920, 15. "New Marshal in Office," *Kansas City* (Mo.) *Star,* 1 Jan. 1921, 8.

[303] "Prisoners Must Be Vaccinated," *Kansas City* (Mo.) *Star,* 17 Nov. 1921, 1.

[304] "Marshal Names Deputies," *Kansas City* (Mo.) *Star,* 17 Dec. 1920, 15. "New Marshal in Office," *Kansas City* (Mo.) *Star,* 1 Jan. 1921, 8.

[305] "New Marshal in Office," *Kansas City* (Mo.) *Star,* 1 Jan. 1921, 8.

[306] "Marshal Names Deputies," *Kansas City* (Mo.) *Star,* 17 Dec. 1920, 15. "New Marshal in Office," *Kansas City* (Mo.) *Star,* 1 Jan. 1921, 8.

[307] **Hines is the only African American Deputy County Marshal the authors located through 1933.** "Marshal Names Deputies," *Kansas City* (Mo.) *Star,* 17 Dec. 1920, 15. "New Marshal in Office," *Kansas City* (Mo.) *Star,* 1 Jan. 1921, 8.

[308] "Marshal Names Deputies," *Kansas City* (Mo.) *Star,* 17 Dec. 1920, 15. "New Marshal in Office," *Kansas City* (Mo.) *Star,* 1 Jan. 1921, 8.

[309] "More Deputy Marshals Sworn In," *Kansas City* (Mo.) *Star,* 6 Jan. 1921, 1.

[310] "Marshal Names Deputies," *Kansas City* (Mo.) *Star,* 17 Dec. 1920, 15. "New Marshal in Office," *Kansas City* (Mo.) *Star,* 1 Jan. 1921, 8.

[311] Ibid.

[312] Ibid.

[313] Ibid.

[314] "More Deputy Marshals Sworn In," *Kansas City* (Mo.) *Star,* 6 Jan. 1921, 1.

[315] "Marshal Names Deputies," *Kansas City* (Mo.) *Star,* 17 Dec. 1920, 15. "New Marshal in Office," *Kansas City* (Mo.) *Star,* 1 Jan. 1921, 8.

[316] Ibid.

[317] "New Marshal in Office," *Kansas City* (Mo.) *Star,* 1 Jan. 1921, 8.

[318] "Marshal Names Deputies," *Kansas City* (Mo.) *Star,* 17 Dec. 1920, 15. "New Marshal in Office," *Kansas City* (Mo.) *Star,* 1 Jan. 1921, 8.

[319] "More Deputy Marshals Sworn In," *Kansas City* (Mo.) *Star,* 6 Jan. 1921, 1.

[320] *Manual of Missouri* for 1923-1924, 161. "Sheriff and Deputies Sworn," *Kansas City* (Mo.) *Star,* 2 Jan. 1925, 4.

[321] The index to the Jackson County Court minutes indicates that on 1 Jan. 1925, John L. Miles' resignation was accepted (60a:6); the author's could not locate the original entry in said ledger. The last and final report of the Jackson County Marshal dated December 1924 was approved by the Jackson County Court on 8 Jan. 1925 (61:11). "Marshal's Star on Shelf," *Kansas City* (Mo.) *Star,* 6 Jan. 1925, p. 5, c. 1. Miles was the last elected County Marshal in Jackson County before the post was abolished by Missouri State Law (Laws of Missouri, 1921, 51st General Assembly, Regular Session, 220-222). Gentry, Sue. "Major Miles Recalls Last Use of the Old County Jail Here," undated, unsourced newspaper clipping in the Jackson County Historical Society Archives. See also, Harry S Truman Library *Oral History Interview with Henry P. Chiles* by J. R. Fuchs.

[322] Hale and Beck, 32-33. "Danger from Bobbed Hair," *Jackson* (Independence, Mo.) *Examiner,* 11 Apr. 1924.

[323] *Manual of Missouri* for 1925-1926, 167. "Sheriff and Deputies Sworn," *Kansas City* (Mo.) *Star,* 2 Jan. 1925, 4.

[324] Hale and Beck, 32-33.

[325] "Sheriff and Deputies Sworn," *Kansas City* (Mo.) *Star,* 2 Jan. 1925, 4.

[326] *Manual of Missouri* for 1927-1928, 168. Gentry, Sue. "Major Miles Recalls Last Use of the Old County Jail Here," undated, unsourced newspaper clipping in the Jackson County Historical Society Archives.

[327] *Manual of Missouri* for 1929-1930, 180.

[328] 1930 and 1932 Independence city directories.

[329] "Remodel of Old Jailer's Home," *Independence* (Mo.) *Examiner,* 9 Feb. 1929, p.1.

[330] *Manual of Missouri* for 1931-1932, 180. Chester Smedley became a prominent attorney in Denver, and also practiced in Kansas City. His wife, Gladys Poe (Waters) Smedley, daughter of Bernard and Susan Frances (Flannery) Waters, wrote the nonfiction novel, *Fairacres.* Chester and Gladys had a daughter, Frances (Smedley) Alshire, born about 1920 in Denver, Colorado. Alshire moved to St. Louis, Missouri. Gladys had been previously married to a Mr. Monfort (prominent in the Greeley, Colorado, area). Mrs. Smedley donated Shepherd family artifacts to the Jackson County Historical Society; she died in 1973.

[331] 1932 Independence city directory.

APPENDIX

B

LEGAL HANGINGS
IN JACKSON COUNTY, MISSOURI
1839-JUNE 1933

Public executions by hanging were sometimes held on Courthouse Squares in some Missouri counties. With the exception of the first legal hanging in 1839 discussed earlier in this text and footnoted below, capital executions in Jackson County, Missouri, were conducted at either the 1859 Jackson County Jail in Independence, or the County's Jail in Kansas City.

It was not uncommon in these times for these events to draw very large crowds, and tickets were often distributed by the County Sheriff.

Below are all the documented, _legal_ hangings (or, judicial executions) in Jackson County from 1839 through June 1933 (when the 1859 Jackson County Jail was decommissioned) that have been proved thus far (2009). Although primarily reliant upon local newspaper articles, of valuable assistance was the appendix of Harriet C. Frazier's _Death Sentences in Missouri, 1803-2005_. (Jefferson, Nc.: McFarland & Co., Inc., Publishers, 2006), 197-213 (although, Jackson County's first legal hanging was inaccurately attributed as "George Goster."). Frazier drew heavily upon the files of Watt Epsy, once the premier collector of the specifics of the death penalty in America. Also consulted but not entirely relied upon was the Internet posting, "Before the Needles" (http://users.bestweb.net/~rg/execution/MISSOURI.htm; as viewed 24 Mar. 2008); but, it contained several entries inaccurately attributed to Jackson County.

Imagine, however, all the many other extralegal executions that transpired throughout Jackson County's tumultuous 175+year history. Frazier contends, for instance, that after the Civil War "from 1866 to 1870, for every two known executions in Missouri, there were approximately nine known lynchings." (Frazier, page 57).

Further description about each event is found in endnotes, or in the articles referenced therein.

Hanged	Where	Convict	Age	Race	Gender	Appeal	Crime	Victim	Age	Race	Gender
May 10, 1839	Indep.	Henry Garster		white	male	No	murder	Williamson Hawkins		white	male[1]

There were no *legal* hangings in Jackson County between 1839 and 1878.

Hanged	Where	Convict	Age	Race	Gender	Appeal	Crime	Victim	Age	Race	Gender
Mar. 1, 1878	KC	Richard Green	27	white	male	Yes	murder	Henry H. Hughes, Deputy County Marshal[2]			
June 24, 1887	Indep.	Edward Calhoun Sneed	27	white	male	Yes	murder	Orlean Harrison Loomis[3]			
Jan. 5, 1894	KC	Martin Reed	65	black	male	Yes	murder	wife Hester Reed	51	black	female[4]
June 29, 1894	Indep.	Harry Jones	30	white	male	No	murder	Madam Jane Wright		white	female[5]
June 29, 1894	KC	William C. Ricksher (alias John Clark)	37	white	male	Yes	murder	Madam Jane Wright		white	female[6]
Feb. 15, 1895	KC	Philip Martin	17-19	black	male	Yes	murder	Eli Stillwell	34		male[7]
Dec. 28, 1898	KC	James Brown	31	black	male	Yes	murder	Henry Prather			male[8]
Mar. 30, 1899	KC	James "Jim" Reed	16-17	black	male	Yes	murder	Susie Blakely	26		female[9]
Jan. 21, 1902	KC	Albert Garth	26	black	male	Yes	murder	Minnie Woods			female[10]
April 11, 1902	KC	James Jackson	24	black	male	Yes	murder	Prophet Everett		black	male[11]
Apr. 17, 1903	KC	John G. "Bud" Taylor	28	white	male	Yes	murder	Ruth Noland	18		female[12]
July 30, 1909	KC	Claude Brooks	22	black	male	Yes	murder	Sidney Herndon	46	white	male[13]
Feb. 8, 1910	KC	John Williams		black	male	No	rape	Mrs. W. H. Jackson	24	white	female[14]
Feb. 8, 1910	KC	George Reynolds	24	black	male	No	rape	Mrs. W. H. Jackson	24	white	female[15]
June 10, 1910	KC	Robert W. Davis	24	black	male	Yes	murder	Harry Evans	17	black	male[16]
Feb. 15, 1915	KC	Wesley Robinson		black	male	Yes	murder	wife Mary Robinson & step-daughter Alma Felton, 11		black	female[17]

Between June 1917 and October 1919, the extreme penalty was life sentence in the state penitentiary.
On October 6, 1919, the death penalty by hanging for capital crimes
(murder, rape, treason, train robbery, kidnapping, and perjury) was re-instituted.

Hanged	Where	Convict	Age	Race	Gender	Appeal	Crime	Victim	Age	Race	Gender
Aug. 17, 1921	KC	Walker Lee	38	black	male	Yes	rape	Mrs. Elizabeth Dahm 73; white; female[18]			
July 25, 1930	KC	Antonio "Tony" "Lollypop" Mangiaracina, Jr.	30	white	male	Yes	murder	James Horace Smith, KCPD 38; male; white[19]			
July 25, 1930	KC	John Messino	29	white	male	Yes	murder	James Horace Smith, KCPD 38; male; white[20]			
July 25, 1930	KC	Carl Nasello	22	white	male	Yes	murder	James Horace Smith, KCPD 38; male; white[21]			
Jan. 15, 1932	KC	Joe Hershon, parolee	26	white	male	Yes	murder	Charles Dingman, KCPD male; white[22]			

[1] Henry Garster was the first *legal* hanging in Jackson County, Missouri. According to Garster's Will, he left his third wife, Ann, and their children, John, Henry and Mary Ann; plus three children from his second marriage, Solomon, Elizabeth and Sarah. Finding records about Garster's widow and surviving children has proved impossible, perhaps because of misinterpretations in the spelling of the pronounced surname. The German derived Gaerster (sometimes Kaerster) has evolved into Gerster, Gaster, Gester, and even Caster; and, as you can see in published accounts cited below, Henry Garster's surname was published years later as "Gastell," "Gaston," and even "Goster." For an in-depth study of this incident, consult William B. Bundschu's *Abuse and Murder on the Frontier: The Trials and Travels of Rebecca Hawkins, 1800-1860.* (Independence, Mo.: Little Blue Valley Publishing Co., 2003). "Day of Doom!" *Kansas City* (Mo.) *Times*, 2 Mar. 1878, 3. "The First Hanging," *Jackson Examiner*, 27 Oct 1905, 6. "That Reminds Me," *Jackson Examiner*, 17 Nov 1905. "Paid Costs of His Own Trial," *Kansas City* (Mo.) *Star,* 29 Dec. 1907, 9. A short account appeared in, "Went Happily to His Death," *Kansas City* (Mo.) *Star*, 28 Dec. 1898 (inaccurately named him as "Gastell"). Frazier, 20, 151-152 (although inaccurately named the perpetrator as "George Goster"). For yet another interpretation of Garster's name ("an old Dutchman named Gaston"), see "Grandfather an Abolitionist: Henry Bundschu Reviews History of Slavery: Jackson County Once Had 3, 944 Slaves," *Jackson County (Mo.) Historical Society JOURNAL*, 1970 (Winter), 13-14. Birdsall, 641. *Westport Historical Society Quarterly*, 1974 (June); *Missouri Historical Review*, 1955 (April), 49:3.

[2] Green's was the first public execution since 1839. He and Frank Miller shot and killed Henry H. Hughes, a deputy under Marshal James Liggett. Miller took a change of venue to Lexington, Lafayette County, Missouri, and was convicted and sentenced to be hanged; but, as Miller did not fire the fatal shot, Governor Phelps commuted his sentence to ten yeas in the penitentiary. Green was hanged on a scaffold built in the open air courtyard against the north wall of the old Jackson County Jail at 2nd and Main Streets in Kansas City, Missouri. Thousands of people stood on the hills north of the jail and saw the hanging. The crowd was so large that Marshal Liggett had to call out the Craig rifles and lined them along the bluff to keep the people from crowding each other over the bluff. Green was remarkably cool and made no speech on the scaffold. "Day of Doom!" *Kansas City* (Mo.) *Times*, 2 Mar. 1878, 3. "Bloody Deeds: The Evening Star Rehearses Jackson County's Murder Record," *Kansas City* (Mo.) *Evening Star,* 8 Aug. 1881. Hughes' death is also discussed in, "Awaiting Their Doom: The Batch of Murderers Confined in the Independence Jail," *Kansas City (Mo.) Star*, 6 Aug. 1886, 1; "Went Happily to His Death," *Kansas City* (Mo.) *Star*, 28 Dec. 1898; and, "In Kansas City Forty Years Ago," *Kansas City (Mo.) Star*, 4 Mar. 1918, 12, where it describes Green's coffin as black walnut with silver mountings…the place of burial is Hamburg, Ia., just opposite Nebraska City." Frazier, 62 (reports the hanging took place in Independence).

[3] Sneed killed Loomis on Southwest Boulevard. He was in jail when Green was hanged, and when Sneed's time came he sent for former Marshal James Liggett and said, "Jim, you made a great success of hanging Green, and I want you to sort of superintend my hanging." "The Penalty Paid: Edward Calhoun Sneed Hanged at Independence Soon after Noonday His Last Day," *Kansas City* (Mo.) *Star,* 24 June 1887, 1. "Went Happily to His Death," *Kansas City* (Mo.) *Star*, 28 Dec. 1898. Frazier, 229.

[4] Martin Reed was the 50+year old father of Jim Reed, who would be hanged for murder in 1899. Both were hanged in Kansas City."Martin Reed is Hanged: The Negro Murderer Pays the Law's Extreme Penalty: He Walked To the Scaffold Unaided…" *Kansas City* (Mo.) *Star*, 5 Jan. 1894. "Went Happily to His Death," *Kansas City* (Mo.) *Star*, 28 Dec. 1898. "A Woman Saw Reed Hanged: The First Instance of the Kind on Record in Jackson County," and "The Hanging of Jim Reed: He Died on the Same Scaffold That His Father Did," *Kansas City* (Mo.) *Star*, 30 Mar. 1899, 2. Frazier, 80.

[5] Clark and Jones were hanged on the same day; Jones in the 1859 Jackson County Jail at Independence; then, Clark in the Jackson County Jail in Kansas City. Madam Jane Wright was an elderly woman who kept an employment office at the Junction. Clark had been out of the Kansas penitentiary only a few weeks. Jones was a cook out of work and met Clark in a saloon where they planned to rob Madam Wright. They went into her office at dusk on 9 Sept. 1893, and strangled her to death. "Two Lives for One," *Kansas City* (Mo.) *Star*, 29 June 1894, 1. "Went Happily to His Death," *Kansas City* (Mo.) *Star*, 28 Dec. 1898. Frazier, 73.

[6] Clark and Jones were hanged on the same day; Jones in the 1859 Jackson County Jail at Independence; then, Clark in the Jackson County Jail in Kansas City. Madam Jane Wright was an elderly woman who kept an employment office at the Junction. Clark had been out of the Kansas penitentiary only a few weeks. Jones was a cook out of work and met Clark in a saloon where they planned to rob Madam Wright. They went into her office at dusk on 9 Sept. 1893, and strangled her to death. "John Clark to Hang June 14," *Kansas City* (Mo.) *Star*, 8 May 1894. "Two Lives for One," *Kansas City* (Mo.) *Star*, 29 June 1894, 1. "Went Happily to His Death," *Kansas City* (Mo.) *Star*, 28 Dec. 1898. Frazier, 73 (reported that it was "this city's first legal execution, but that doesn't compute; see execution of Martin Reed above).

[7] Martin's name had first appeared in the jail record book on 13 June 1890, when he was sentenced for 10 days for petty larceny. Then, on 10 Sept. 1890, he was sentenced to jail for burglary. "His aged saved him from the penitentiary then; he was only a boy." On 1 Sep. 1891, Martin was again sentenced for burglary; and on 16 Feb. 1893, another sentence. Then, on the night of 4 July 1893, Martin, who was then a bellboy at the Midland Hotel "and a negro companion named Lyle were walking together on East 18th Street near Harrison," when they passed Eli Stillwell, "who was intoxicated and jostled against them in passing. Angry words passed between the two negroes and Stillwell, who was a white man." Martin stabbed Stillwell in the heart. Before he was hanged he broke down and wept and shrieked and pleaded for a few more minutes to live. "A Stay of Life for Martin," *Kansas City* (Mo.) *Star*, 8 Dec. 1894. "May Hang Feb. 3," *Kansas City* (Mo.) *Star*, 22 Jan. 1894. "Philip Martin to Hang," *Kansas City* (Mo.) *Star*, 5 Nov. 1894. "Stolid with Death Near," *Kansas City*

(Mo.) *Star*, 12 Feb. 1895, 1. "Went Happily to His Death," *Kansas City* (Mo.) *Star*, 28 Dec. 1898. Frazier, 125.

[8] Brown shot Henry Prather, "another negro," on April 1, 1896, after the two quarreled at the home of Prather's love interest, Mrs. Ella Williams, who lived at 9th and Wyoming. Brown first shot Prather in the leg; but Brown's second shot pierced Prather's heart as he attempted to run away. Brown fled first to Argentine, then Hutchinson, Kansas before making it to Quincy, Illinois, where he fell in love with a woman. The woman, however, had a lover whom Brown had had arrested on a trivial charge. This man knew of Brown's killing Prather, and while in jail wrote Chief Hayes of the murderer's whereabouts. Brown was sentenced to be hanged on July 13, 1897, but received a stay of execution while the Missouri Supreme Court considered his case. That court affirmed the decision and set the hanging for December 13, 1898. Lieutenant Governor Bolte granted a respite until Governor Stephens, who was ill at Hot Springs, had a chance to consider the case. Stephens refused to interfere. "Went Happily to His Death," *Kansas City* (Mo.) *Star*, 28 Dec. 1898. Frazier, 232.

[9] After a Missouri Supreme Court decision, Reed was hanged on the same scaffold as his father. "Went Happily to His Death," *Kansas City* (Mo.) *Star*, 28 Dec. 1898. "A Woman Saw Reed Hanged: The First Instance of the Kind on Record in Jackson County," and "The Hanging of Jim Reed: He Died on the Same Scaffold That His Father Did," *Kansas City* (Mo.) *Star*, 30 Mar. 1899, 2. Frazier, 80, 125-126.

[10] "This Negro Must Hang," *Kansas City* (Mo.) *Star*, 4 Jan. 1902. "Reading His Bible Now," *Kansas City* (Mo.) *Star*, 9 Jan. 1902. "The Case of Albert Garth," *Kansas City* (Mo.) *Star*, 16 Jan. 1902, 4. "The Governor Again Refuses…" *Kansas City* (Mo.) *Star*, 19 Jan. 1902. "From Cell to Scaffold…" *Kansas City* (Mo.) *Star*, 25 Jan. 1902.

[11] "Murder in the First Degree," *Kansas City* (Mo.) *Star*, 17 Apr. 1901; "By the Neck Until Dead," *Kansas City* (Mo.) *Star, 3 Jul 1901;* "Religion His only Staff," *Kansas City* (Mo.) *Star*, 8 April 1902. Frazier, 233.

[12] "Bud Taylor Case Tuesday," *Kansas City* (Mo.) *Star*, 12 Oct. 1902. Frazier, 84.

[13] "Ready to Hang Brooks," *Kansas City* (Mo.) *Star*, 28 June 1909, 4. "A Slayer Pays the Penalty," *Kansas City* (Mo.) *Star*, 30 July 1909, 1. Frazier, 89.

[14] "Is the Confession a Ruse?" *Kansas City* (Mo.) *Star*, 18 Jan. 1910. "The Marshal Will Officiate," *Kansas City* (Mo.) *Star*, 19 Jan. 1910, 2. Also, "Negroes to Die Next Tuesday," *Kansas City* (Mo.) *Star*, 1 Feb. 1910. Oddly, "Mrs. J. H. [Blanche D.] Williams, the wife of John H. Williams, the negro officer who arrested the assailants of Mrs. W. H. Jackson, died last night at her home," *Kansas City* (Mo.) *Star*, 30 Jan. 1910, 7. Also, her Missouri Death Certificate Number 601. Frazier, 137-139.

[15] "Is the Confession a Ruse?" *Kansas City* (Mo.) *Star*, 18 Jan. 1910. "The Marshal Will Officiate," *Kansas City* (Mo.) *Star*, 19 Jan. 1910, 2. Also, "Negroes to Die Next Tuesday," *Kansas City* (Mo.) *Star*, 1 Feb. 1910. Reynolds was buried in Highland Cemetery. Missouri Death Certificate Number 1921. Frazier, 137-139.

[16] Davis, a quarry worker, was convicted of brutally and grotesquely "slaying…a crippled benefactor," Harry Evans, "another negro." Davis was buried in Highland Cemetery. "A Slayer Pays the Penalty," *Kansas City* (Mo.) *Star*, 30 Jul. 1909. "Davis to the Death Cell," *Kansas City* (Mo.) *Star*, 4 June 1910. "Ghosts in the Death Cell?" *Kansas City* (Mo.) *Star*, 7 June 1910. Missouri Death Certificate Number 16625. Frazier, 89.

[17] "Robinson to Die Feb. 15," *Kansas City* (Mo.) *Star*, 4 Jan. 1915. "Negro to Death Cell," *Kansas City* (Mo.) *Star*, 9 Feb. 1915. "Hanging Up to the Public," *Kansas City* (Mo.) *Star*, 10 Feb. 1915. "Negro's Fate is Sealed," *Kansas City* (Mo.) *Star*, 11 Feb. 1915. "Little Hope for Negro," *Kansas City* (Mo.) *Star*, 12 Feb. 1915. "Awaits the Noose Calmly," *Kansas City* (Mo.) *Star*, 13 Feb. 1915. "Negro Pays Life Penalty," *Kansas City* (Mo.) *Star*, 15 Feb. 1915. Also, "Death Penalty in Today," *Kansas City* (Mo.) *Star*, 6 Oct. 1919. Also, Frazier, 89-90.

[18] Lee, a section hand on the railroad near the Independence, Missouri, entered the home of widow Elizabeth (Mrs. Barney) Dahm, and brutally attacked her; she later died 13 Mar. 1921; Missouri Death Certificate Number 6657. Dahm was listed in the 1910 U.S. Census for Kansas City, Jackson County, Missouri. At that time she was 63. Her husband was 61, and they had been married for 35 years. Three of their four children were living with them: Mary M., 32; Philip A., 28; and, Louis L., 26. Lee was hanged at Kansas City and removed and buried in Maple Hill Cemetery, likely in Glasgow, Missouri, where he was from; Missouri Death Certificate 20658. "Negro's Hanging Date Soon," *Kansas City* (Mo.) *Star*, 13 June 1921; "Negro Pleads to Escape Noose," *Kansas City* (Mo.) *Star, 26 Jul. 1921;* "Walker Lee Must Hang," *Kansas City* (Mo.) *Star* , 30 July 1921; "Walker Lee to Death Cell," *Kansas City* (Mo.) *Star* , 8 Aug. 1921; "See Tickets for Hanging," *Kansas City* (Mo.) *Star,* 14 Aug. 1921, 10; "He Sang on the Gallows," *Kansas City* (Mo.) *Star, 17 Aug. 1921, 2. Frazier, 139.

[19] The 30-year-old was hanged in Kansas City and laid to rest in St. Mary's Cemetery, Kansas City, Missouri. Missouri Death Certificate Numbers 20749 and 23092. Smith was a traffic police officer who left behind his wife Velma Gossett Smith. Frazier, 97-99.

[20] Missouri Death Certificate Numbers 20749 and 23104. Smith was a traffic police officer who left behind his wife Velma Gossett Smith. Frazier, 97-99.

[21] Missouri Death Certificate Numbers 20749 and 23095. Smith was a traffic police officer who left behind his wife Velma Gossett Smith. Frazier, 97-99.

[22] The 26-year-old Russian immigrant was hanged in Kansas City and buried in Mt. Carmel Cemetery. Missouri Death Certificate Number 1113. Frazier, 99 (who documents Hershon as the only known Jew ever executed in Missouri).

APPENDIX

C

UNITED STATES MARSHALS, 1813-PRESENT SERVING JACKSON COUNTY AREA (WESTERN DISTRICT, WESTERN DIVISION OF MISSOURI)

The Territory of Missouri was created on March 3, 1805. The District of Missouri was created on March 16, 1822. The District was divided into Eastern and Western Districts in 1857. The following is a listing of former United States Marshals for the Western District of Missouri.
(Reprinted with courtesy from http://www.usmarshals.gov/district/mo-w/general/history.htm)

NAME	DATE	VICE
TERRITORY OF MISSOURI		
Henry Dodge	July 27, 1813 (S)	Original Appointment
Alexander McNair	April 13, 1813 (S)	Dodge (Resigned)
Henry Dodge	February 9, 1817 (S)	McNair (Resigned)
DISTRICT OF MISSOURI		
Henry Dodge	April 25, 1822 (S) December 22, 1825 (S)	Himself as Marshal of the Territory of Missouri
John Simonds, Jr.	May 21, 1827 (R) December 27, 1827 (S)	Dodge (Resigned)
Augustus Jones	August 14, 1829 (R) March 18, 1830 (S) March 6, 1834 (S)	Simonds (Removed)
James H. Relfe	October 18, 1836 (R) March 2, 1837 (S) February 17, 1841(S)	Jones (No reason given)
William H. Russell	April 13, 1841 (R) July 22, 1841 (S)	Relfe (Removed)
Weston F. Birch	March 29, 1843 (R)	Russell (Removed)
Robert C. Ewing	September 4, 1844 (R) January 15, 1845 (S) January 8, 1849 (S)	Birch (Rejected by Senate) Anderson (Decline)
John W. Twitchell	April 25, 1850 (S)	

Hiram H. Baber	September 27, 1852 (R) December 28, 1852 (S)	Twitchell (Deceased)
Thomas S. Bryant	August 13, 1853 (R) March 14, 1854 (S)	Baber (Removed)
WESTERN DISTRICT OF MISSOURI		
James L. Jones	March 3, 1857 (S)	Original Appointment
James O. Sitton	June 1, 1861 (R) July 22, 1861 (S)	Jones (Removed)
Thomas B. Wallace	February 17, 1862 (S)	Sitton (Resigned)
Smith O. Scofield	March 10, 1865 (S)	
Thomas B. Wallace	March 1, 1867 (S)	
George Smith	April 15, 1869 (S) March 20, 1873 (S)	Wallace (Removed)
Charles C. Allen	November 20, 1877 (S) March 15, 1882 (S)	Smith (Term Expired)
Joseph H. McGee	March 9, 1883 (R) January 21, 1884 (S)	Allen (Resigned)
Elijah Gates	November 24, 1885 (R) August 2, 1886 (S)	McGee (Suspended)
John P. Tracey	February 4, 1890 S)	Gates (Removed)
Joseph Orville "Jo" Shelby	February 21, 1894 (S)	Tracey (Term Expired)
Giles Y. Crenshaw	March 1, 1897 (S)	Shelby (Deceased)
Edwin R. Durham	April 19, 1898 (S) May 27, 1902 (S) June 28, 1906 (C)	Crenshaw (Resigned)
Albert J. Martin	September 29, 1910 (R) December 13, 1910 (C)	Durham (Term Expired)
Henry C. Miller	February 18, 1914 (C.A.)	Martin (Resigned)
William A. Shelton	March 10, 1915 (R) May 10, 1916 (C)	Miller (C.A.)
I. K. Parshall	November 22, 1921 (C)	Shelton (Term Expired)
Asa W. Butler	May 17, 1926 (C) July 3, 1930 (C)	Parshall (Term Expired)
Henry L. Dillingham	March 1, 1934 (C) August 3, 1939 (C)	Butler (Resigned)
Fred A. Canfil	January 17, 1944 (C)	Dillingham (Term Expired)
William B. Tatman	April 1, 1953 (C.A.)	Canfil (Deceased)
John B. Dennis	June 10, 1954 (C) May 27, 1959 (C)	Tatman (C.A.)
Francis M. Wilson	April 14, 1961 (C) May 22, 1965 (C)	Dennis (Term Expired)
John T. Pierpont	February 6, 1970 (C) May 14, 1974 (C)	Wilson (Term Expired)
Emmett W. Fairfax	June 30, 1977 (C)	Fairfax (Term Expired)
Lee Koury	December 9, 1981 (C) March 10, 1986 (C)	Koury (Term Expired)
Larry J. Joiner	May 14, 1991 (C)	Joiner (Resigned)
Robert Bradford English	October 11, 1994 (C)	
C. Mauri Sheer	May 5, 2002	English

APPENDIX

D

PROVOST MARSHALS OF THE CIVIL WAR ERA

HISTORY OF THE PROVOST MARSHAL

On July 18, 1861, Union General Irvin McDowell issued General Order No. 18, defining the authority of the provost marshal in the Army of Northeast Virginia, as the troops moved southward on campaign. In 1862, General George B. McClellan assumed command of the newly formed Division of the Potomac, which included the departments of Northeast Virginia and Washington. He issued the first orders describing the duties of provost marshals within a field army during the Civil War. For the duration of the war, each division, brigade, and corps of the Union Army included a provost marshal. Guards were assigned to the provost marshal to assist in carrying out assigned functions, chief of which was preservation of order.

In September 1862, the federal Adjutant General's office issued General Order No. 140, appointing special provost marshals for each state. The special provost marshal had many responsibilities, which included investigating charges or acts of treason and arresting deserters, spies, and persons deemed disloyal. A reorganization of the War Department in 1863 eliminated the position of special provost marshal, but appointed an assistant provost marshal general (APMG) for each state, a provost marshal for each congressional district and a deputy provost marshal for each county. The duties remained much the same. In addition, the provost marshal assigned to the district was responsible for maintaining troop discipline, assuming custody of prisoners and deserters, administering punishment, and suppressing any depredations and disturbances caused by Army troops or individual soldiers.

These provost marshals were assigned regardless of the level of active warfare within a state or district. In districts with active fighting, the provost marshal's primary duty was to limit marauding against citizens, prevent stragglers on long marches, and generally suppress gambling or other vices not conducive to good order and discipline. However, in many districts, the war's fighting was somewhat removed and the area did not see battles. In these areas, the provost marshal's duties were more magisterial. The provost marshal had the power to administer and enforce the law when it came to regulating public places; conduct searches, seizures, and arrests; issue passes to citizens for movement in and out of Union lines; and record and investigate citizen complaints. It was not uncommon for the law to be suspended in many cases and for the provost marshal, mostly independent of any real supervision, to dispense with the rules of civil procedure.

RECORDS OF THE PROVOST MARSHAL

The Provost Marshal Papers for the state of Missouri are part of Record Group 109, War Department Collection of Confederate Records in the National Archives and Records Administration (NARA). Although they are records of the Union Army, they were associated with Confederate records in the War Department because they relate, in part, to Confederate citizens and sympathizers. This collection is divided into two series: 1) *Union Provost Marshals' File of Papers Relating to Individual Citizens* (on 300 rolls of microfilm), and 2) *Union Provost Marshals' File of Papers Relating to Two or More Civilians* (on 94 rolls of microfilm).

The series was assembled in the War Department from documents that were extracted from the files of the Union Army provost marshals and from other records of Army territorial commands. The documents here reproduced relate to civilians, or "citizens," as they were called during the Civil War, who came in contact with the Army. They included correspondence, provost court papers, lists of prisoners, orders, passes, paroles, oaths of allegiance, transportation permits, and claims for compensation for property used or destroyed by military forces.

The microfilm collection contains thousands of pages of documents detailing the way the provost marshal affected the lives of Missouri citizens who came into contact with the Union Army. The office of provost marshal generated much paperwork which offers a unique look at a state divided in loyalty and beliefs, and the war society that resulted. Far from being solely a resource for military research, the provost marshal papers provide information about the role of women during the war, its effect on Missouri's slavery institution, and the difficulties experienced by war refugees.

The documents on film include correspondence, provost marshal court papers, orders, passes, paroles, oaths of allegiance to the United States, transportation permits, and claims for compensation for property used or destroyed by military forces. Charges could be initiated by anyone, civilian or military. Statements by accusers or witnesses were taken down as evidence; citizens could be arrested, however, simply on suspicion.

An online database created by the Missouri State Archives (link below) is an index of the Missouri portion of the collection.

PROVOST MARSHAL DATABASE INDEX PROJECT
http://www.sos.mo.gov/archives/provost

The Missouri State Archives database index began in 2000. Volunteers and student interns extracted discrete information, such as name and subject matter, from a review of microfilm with the goal of creating a finding aid for the Missouri portion of the document collection. The database contains nearly 67,000 searchable entries relating to Missouri. In addition to the index, digital images of the documents in the Two or More Civilians series are available online, except for 10 rolls containing prisoner lists. Records of the much larger Individual Citizens series are being digitized and will be placed online as they become available. This represents a virtually unknown manuscript collection detailing the national experience in the trans-Mississippi West.

USING THE PROVOST MARSHAL DATABASE INDEX

The database index can be searched by name, county, and subject. Place names and dates were not readily identifiable for a small percentage of the county, city, and date fields. The results that are returned from the search are:

- name (be alert to alternate spellings of proper names)
- subject (subjective main topic phrase assigned by indexer)
- county (name of Missouri county)
- city (name of Missouri town/city)
- date
- reel number (State Archives microfilm reel number)

Please note this database is simply an index to assist researchers in locating information found in the original microfilmed records. The database index provides a microfilm reel number(s) where researchers can locate the original record.

MORE ABOUT RECORD GROUP 109

Publications and pamphlets on Microfilm Publications in the National Archives Library (Civil War-Era) for **Record Group 109** (War Department Collection of Confederate Records). *Note:* A pamphlet date indicates reference to a microfilm publication/pamphlets in the Archives Library Information Center libraries. The library call number is CD 3027. M5 N3 (plus the pamphlet number).

For the complete federal description of the collection, see the National Archives Microfilm Publications, Pamphlet Accompanying Microcopy Nos. 345 and 416. Other series of specific relation to Missouri are **bolded**, *italicized,* and underlined.

TITLE	MICROFILM/ PAMPHLET NO.	PAMPHLET DATE	PAGES OR #ROLLS/FICHE
Morning Reports, 3rd Regiment of Mississippi Volunteers, Nov 14, 1861-June 3, 1862 and of Company H, 7th Mississippi Volunteers, Oct 1861-May 1864.	A 39		1
Registers of Applications for Appointment of Brigadier Generals and for Regimental Promotions, 1863-1865.	A 47		1
Letters sent by Lt. Col. G.H. Hill Commander of the Confederate Ordnance Works at Tyler, Texas 1864-1865	M 119	1973	1
Index to Compiled Service Records of Confederate Soldiers who Served in Organizations From the State of Florida	M225		9
Index to Compiled Service Records of Confederate Soldiers Who Served in Organizations From the State of Georgia	M 226		67
Index to Compiled Service Records of Confederate Soldiers Who Served in Organizations From the State of Texas	M 227		41
Index to Compiled Service Records of Confederate Soldiers Who Served in Organizations From the State of North Carolina	M 230		43
Index to Compiled Service Records of Confederate Soldiers Who Served in Organizations From the State of Tennessee	M 231		48
Index to Compiled Service Records of Confederate Soldiers Who Served in Organizations From the State of Mississippi	M 232		45
Compiled Service Records of Confederate Soldiers Who Served in Organizations From the State of Florida	M 251		104
Consolidated Index to Compiled Service Records of Confederate Soldiers (1-200)	M 253A		200
Consolidated Index to Compiled Service Records of Confederate Soldiers (201-400)	M 253B		200
Consolidated Index to Compiled Service Records of Confederate Soldiers (401-453)	M 253C		135
Compiled Service Records of Confederate Soldiers Who Served in Organizations Raised Directly by the Confederate Government	M 258		123
Records Relating to Confederate Naval and Marine Personnel	M 260		7
Compiled Service Records of Confederate Soldiers Who Served in Organizations From the State of Georgia	M 266 A through C		607
Compiled Service Records of Confederate Soldiers Who Served in Organizations From the State of South Carolina	M 267 A through B		392
Compiled Service Records of Confederate Soldiers Who Served in Organizations From the State of Tennessee	M 268 A through B		359
Compiled Service Records of Confederate Soldiers Who Served in Organizations From the State of Mississippi	M 269 A through C		427
Compiled Service Records of Confederate Soldiers Who Served in Organizations From the State of North Carolina	M 270 A through C		580
Compiled Service Records of Confederate Soldiers Who Served in Organizations From the State of Alabama	M 311 A through C		508
Compiled Service Records of Confederate Soldiers Who Served in Organizations From the State of Arkansas	M317 A through B		275
Compiled Service Records of Confederate Soldiers Who Served in Organizations From the State of Arizona	M318		1
Compiled Service Records of Confederate Soldiers Who Served in Organizations From the State of Kentucky	M319		136
Compiled Service Records of Confederate Soldiers Who Served in Organizations From the State of Louisiana	M 320 A through C		414
Compiled Service Records of Confederate Soldiers Who Served in Organizations From the State of Maryland	M321		22
Compiled Service Records of Confederate Soldiers Who Served in Organizations From the State of Missouri	***M322***		***193***
Compiled Service Records of Confederate Soldiers Who Served in Organizations From the State of Texas	M323 A through C		445
Compiled Service Records of Confederate Soldiers Who Served in Organizations From the State of Virginia	M 324A through F		1075
Compiled Service Records of Confederate General and Staff Officers, and Non-Regimental Enlisted Men	M 331 A through B		275

TITLE	MICROFILM/ PAMPHLET NO.	PAMPHLET DATE	PAGES OR #ROLLS/FICHE
Union Provost Marshal's File of Papers Relating to Individual Civilians (Rolls 1-200)	_M 345 A_		_100_
Union Provost Marshal's File of Papers Relating to Individual Civilians (Rolls 201-300)	_M 345 B_		_100_
Confederate Papers Relating to Citizens or Business Firms	M 346 A through F	1982	1158
Unfiled Papers and Slips Belonging in Confederate Compiled Service Records	M 347 A through C		442
Records of the Louisiana State Government, 1850-88, in the War Department Collection of Confederate Records	M 359	1962	24
Index to Compiled Service Records of Confederate Soldiers Who Served in Organizations From Alabama	M 374		49
Index to Compiled Service Records of Confederate Soldiers Who Served in Organizations From Arizona	M 375		1
Index to Compiled Service Records of Confederate Soldiers Who Served in Organizations From Arkansas	M 376		26
Index to Compiled Service Records of Confederate Soldiers Who Served in Organizations From Kentucky	M 377		14
Index to Compiled Service Records of Confederate Soldiers Who Served in Organizations From Louisiana	M 378		31
Index to Compiled Service Records of Confederate Soldiers Who Served in Organizations From Maryland	M 379		2
Index to Compiled Service Records of Confederate Soldiers Who Served in Organizations From Missouri	_M 380_		_16_
Index to Compiled Service Records of Confederate Soldiers Who Served in Organizations From South Carolina	M 381		35
Index to Compiled Service Records of Confederate Soldiers Who Served Organizations From Virginia	M 382		62
Index to letters Received by the Confederate Secretary of War 1861-65	M 409	1962	34
Index to letters Received by the Confederate Adjutant and Inspector General and the Confederate Quartermaster General 1861-1865	M 410	1962	41
Union Provost Marshals' File of Papers Relating to Two or More Civilians	_M 416_	_1969_	_94_
Letters received by the Confederate Secretary of War 1861-1865	M 437	1965	151
Letters received by the Confederate Quartermaster General	M 469	1963	14
Letters received by the Confederate Adjutant and Inspector General 1861-1865	M 474	1964	164
Letters sent by the Confederate Secretary of War 1861-1865	M 522	1964	10
Telegrams sent by the Confederate Secretary of War to the President 1861-1865	M 523	1964	2
Telegrams sent by the Confederate Secretary of War 1861-1865	M 524	1964	1
Selected records of the War Department Relating to Confederate Prisoners of War 1861-1865	M 598	1966	145
Telegrams received by the Confederate Secretary of War 1861-65	M 618	1966	19
Letters and telegrams sent by the Confederate Adjutant and Inspector General 1861-1865	M 627	1965	6
Letters and telegrams sent by the Engineer Bureau of the Confederate War Department, 1861-1864	M 628	1965	5
Index to Compiled Service Records of Confederate Soldiers Who Served in Organizations Raised Directly by the Confederate Government and of Confederate Officers and Non-Regimental Enlisted Men	M 818		26
Confederate States Army Causalities: Lists and Narrative Reports 1861-1865	M 836	1971	7
Compiled Records Showing Service of Military Units in Confederate Organizations	M 861		74
Letters and telegrams sent by the Confederate Quartermaster General 1861-1865	M 900	1976	8

TITLE	MICROFILM/ PAMPHLET NO.	PAMPHLET DATE	PAGES OR #ROLLS/FICHE
General orders and circulars of the Confederate War Department 1861-1865	M 901	1975	3
Papers Pertaining to Vessels of or Involved With the Confederate States of America: 'Vessel Papers'	M 909		32
Orders and circulars issued by the Army of the Potomac and the Army and Department of Northern Virginia C.S.A. 1861-1865	M 921	1974	4
Inspection Reports and Related Records Received by the Inspection Branch in the Confederate Adjutant and Inspector General's Office	M 935		18
Records of the Virginia Forces 1861	M 998	1976	7
Muster Rolls and Lists of Confederate Troops Paroled in North Carolina	M 1781		7
Lists of Confederates Captured at Vicksburg, Mississippi, July 4, 1863	M 2072		1
Reference File Relating to Confederate Organizations from Georgia	T 455		1
Reference File Relating to Confederate Medical Officers	T 456		3
Copies of Letters and Telegrams Received and Sent by Governor Zebulon B. Vance of North Carolina, 1862-1865	T 731		1
Correspondence and Reports of the Confederate Treasury Department, 1861-1865	T 1025		2

APPENDIX

E

ROGUES' GALLERY - MUG SHOTS FROM THE 1859 JACKSON COUNTY JAIL

These images…mug shots…were presumably taken by the jailor or other deputy at the 1859 Jackson County Jail. From dates of articles relating to these individuals, the photographs date from 1896-1898. James Bruce Ross was Jailor through December 1896 and Joseph W. Potts assumed the duty on January 1, 1897 and served through December 1898.

Each 2.5" x 4.5" card has the image glued to the front. Stamped on the back are the following categories, most of which were never completed: [Inmate] Number; Name; Alias; Color; Height; Eyes; Hair; Weight; marks; Nativity; Shoe; Comp[lexion]; Teeth; Beard; Remarks.

All 28 cards are identified, except two. All but one are represented here; one of two unidentified cards is too faint to procure a reproduction. These were an anonymous donation to the Jackson County Historical Society's collections. Three additional "mug shots" presented here (J, L & R) were *not* part of this donation; the authors found reproductions on exhibit at the 1859 Jail, Marshal's Home and Museum; the location of the originals is unknown.

In some cases the background matter reveal interesting details such as the limestone blocks and grated windows of the 1859 Jackson County Jail. Others show outbuildings (livery; woodshed) that were, at that time, in the yard behind (to the east of) the Jail proper. One image reveals minute details of the 1887 County Courthouse and Independence Square.

The authors located newspaper articles for eight of these alleged perpetrators held in the County Jail awaiting trial, or sentenced convicts serving time.

 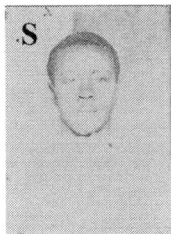  

 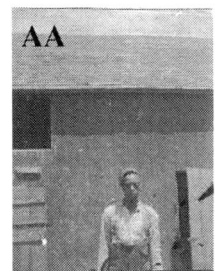

APPENDIX E - ROGUES' GALLERY

	NUMBER	NAME	ALIAS	COLOR	HEIGHT	EYES	HAIR	WEIGHT	MARKS
A	145	Arden, Frank		White	5' 3.5"	Blue	Black	130	Last finger on right hand broken
B	433	Allen, C. J.	Clark, George	White	5' 6.5"	Pale Blue	Dark Brown; little Gray	160-170	
C	146	Avery, Charles[1]	Smith, Charles Sinclair, Harry	White	5' 4"	Brown	Light	145	
D		Bennett, James[2]		Black		Black	Black	160-170	
E	126	Boyd, Phillipp		Black	5' 7.75"	Black	Black	160	
F	142	Brockway, Joseph		White	5' 9"	Black	Black	160	
G		Douglas, William		Black	5' 7.75"	Black	Black	160	
H	183	Edmonson, Jack		White	5' 5.25"	Black	Light; sandy	140-150	Scar on nose
I		Field, John		Black		Black	Black		
J		Franklin, James[3]		White					
K	184	Gilliam, Bart		White	5' 7.25"	Blue	Dark	165-175	
L		Hayns, Alix "Munk"[4]		Black					
M	147	Hutchens, Seymore		White	5' 7"				
N		Israel, Bert		Black	5' 6"	Black	Black	160	
O		Jenkins, Rose							
P	174	Lawson, Ed		Black	5' 6"	Black	Black	150	
Q	144	Lobb, Alex		Black	5' 4.25"	Black	Black	160	
R		Lonager, John[5]		White					
S	258	Mabry, Thomas[6]		Black	5' 5"	Black	Black	150	
T		Mathiews, Albert		Black	5' 11.75"	Black	Black	170-180	Dimple in chin
U	216	McFadden, Lon		White	6' 1"	Brown	Black	170-180	
V	439	Moore, Bert[7]		Yellow	5' 6"	Black	Black	150-160	
W	71	Moore, Roy[8]		Black	5' 7.25"	Black	Black	165-170	Bullet scar near navel on right side
X		Smith, Richard		Black					
Y	132	Sullivan, Claud		Yellow		Brown	Blackish yellow	130	
Z	67	Webb, James	French, James	White	5' 11.25"	Brown	Dark Brown	170	
AA	127	Williams, William[9]		Black	5' 7.25"	Black	Black	150	
BB	255	Wright, Arthur[10]		White	5' 6"	Blue	Dark Brown	160	
CC	256	Wright, Harry		White	5' 6"	Black	Black	150	

	NATIVITY	SHOE	COMP	TEETH	BEARD	REMARKS	AGE
A		#7	Dark	Regular	Small; dark	Arrested for burglary	24
B		#7	Sandy	Upper good; 3 lower out in center	Mustache heavy		
C		#6	Fair	Regular	Light	Arrested for burglary & larceny	23
D	Canada	#8	Good; light	Good	Light	5 years for assault	
E	Illinois	#9		Regular	Medium	Petit larceny	20
F	New York	#9	Dark	Regular	Dark	Supposed to be crazy at times	24
G	Missouri	#9	Black	Regular		Assault	
H	Kentucky	#7	Fair	Regular	Medium weight	All round crook was running picture wagon	34
I						Rape	
J							
K	Indiana	#9	Dark	Regular		Drunkard and a black smith	26
L							
M							20
N	Missouri	#9	Black	Regular	Medium	Arrested generally for disturbing the peace	21
O							
P	Missouri	#8	Black	Regular	Thin	All around crook; good talker	21
Q	Missouri	#8		Regular	Medium	General crook	44
R	Missouri	#7	Rather light	Good	Very little	Murder first degree	24
S							
T		#10	Black	Regular		Burglary and larceny	23
U	Missouri	#9	Dark	Regular		Served one term in Jefferson City for horse stealing	27
V	Missouri	#9		Good	Light	All around crook	18-20
W		#9		Regular	Medium	All around crook	23
X							
Y	Missouri	#8		Regular		Arrested for burglary and larceny	18
Z	New York	#8	Dark	Regular	Dark	Assault	34
AA	Missouri	#9		Regular	Thick	Arrested for assault	19
BB	Missouri	#5	Fair	Regular	No	Murder in first degree	20
CC	Missouri	#7	Dark	Good	Very little	Murder in first degree	22

[1] "Wants to Marry in Jail," *Kansas City* (Mo.) *Star*, 17 June 1896: *Miss Sylvia V. West and her mother went to the county jail today and asked permission to marry Charles Avery, who is serving a six months sentence for stealing, and will be released in October. The marshal advised miss West, who was young and unsophisticated looking, to wait till Avery got out. "No, sir," she said," we were engaged before he was arrested, and this was the day set for our marriage. I would keep my promise if he was sentenced to be hanged." The marshal told her to bring a license and a minister and she could marry Avery.* "Romances in Jail Life," *Kansas City* (Mo.) *Star*, 21 June 1896: *It developed yesterday that Avery had promised to marry Fanny Battle, and that he had written letters regularly to her since he has been in jail. Fanny called at the marshal's office yesterday afternoon and left a package which she wished delivered to Avery. One standing rule of the marshal's is to examine everything sent in to prisoner, and as soon as Miss Fanny had gone he opened the parcel she had left. It contained a large book of sermons and scriptural lessons, profusely illustrated. It was named, "Light on Life's Highway." On the fly leaf was written, "Charle Averry, from Fanny Battle, in the year 1896." On the next leaf was written in lead pencil: "Charle look at his book and see what Crist had to say a bought forgiving one another. Now I hope you will forgive me and try me once more in life." Besides the book there was a large package of fervent love letters which Avery had written her from the jail. They were tied in awide strip of black crape. Pinned to the crape was a letter from Miss Fanny. It began: "My Averry Deer Cur, I guess the fontain springs of love for me in your hart has run dry Charle." Fanny went on to say that she had read of his marriage, asked him if he intended to 'rekognisss' his wife when he got out of jail. She returned him his letters and kisses, said that the crape on the letters was her heart, and ended her missive this way: "I will reform rite away from this day on if you will tak me bak, and if not I will mak myself a watter grave in the bottom of the Kansas City river. Your broking hartde girl." Miss Fanny Battle recently served a term of fifteen days in jail for disturbing the peace.* Jackson County marriage records show a marriage between Sylvia V. West and Harry Sinclair on 17 June 1896. The marriage ceremony was performed by Judge Guinotte in the office of the County Jail. Finally, "Avery Again in Trouble," *Kansas City* (Mo.) *Star*, 17 Nov. 1896: *Charles Avery, who was sent to the county jail a year ago for stealing brass from the railroad yards, and who, while in jail, was married to Miss Silvia West of Jasper County, Mo., was sentenced to 200 days in the workhouse today by Police Judge Gifford for stealing $28 worth of brasses from the Missouri Pacific freight yards. Avery steals brass while pretending to be a car inspector....*

[2] "Jail Prisoners Fight," *Kansas City* (Mo.) *Star*, 13 Mar. 1898: *In a fight in the county jail at Independence yesterday afternoon James Bennett, a negro, made a vicious assault with a knife of H. Clay Lewis, a white prisoner. Lewis was badly cut about the face. The fight was over a game of cards. Bennett would have finished a four months' sentence for petit larceny Monday. Now he will be held for assault with intent to kill.*

[3] A **reproduction** of the "mug shot" for James Franklin was found by the authors in a display at the 1859 Jail, Marshal's Home and Museum. At the time of this printing, the location of the original card is unknown. It was not part of the anonymous donation of other "mug shots" represented here.

[4] A **reproduction** of the "mug shot" for Alix "Munk" Hayns was found by the authors in a display at the 1859 Jail, Marshal's Home and Museum. At the time of this printing, the location of the original card is unknown. It was not part of the anonymous donation of other "mug shots" represented here.

[5] A **reproduction** of the "mug shot" for John Lonager was found by the authors in a display at the 1859 Jail, Marshal's Home and Museum. At the time of this printing, the location of the original card is unknown. It was not part of the anonymous donation of other "mug shots" represented here.

[6] "Grand Jury Makes a Report," *Kansas City* (Mo.) *Star*, 12 Dec. 1897; "How his 'Mammy' Took It," *Kansas City* (Mo.) *Star*, 12 Dec. 1897 (mentioning William Williams' cell adjoining Tom Mabry, *the negro murder who killed his sweetheart, brought in last night from Independence;*" and, "The Mabry Murder Trial," *Kansas City* (Mo.) *Star*, 4 Jan. 1899: *The trial of Thomas Mabry, negro, for the killing of Hattie Lawson, his negro sweetheart, at Independence, November 14, 1897, began in the criminal court today. The entire forenoon was consumed in the selection of the jury. T. A. J. Mastin, deputy prosecutor, and Prosecutor Reed, are conducting the case for the state, and Joseph McCoy is defending Mabry. The dead girl and three or four friends were talking together at midnight near the Independence electric light plant when Mabry walked up, grasped the girl and turned her around facing him. He said something to her in an undertone, that the others did nor hear, placed the revolver to her breast and fired. He claims the shooting was accidental. When he found he had killed the girl Mabry fell on her dead body and cried aloud. The trial will occupy all of tomorrow.*

[7] "County Board Grants Five Paroles," *Kansas City* (Mo.) *Star*, 27 Sep. 1919: *Bert Moore, sentenced to six months in the county jail for petit larceny*. Given the date, this news item was likely for a later crime, since most of the "mug shots" are for inmates dating 1896-1898.

[8] "Roy Moore's Tale Was False," *Kansas City* (Mo.) *Star*, 14 Mar. 1897: *Roy Moore, a notorious negro thief, was sent to jail for one year by Justice Krueger yesterday afternoon for stealing two rings from a couple of dusky beauties. When put on the stand Moore swore that he had not known either of the women fifteen minutes before they voluntarily gave him their rings. Justice Krueger looked him over, decided that he was not possessed of personal magnetism, and gave him twelve months in which to think over his deed.*

[9] "Murder is Not a Fine Art," *Kansas City* (Mo.) *Star*, 12 Dec. 1896: *Eight prisoners in the county jail are charged with murder in the first degree.... William Williams, a negro, who shot Lawrence Schueble because he shouted for Bryan*; "Railroaded to Death, He Says," *Kansas City* (Mo.) *Star*, 21 Nov. 1897: "I'm a negro without a cent, and they railroaded me through quick;" "To Save A Murderer's Life," *Kansas City* (Mo.) *Star*, 29 Nov. 1897: a lengthy article about Rev. Dr. Roberts of The Church of This World pleading for justice for William Williams; "How His 'Mammy' Took It," *Kansas City* (Mo.) *Star*, 12 Dec. 1897: a lengthy article about Williams' death sentence being commuted by Governor Stephens to fifty years in the penitentiary; and, an interview with and sketch of Williams' mother.

[10] "Wright Held for Murder," *Kansas City* (Mo.) *Star*, 9 Nov. 1897 and "Grand Jury Makes a Report," *Kansas City* (Mo.) *Star*, 10 Dec. 1897 charges against Arthur and Harry Wright for the murder of J. P. Hess, near Lee's Summit November 7; "Another Murder Case in Court," *Kansas City* (Mo.) *Star*, 14 Feb. 1898; "Its Close Most Dramatic," *Kansas City* (Mo.) *Star*, 20 Feb. 1898, giving accounts of the trial, including having a buggy in the courtroom; and, "The Wright Boys Go Free," *Kansas City* (Mo.) *Star*, 21 Feb. 1898.

APPENDIX F

1859 JACKSON COUNTY JAIL SITE - EVOLUTION
SANBORN FIRE INSURANCE MAP, AUGUST 1885

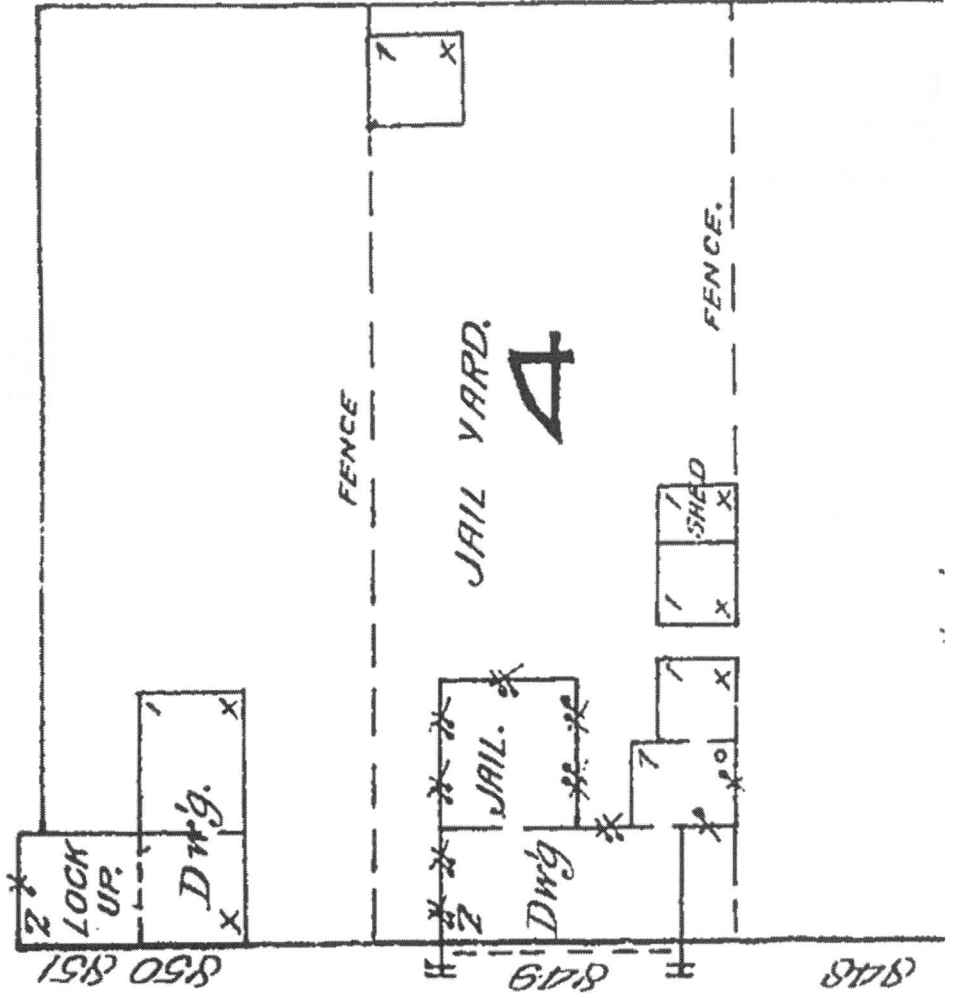

This shows the location along Main Street (at the corner of present-day Truman Road) where the 1841 Jackson County Jail structure remained in 1885 at this location, and was denoted as a Lock Up. The structure next to it was a dwelling (Dw'g).

This shows the location along Main Street (at the corner of present-day Truman Road) where the 1841 Jackson County Jail structure remained in 1885 at this location, and was denoted as a Lock Up. The structure next to it was a dwelling (Dw'g).

This shows the location along Main Street (at the corner of present-day Truman Road) where the 1841 Jackson County Jail structure remained in 1885 at this location, and was denoted as a Lock Up. The structure next to it was a dwelling (Dw'g).

1859 JACKSON COUNTY JAIL SITE - EVOLUTION
SANBORN FIRE INSURANCE MAP, DECEMBER 1892

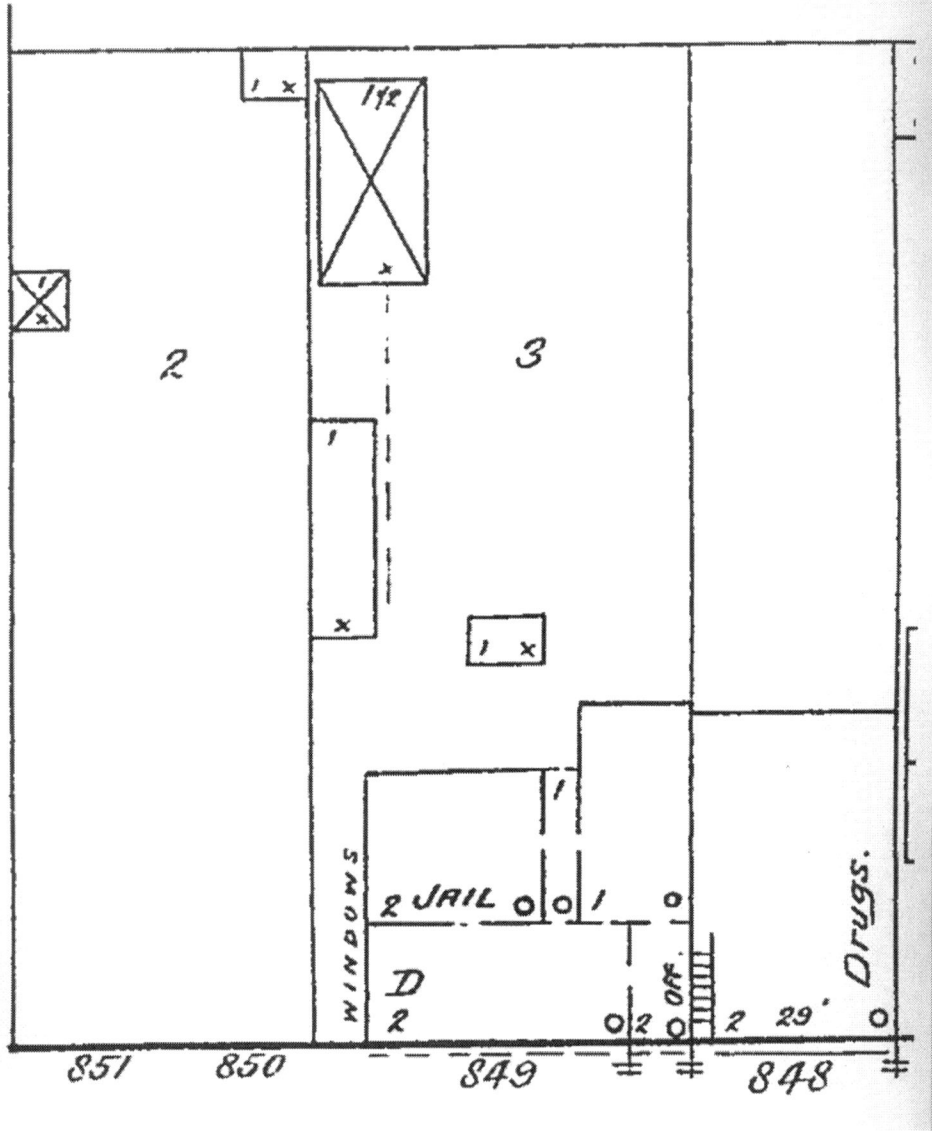

This shows the location along Main Street of the 1841 Jackson County Jail at or near the corner of Main Street and Truman Road. Oddly, it was not drawn on this map. See the next map, which shows it remained as of 1898.

This shows the location of the 1859 Jackson County Marshal's Home and Jail, with out-buildings. An enclosed office appears in the location of the present-day front courtyard.

The footprint of the present-day gift shop is not the same building as outlined here.

By 1892 a drugstore abutted the south side of the kitchen (present-day gift shop), where a south-facing window faces the ca 1892 brick wall.

1859 JACKSON COUNTY JAIL SITE - EVOLUTION

SANBORN FIRE INSURANCE MAP, SEPTEMBER 1898

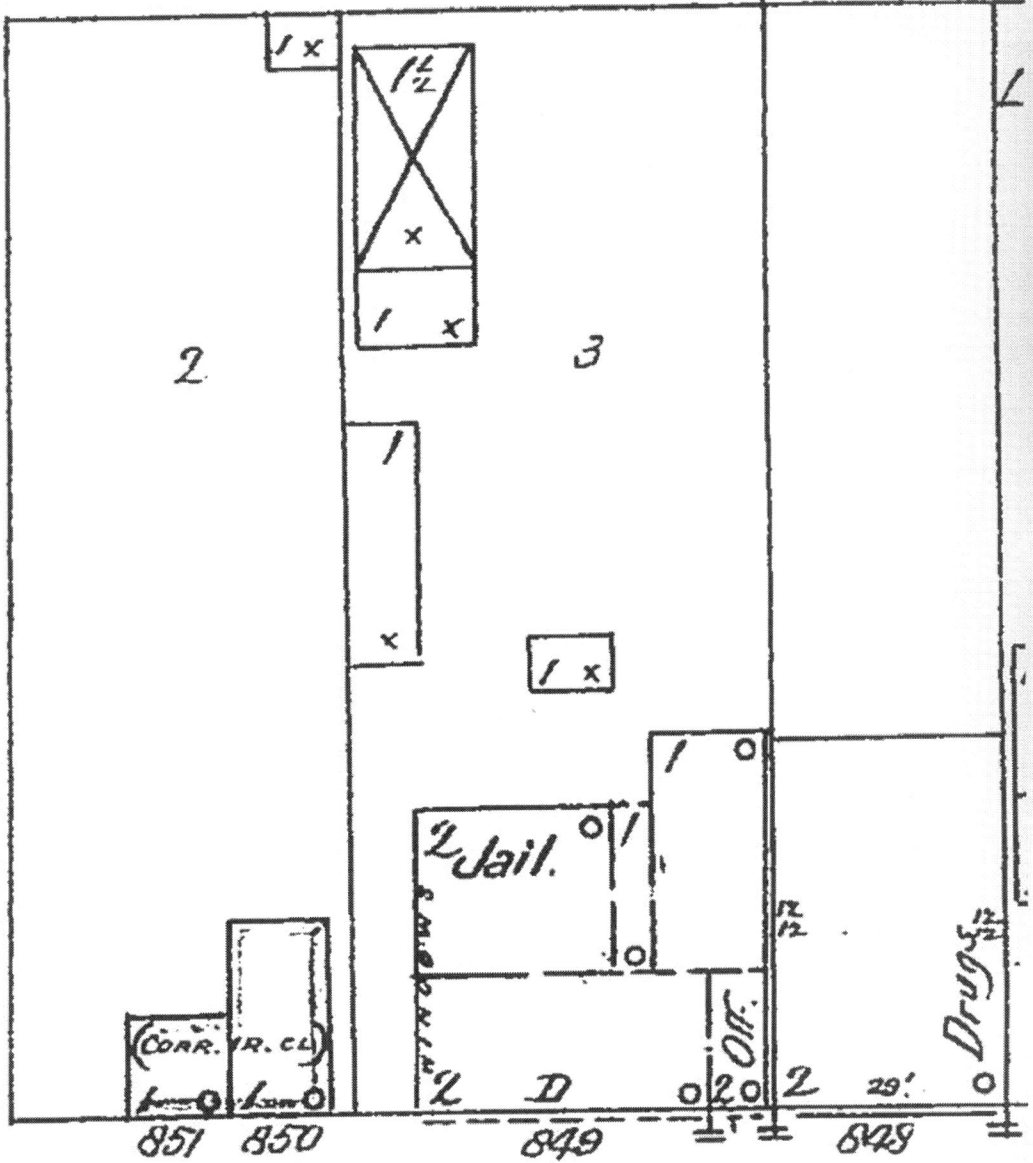

This shows the location along Main Street near present-day Truman Road where the 1841 Jackson County Jail remained, and is denoted here as "IR. CL.," which stands for 'iron clad on a wood frame.'

This shows the location of the 1859 Jackson County Marshal's Home and Jail, with out-buildings.

This lot, and the lot to the south, is quite similar to the 1892 map, though the placement of windows and doorways (hollow circles) differ slightly.

1859 JACKSON COUNTY JAIL SITE - EVOLUTION
SANBORN FIRE INSURANCE MAP, SEPTEMBER 1907

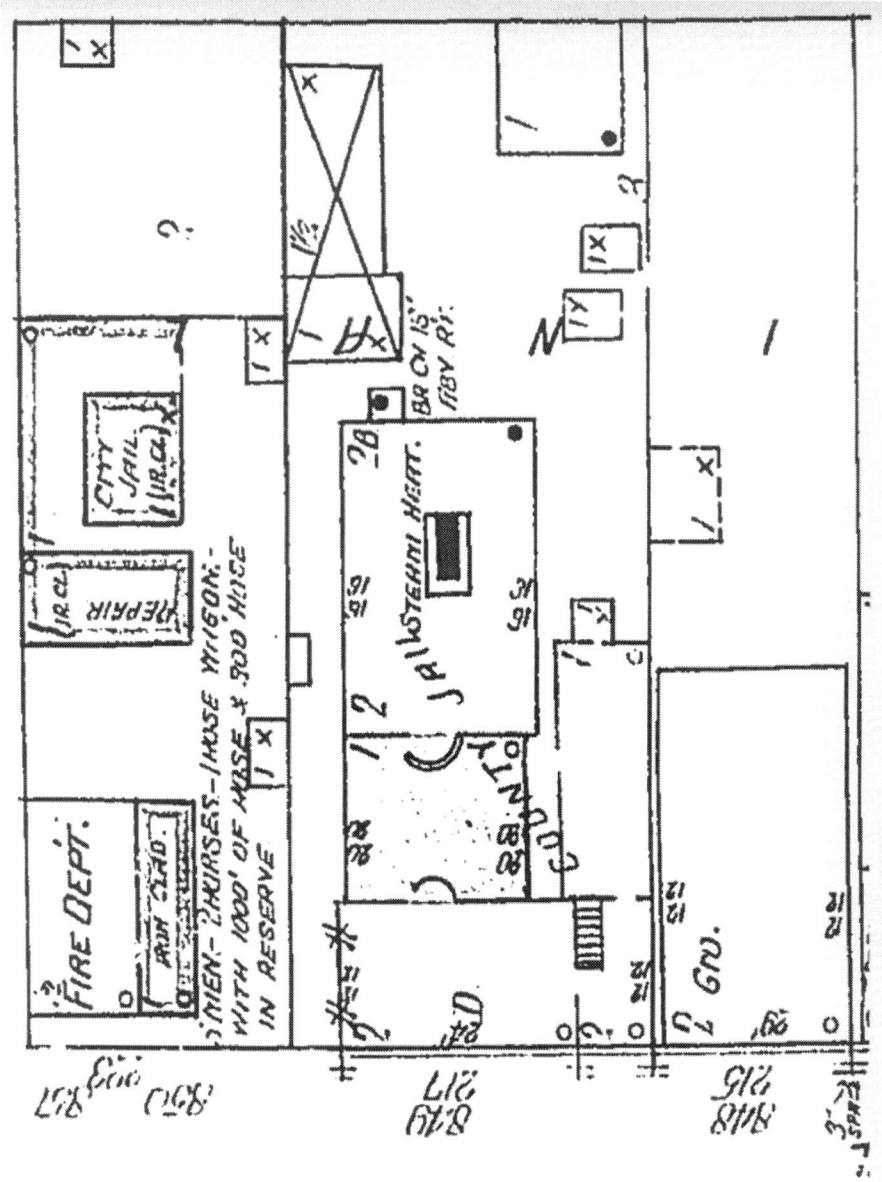

This shows the location along Main Street at present-day Truman Road, where the iron clad portion of the 1841 Jackson County Jail remained. The Fire Department had located to the lot by this time; and, the City had constructed iron clad structures on the east portion of the lot (one as a repair shop; another for a City Jail.

This shows the location of the 1859 Jackson County Marshal's Home and Jail, with out-buildings, including the 1907 addition featuring steam heat. The hollow circles identify location of doorways. The south wall of the Marshal's Home *should* have encompassed the staircase; it appears here to be part of the present-day front courtyard.

The drugstore from the 1892 and 1898 maps was by 1907 a grocery store.

1859 JACKSON COUNTY JAIL SITE - EVOLUTION
SANBORN FIRE INSURANCE MAP, AUGUST 1916

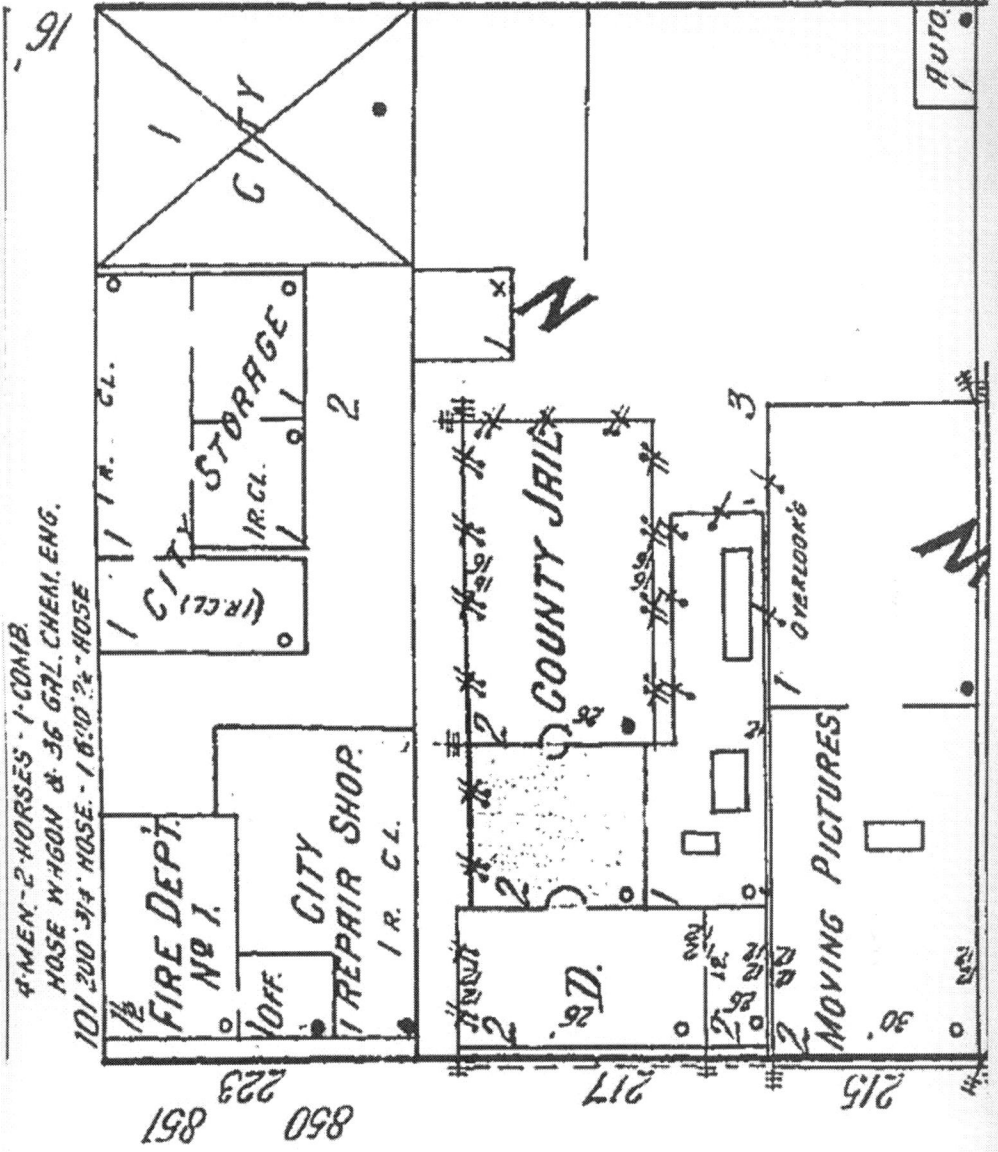

This shows the location along Main Street at present-day Truman Road where the iron clad portion of the 1841 Jackson County Jail remained, and was by 1916 used as the City Repair Shop. The Fire Department remained adjacent; and, the City's storage included the former iron clad structures (see 1907) on the east portion of the lot.

This shows the location of the 1859 Jackson County Marshal's Home and Jail, with out-buildings, including the 1907 addition. The hollow circles represent doors; black circles, fire protection.

The footprint of the present-day gift shop does not show as such on this map, and appears to be incorporated into a much larger structure (possible a "lean-to") that extends east on the lot.

The grocery store from the 1907 map was by 1916 a silent motion picture movie house.

1859 JACKSON COUNTY JAIL SITE - EVOLUTION

LEO H. KOEHLER SURVEY, JANUARY 1925

Deeded to Independence, 1881.

'.01

32.33

82.5'

Deed distance

33.5'

50.0'

16.5'

155'

Lot 2

Fence
Line of possesion

Frame Bldg.

19.2'

Fence

Lot 3.

66.0'

S.W.Cor.Lot 2. O.T.

Jail Bldg.

'.01

'02.1

32.33'

An August 1926 Sanborn Fire Insurance map closely aligns with the 1916 map *(copyright prevents its reproduction here)*. The most noticeable absence on the 1926 map is the "iron clad" features of the 1841 Jackson County Jail previously denoted. The iron clad structures may likely have still been there; but, the details were not provided.

This shows the location of the 1859 Jackson County Marshal's Home and Jail complex, complete with a fence running the perimeter of the lot denoting the "line of possession" *that a frame building appears to have been built upon.* The present-day gift shop does not show as such on this map; it is engulfed within a much larger structure of some kind (possibly a 'lean-to') that runs east midway to the 1907 addition.

The building to the south of the 1859 Jackson County Jail site remained a "moving pictures" establishment on the 1926 Sanborn Fire Insurance map.

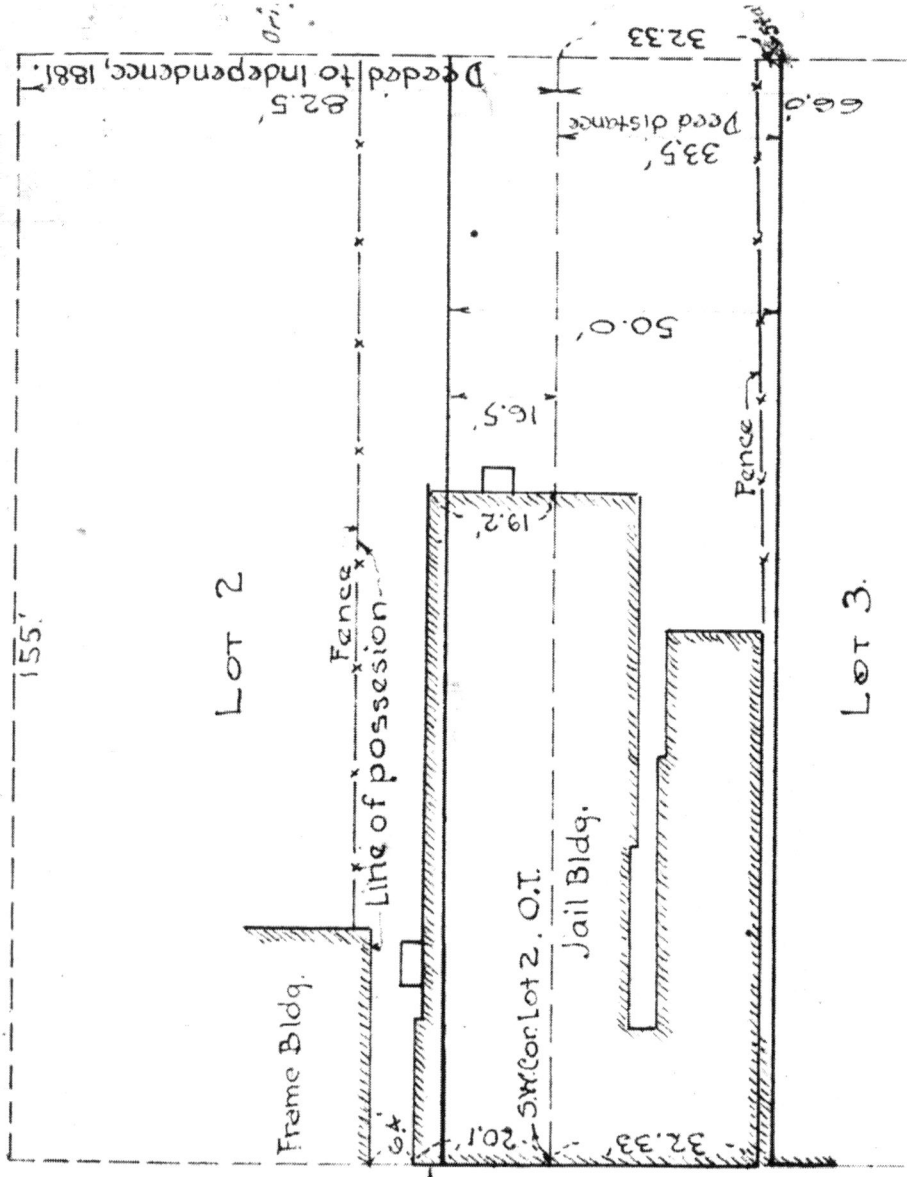

ABOUT YOUR
JACKSON COUNTY HISTORICAL SOCIETY

The first recorded activity of the Jackson County Historical Society was the Independence Day celebrations of 1909 when a picnic was held on the shaded lawn of the John B. Wornall House in Kansas City, Missouri.

The Jackson County Historical Society formally organized January 19, 1940, with its headquarters at the County Seat in Independence. Its historical records (now the Society's *Archives and Research Library)* were then maintained in a single cabinet at the Jackson County Library located on Independence Square.

The Society became more active and formally incorporated in 1958 when the oldest structure on Independence Square was slated for demolition . . . the 1859 Jackson County Jail and adjoining Marshal's Home. After a fervent capital campaign under the leadership of Society President W. Howard Adams, the *1859 Jail, Marshal's Home and Museum* (217 North Main Street, Independence, Missouri) opened to the public in June 1959, in the building's 100th year. A one-room schoolhouse used for 90 years on the William Bullitt Howard estate near Lee's Summit, Missouri, was also relocated to the museum site for preservation and interpretation. The restored structures and period rooms were furnished with significant Jackson County-related artifacts from the 19th Century.

Membership grew from 700 in 1958 to 2,351 a decade later. During this period, the Society acquired the John B. Wornall House on the 100th anniversary of the Battle of Westport (an event significant to that site's history) in October 1964. Although the home was open by 1969 for "under restoration" tours, it took another three years of research, planning, fund-raising, and restoration before the historic house museum opened to the public in September 1972. In 1998, the Wornall House, became a separate, independent organization.

By 1972, the Society's *Archives and Research Library*, had outgrown temporary quarters located in the basement of the Harry S Truman Presidential Museum and Library. The *Archives and Research Library* were relocated to space provided by Jackson County government in the historic Truman Courthouse on

Independence Square. Today (2009), we are streamlining our archives cataloging and indexing systems, and building an Internet-based, key-word searchable database. We are making plans to digitize selections from our collections. Each of these two major projects will one day be available online.

A growing audience makes use of the Historical Society's products, services and programs. For instance, around 1972 our Archives served about 100 people annually. Since 2000, the Archives have consistently assisted thousands of patrons, and have accepted more than 100 collections annually. The quantity and quality of the Society's products, services, sites, and programs are adapted to meet the needs of its patrons. Generous benefactors have also helped establish permanent endowment funds for the long-term care of the Society's historic sites and collections.

We encourage readers with family connections to the former occupants and workers at the 1859 Jackson County Jail to donate related materials to the Jackson County Historical Society for continued preservation and exhibition at the 1859 Jail, Marshal's Home and Museum.

And, consider that routine upkeep of a 150+year-old historic structure requires on-going dedication to maintenance and repair. *Your pledge of financial support is most welcomed.* We appreciate and thank you in advance for doing what you can to help keep this remarkable site open to the public for another half century . . . and beyond!

Feel free to inquire with the "Marshal" or one of his "deputies" for more information about the Jackson County Historical Society's products, services, sites and programs:

1859 JAIL, MARSHAL'S HOME & MUSEUM
217 North Main Street
Independence, Missouri 64050
816.252.1892

ARCHIVES, RESEARCH LIBRARY & BOOKSHOP
HARRY S TRUMAN OFFICE & COURTROOM
In the Jackson County Truman Courthouse
On historic Independence Square
816.252.7454

ADMINISTRATION
P.O. Box 4241
Independence, Missouri 64051
816.461.1897

INFO@JCHS.ORG
JCHS.ORG

ABOUT THE AUTHORS

David W. Jackson has served the Jackson County Historical Society as Archives and Education Director, and *Jackson County Historical Society JOURNAL* editor, since November 2000. He directs more than 20 volunteers who help with a multitude of tasks in the administration of the various functions of the Archives and non-circulating Research Library; physical and online Bookshop; Harry S Truman Office and Courtroom; and, educational programs that include a speaker's bureau, lecture series, and website improvement and maintenance.

Jackson is founder and director of The Orderly Packrat (orderlypackrat.com). Under The Orderly Pack Rat imprint, Jackson is also author and publisher of *Direct Your Letters to San Jose: The California Gold Rush Letters of James and David Lee Campbell, 1849-1852* (2000); *Lost Souls of the Lost Township: Untold Life Stories of the People Buried in the Davis-Smith Cemetery, Kansas City, Missouri* (co-authored with Paul R. Petersen, 2011); *Changing Times: Almanac and Digest of Kansas City's Gay and Lesbian History* (2011); and, *Recipes of our Past: Morsels from Our Grandmothers' Recipe Boxes* (2005; revised and enlarged 2011).

Jackson has guided the creation of full-name indices to commemorate anniversary editions for two important Jackson County resources: *Illustrated Historical Atlas of Jackson County, Missouri* (2007 reprint of an original 1877 edition); and, *Vital Historical Records of Jackson County, Missouri, 1826-1876* (2009 reprint of a 1934 original genealogical resource).

In addition to contributing occasional feature articles to the *Jackson County Historical Society JOURNAL* and writing or editing copy for various products on behalf of the Historical Society, Jackson's history-related columns appear regularly in both *the Kansas City Star* and *Independence Examiner* newspapers.

In 2010, The History Press released a compilation of adaptations of Jackson's aforementioned newspaper columns in a book titled, *Kansas City Chronicles: An Up-to-Date History*. To celebrate the bicentennial of the birth of Missouri's famous painter, George Caleb Bingham, Jackson assisted in the 2011 production of two books that peripherally touch on Bingham's life (*Missouri Star: The Life and Times of Martha A. "Mattie" (Livingston) Lykins Bingham,* and *Borderland Families: Always on the Edge*, both authored by Rose Ann Findlen. These products highlight the life and recollections of Bingham's second wife, "Mattie" Bingham, who had previously been married to Kansas City physician, Dr. Johnston Lykins.

Paul Kirkman, after receiving his B.A. in History from Columbia College, entered the archival internship program for the Jackson County Historical Society. While in the program, Paul volunteered at the 1859 Jail, Marshal's Home and Museum. He also authored, "Jackson County's Little Blue River Valley: Balancing Development and Preservation of an Historic Rural Landscape," in the Autumn 2005 issue of the *Jackson County Historical Society JOURNAL*.

Upon completion of his internship, Kirkman began work as an archival assistant for the Kansas City Parks and Recreation Department. Kirkman is an independent scholar for the State Historical Society of Missouri's Speakers' Bureau, and presents programs on, "Frontier Justice," and "Social Outlaws and Notorious Persons of the Missouri–Kansas Border Area, 1860–1880." Kirkman lives with his family in Independence, just a few short blocks away from the 1859 Jackson County Jail.

ACKNOWLEDGEMENTS

Our gratitude is extended to Gay Clemenson, former 1859 Jail, Marshal's Home and Museum director, for giving permission for us to rely upon her detailed, 33-page manuscript account of law and order on the Missouri frontier, "Keeping the Peace in Jackson County, Missouri, 1827-1887." Gwen L. Myers' 92-page manuscript about the history of Jackson County's Sheriffs was invaluable as a benchmark for research continued and presented here.

Linda Camp's article, "Jackson County's Jail and Its Jailers: Early Sheriffs Enforced the Law to 1859," in the Society's Spring 2004 *Jackson County Historical Society JOURNAL* provided insights into the pre-1859 Jackson County officials. Research by Kathleen Tuohey also helped to flesh out the life stories of these early sheriffs. Highlights of the Jail's history from 1859-1933 were brought up-to-date in an abbreviated fashion by David W. Jackson in his Autumn 2004 *Jackson County Historical Society JOURNAL* article, "Unlocking the Shackled Past of Jackson County's Jail in Independence."

The booklet, *History of the 1859 Jail and other Early Jails Located in Independence, Missouri,* by Donald R. Hale and Vicki P. Beck (Independence, Mo.: Blue & Grey Bookshoppe, 2001) provided insights into some of the more notorious prisoners incarcerated in Jackson County's early jail facilities. Harriet C. Frazier's *Death Sentences in Missouri, 1803-2005*, is an extraordinary study on the subject, and was helpful in cross-checking the appendix we compiled on *legal* hangings in Jackson County. Terry L. Anderson's *Jackson Examiner* newspaper abstracts, published in eight volumes as, *Come and Spit on the Floor and Make Yourself at Home*, was also illuminating and useful in recording printed, secondary matter that complemented the Jackson County Historical Society's newspaper clipping files about the Jail.

A special thanks to Paul Kirkman's step-son, Steven W. Williams III, for acting as "research assistant," and faithfully transcribing notes from microfilmed records; and, to volunteer Pati Kidwell who assisted by checking (and double checking) our indexing.

The minutes of the Jackson County Court (predecessor of the Jackson County Legislature) were indispensable in finding and documenting primary citations for events that have either been written about, or alluded to by authors in the past. The time consuming task of reading the minutes day-by-day was made somewhat easier because of the Great Depression era Historical Records Survey of the Works Projects Administration that produced typewritten transcriptions of the original, handwritten ledgers (14:141). The indices to this record group remain in *handwritten* format, and don't always provide the level of detail researchers might expect. The *typewritten minutes* and *handwritten indices* have been preserved on microfilm. To the best of our knowledge, these ledgers are in storage at the Jackson County Records Center. It is not believed that the original, *handwritten* minute ledger books were maintained after the transcriptions were made in the 1930s. The only known, surviving, original, *handwritten* ledger is the very first one dating from 1827-1833 that was bestowed to the Jackson County Historical Society by Harry S Truman. The entries provided as source material in this work are referenced by either a two or three digit numeral (ex. 11:127:98599). The first digit signifies the volume number; the second represents the page number; the third is a sequential, item-level number that was stamped beside each entry, or action (in most, but not all instances, we attempted to capture this identifier as well). The authors uncovered in their research endless detail, and painstakingly cited sources for accuracy and credibility; only a few end-note citations in this work were included that were not personally viewed by the authors; these instances were clearly delineated.

ILLUSTRATIONS

All illustrations courtesy the Jackson County Historical Society Archives, unless otherwise noted. "Anon." indicates widely available photo stock, believed to be in the public domain.

PAGE	DESCRIPTION	COURTESY
cover	1859 Jail cellblock, first floor	Photo courtesy Nick Vedros
3	Captain Meriwether Lewis, as drawn by muralist Charles Goslin	Jackson County Historical Society Art Collection
3	Captain William Clark by Charles Goslin	Jackson County Historical Society Art Collection
3	Soldat Du Chene, "Soldier of the Oak," Second Chief of the Little Osage Nation (jchs003738l)	
5	Fort Osage Blockhouse, cropped and digitally enhanced to resemble what the 1827 Jackson County Jail might have looked like (jchs001910s)	
7	Joseph Reddeford Walker (jchs001295l)	Alfred Jacob Miller, "Portrait of Captain Joseph Reddeford Walker," Josyln Art Museum, Omaha, Nebraska.
8	Santa Fe Trail	Anon.
10	Cover of book, Abuse and Murder on the Frontier	William B. "Bill" Bundschu, from original artwork by Ernst Ulmer
11	Temple Lot, 1907, by George Edward Anderson	Scot Facer Proctor. "Another Witness of the Light: The Museum of Church History and Art Showcases Two Twentieth Century Photographers." [Missouri Gallery] Meridian Magazine (as viewed at http://www.meridianmagazine.com/images/churhistart/andersonindptmplsite.jpg)
12	Rebecca Littleton Hawkins in her later years (jchs004709s)	
13	Handcuffs and Ball and Chain	Anon.
14	Orrin Porter Rockwell	Anon.
14	Lilburn W. Boggs (jchs003736m)	State Historical Society of Missouri
16	Samuel Combs Owens (jchs009069xxx)	
18	Colonel Alexander William Doniphan	Library of Congress, Prints and Photographs Division (DAG no. 124; LC-USZ62-109945, or LC0USZ62-62670)
18	Old Plantation (Benjamin Franklin Thomson estate) (jchs003518l)	
19	Old Plantation (Benjamin Franklin Thomson estate) (jchs003520l)	
20	Mariah Louisa Thomson by George Caleb Bingham (jchs003517l)	
20	Benjamin Franklin Thomson, by George Caleb Bingham (jchs003516l)	
20	George W. Buchanan (jchs003647)	
21	Scene as it would have appeared around Independence Square [The old French Market, New Orleans, attributed to William Henry Jackson]	Library of Congress, Prints and Photographs Division, Detroit Publishing Company Collection (LC-D418-8113 DLC (b&w glass neg.))
21	Captain John A. Sutter (Johann Augustus Sutter)	Anon.

22	William Botts (attributed) (jchs004129s)	
23	Missouri-Kansas Border	Anon. Drawn under the supervision of James C. Malin
24	Major John W. Burrus (jchs001660m)	
31	Asa Beebe Cross office (first door on left); looking east on Missouri Avenue from Delaware, downtown Kansas City	Missouri Valley Special Collections, Kansas City Public Library, Kansas City, Missouri (Barcode 10007653)
31	Asa Beebe Cross	Bryan, John. *America's Contribution to American Architecture* (St. Louis, Mo.: St. Louis Press Club, 1928), 79.
32	1859 Marshal's Home (and Jackson County Jail to the rear), as represented in the *Illustrated Atlas of Jackson County, Missouri, 1877*. This is the earliest view of the 1859 Marshal's Home. See also image on page 107 showing a later, 2-story addition on the south end of the building, which may have been added between 1885 and 1892, according to the maps in Appendix F. (jchs011133l)	The 1877 *Atlas* containing the earliest, detailed maps of Jackson County, was reprinted in 2007 with a full-name index, and is available for sale by the Jackson County Historical Society.
32	Specifications for 1859 Jackson County Jail (jchs005252al)	
33	Sketch of the 1859 Marshal's Home, 217 N Main Street, Independence, Missouri by Virginia Jennings (attributed) (jchs003144l)	
34	1859 Marshal's Home, office (jchs002980l)	
35	1859 Marshal's Home, parlor (jchs011092l)	
35	1859 Marshal's Home, child's bed chamber (jchs011091l)	
36	1859 Jail cellblock, first floor	Photo courtesy Steve Noll
37	Where the 1859 Jackson County Jail abuts the rear of the Marshal's Home (jchs002981l)	
38	1859 Jail cellblock, second floor	Photo courtesy Steve Noll
38	Shackles	Anon.
39	1859 Jail cellblock, first floor (jchs011120l)	
43	William Clarke Quantrill, portrait in charcoal on paper, which was prominently displayed in a frame for years at Quantrill reunions (jchs009241xx)	
44	Restraints in a cell of the 1859 Jackson County Jail (jchs010945s)	
45	Elderly African American couple posed outside of building, near Hampton Institute, Hampton, Va., by Frances Benjamin Johnston	Library of Congress, Prints and Photographs Division, (LC-USZ62-118921 (b&w film copy neg.)
46	Colonel Upton B. Hays (jchs007765m)	
46	Locks and keys	Anon.
47	Locks and keys	Anon.
47	Quantrill reunion, with framed Quantrill portrait on display (jchs002556l)	
48	Engraving of "Lawrence Massacre"	*Harper's Weekly*, 19 September 1863
48	General Thomas Ewing	Kansas State Historical Society

50	Martial Law, or Order No. 11 by George Caleb Bingham, from a an original engraving in the Jackson County Historical Society's collections that is signed by Bingham (jchs004009l)	In recognition of the 140th anniversary of the issuance of Order No. 11, the Jackson County Historical Society in 2003 reprinted its original engraving; copies are available for sale.
51	1848 Jackson County Courthouse on Independence Square (actually between June 1852 and May 1853), as taken from the 1868 Bird's Eye View, Independence, Missouri, by A. Ruger (jchs004816s)	See the Autumn 2007 issue of the Jackson County Historical Society JOURNAL.
52	Major General Sterling Price	Anon.
55	Kizzie, the only image of an African-American slave yet donated to the Jackson County Historical Society's collections (jchs002557l)	
56	1859 Jackson County Jail cellblock (jchs010957s)	
57	1860 U.S. Census of Henry Bugler and family, with Jail inmates	National Archives and Records Administration, 1860 U.S. Population Schedules, Independence, Blue Township, Jackson County, Missouri; M653-625, page 26.
58	"Bloody" Bill Anderson (jchs004908l)	
58	General Joseph Orville "Jo" Shelby (jchs008875m)	
58	Diagram of points of fight between Peacock and Chiles and their two sons on the Independence Public Square, in 1872	*Kansas City* (Mo.) *Star*, 31 Mar. 1912.
61	Hold Up (re-enactment at Selsa Station) (jchs011078l)	
62	Henry Bugler, postmortem (jchs003807s)	
62	Henry Bugler's tombstone, Woodlawn Cemetery	Photo courtesy David W. Jackson
63	Rev. Abner Holton Deane, copied from a George Caleb Bingham original in the possession of William Jewell College, as painted by muralist Charles Goslin, and displayed at the 1859 Jail, Marshal's Home and Museum	Photo courtesy Steve Noll
63	Richard Green	*Kansas City* (Mo.) *Times*, 2 Mar. 1878, 3.
64	Gallows where Green was hung	*Kansas City* (Mo.) *Times*, 2 Mar. 1878, 3.
67	1870 Jackson County Courthouse, designed by Asa Beebe Cross, downtown Kansas City, 2nd and Main Streets (jchs000716al)	
69	Jesse Woodson James (jchs005029l)	
69	Major Granville Dyson Page (jchs015961s)	
70	Overfelt-Johnston House (aka. Cammie Johnston House), where the first Jackson County Marshal, Granville Dyson Page, lived during the Civil War (jchs014266m)	
71	Major Granville Dyson Page tombstone, Woodlawn Cemetery	Photo courtesy David W. Jackson
71	1871 Jackson County Courthouse, downtown Kansas City at 2nd and Main Streets, destroyed by cyclone in 1886 (jchs000716al)	
75	Jesse Woodson James (jchs005494l)	
75	Missouri Governor Thomas Theodore Crittenden	Anon.
76	Frank James (jchs004166l)	
77	Frank James cell in the 1859 Jackson County Jail (restored)	Photo courtesy David W. Jackson

107	Derelict 1859 Marshal's Home. This image shows a 2-story structure at the south end of the original building (possibly added between 1885 and 1892) where today there is a courtyard, as in the original plan. The lower window appears to have originally been a door. This entire part of the structure was removed during the renovation to revert to the original 1859 footprint. (jchs005177l) Compare with image on page 32. See also maps in Appendix F.	
108	In the doorway, left to right: Judge Henry Bundschu, JCHS member; Mrs. Norman Davidson, President, Junior Service League; and, Phil Davis, Holiday Inn. Standing: Coburn Jones, Secretary, Chamber of Commerce; Jerry Surber, President, Junior Chamber; Dale Williamson, President, Chamber of Commerce; Homer M. Clements, Superintendent of School; and, Richard Graba, JCHS member. Kneeling: Keith Wilson, attorney at law; T. Hall Collison, *The Independence Examiner*; and, James Shaffer, attorney.	*Independence* (Mo.) *Examiner*, 14 Aug. 1856, 1.
109	Signing title of the 1859 Jackson County Jail from the American Legion to the Jackson County Historical Society. Seated: W. Howard Adams, President of JCHS; Mayor William Sermon. Standing: Roy Layland, Treasurer of JCHS; Edgar G. Hinde, Sr. and Warren Gray, representing the American Legion. (jchs002996l)	
110	Jackson County Assessment Map (26-230)	Jackson County Recorder of Deeds
110	W. Howard Adams in the Marshal's office (jchs005143l)	
111	Former U.S. President Harry S Truman kicks off capital campaign to restore the 1859 Jackson County Jail (jchs05175l)	
111	Hanging the sign to the 1859 Jail, Marshal's Home and Museum. Dwight Potts is on the left. (jchs010896s)	
112	William Bullitt Howard Schoolhouse installed at the 1859 Jackson County Jail site (jchs005269l). Visible on the north wall of the building to the south of the site are the outlines of former structures that once comprised the jail facility. See maps in Appendix F.	
113	4 images of students in the Howard Schoolhouse (jchs011011; 011012; 011014; 011071)	
113	Letter of Harry S Truman congratulating the Jackson County Historical Society on their rescue and restoration efforts (JCHS Document ID L57.002F21)	
113	Harry S Truman at 1859 Jail, Marshal's Home and Museum dedication ceremonies (jchs005195l)	
114	Friendly Persuasion movies set (jchs010962s). The 1859 Marshal's Home as a 'cast member.' Note the temporary addition of a sign over the north door, and 'bars' in front of the lower windows.	
114	Unidentified youth looks at exhibit at the 1859 Jail, Marshal's Home and Museum (jchs005193s)	
115	Roger "T" Sermon, Jr. (jchs005968s)	
117	1859 Marshal's Home (jchs011093l)	
117	Restoration work on the 1859 Marshal's Home (jchs011116l)	
118	2 photos of exhibit cases in the 1859 Jail, Marshal's Home and Museum	Photo courtesy David W. Jackson
118	Unidentified patron entering the 1859 Jail, Marshal's Home and Museum (jchs011123l)	

119	Jesse Woodson James (jchs0054941)	
120	Prisoners being taken to Jefferson City by Riverboat "Chester;" Harry C. Hoffman was Marshal (jchs0054501)	
120	County Sheriff business card of Overton H. Gentry, Jr. (JCHS Document ID 32F19)	
121	Joseph Reddeford Walker (jchs001295s)	
121	Benjamin Franklin Thomson (jchs0035171)	
121	William Botts (attributed) (jchs004129s)	
121	Major John W. Burrus (jchs001660m)	
122	C. B. L. Boothe (jchs008875m)	
123	William S. Sitlington (jchs006972s)	
123	Robert S. Stone	
124	Winfred S. Pontius	Marshall and Morrison. *Political History of Jackson County, Missouri.* (n.p., 1902), 25.
124	John P. Gilday	Marshall and Morrison. *Political History of Jackson County, Missouri.* (n.p., 1902), 197.
124	Thomas J. "Tom" Pendergast	Marshall and Morrison. *Political History of Jackson County, Missouri.* (n.p., 1902), 47.
125	John M. Rood	
125	Shield of John Riley Jones, Deputy Sheriff	Photo courtesy Beverley (Jones) Zimmerman
126	Overton H. Gentry (jchs001294s)	
127	Major John L. Miles (jchs003946m)	
151	Frank Arden (jchs013970s)	
151	C. J. Allen (jchs013971s)	
151	Charles Avery (jchs013972s)	
151	James Bennett (jchs013973s)	
153	Phillipp Boyd (jchs013974s)	
153	Joseph Brockway (jchs013975s)	
153	William Douglas (jchs013976s)	
153	Jack Edmonson (jchs013977s)	
153	John Field (jchs013978s)	
153	James Franklin (jchs016976s)	
153	Bart Gilliam (jchs013979s)	
153	Alix "Munk" Hayns (jchs016977s)	
153	Seymore Hutchens (jchs013980s)	
153	Bert Israel (jchs013981s)	
153	Rose Jenkins (jchs013982s)	
153	Ed Lawson (jchs013983s)	

153	Alex Lobb (jchs013984s)
153	John Lonager [sic.] (jchs016978s)
153	Thomas Mabry (jchs013985s)
153	Albert Matthiews (jchs013986s)
153	Lon McFadden (jchs013987s)
153	Bert Moore (jchs013988s)
153	Roy Moore (jchs013989s)
153	Richard Smith (jchs013990s)
153	Claud Sullivan (jchs013991s)
153	James Webb (jchs013992s)
153	William Williams (jchs013993s)
153	Arthur Wright. Not pictured; image too light to reproduce without significant enhancements (jchs013994s)
153	Harry Wright. Not pictured; image too light to reproduce without significant enhancements (jchs013995s). There is also one unidentified "mug shot" in this collection not pictured.
159	Independence, Missouri [map]. August 1885, Sheet 1. Scale not given. "Sanborn Fire Insurance Maps, 1867-1970 – Missouri." ProQuest Information and Learning, through Mid-Continent Public Library System. <http://sanborn.umi.com.proxy.mcpl.lib.mo.us/mo/4709/dateid-000001.htm?CCSI=45n > (14 Mar. 2009).
160	Independence, Missouri [map]. December 1892, Sheet 3. Scale not given. "Sanborn Fire Insurance Maps, 1867-1970 – Missouri." ProQuest Information and Learning, through Mid-Continent Public Library System. <http://sanborn.umi.com.proxy.mcpl.lib.mo.us/mo/4709/dateid-000002.htm?CCSI=45n> (14 Mar. 2009).
161	Independence, Missouri [map]. September 1898, Sheet 4. Scale not given. "Sanborn Fire Insurance Maps, 1867-1970 – Missouri." ProQuest Information and Learning, through Mid-Continent Public Library System.<http://sanborn.umi.com.proxy.mcpl.lib.mo.us/mo/4709/dateid-000003.htm?CCSI=45n> (14 Mar. 2009).
162	Independence, Missouri [map]. September 1907, Sheet 7. Scale not given. "Sanborn Fire Insurance Maps, 1867-1970 – Missouri." ProQuest Information and Learning, through Mid-Continent Public Library System.<http://sanborn.umi.com.proxy.mcpl.lib.mo.us/mo/4709/dateid-000003.htm?CCSI=45n> (14 Mar. 2009).
163	Independence, Missouri [map]. August 1916, Sheet 8. Scale not given. "Sanborn Fire Insurance Maps, 1867-1970 – Missouri." ProQuest Information and Learning, through Mid-Continent Public Library System.<http://sanborn.umi.com.proxy.mcpl.lib.mo.us/mo/4709/dateid-000003.htm?CCSI=45n> (14 Mar. 2009).
164	Independence, Missouri [map]. January 1925. Leo H. Koehler survey for Jackson County. Original is in the offices of the Jackson County Public Works Department.
165	Picnic on the lawn of the John B. Wornall House (jchs007361x)
165	John Cianciolo, as the Jackson County Marshal — Photo courtesy John and Lottie Cianciolo
166	Unidentified living historian at the 1859 Jail Museum (jchs010964s)

177

INDEX

180

185

188

Made in the USA
Columbia, SC
13 May 2017